A Celebration of Young Poets

Illinois and Indiana – Fall 2007

Creative Communication, Inc.

A Celebration of Young Poets
Illinois and Indiana – Fall 2007

An anthology compiled by Creative Communication, Inc.

Published by:

CREATIVE COMMUNICATION, INC.
1488 NORTH 200 WEST
LOGAN, UT 84341

ISBN: 978-1-60050-157-9

Foreword

The poets between these pages are not famous...yet. They are still learning how language creates images and how to reflect their thoughts through words. However, through their acceptance into this publication, these young poets have taken a giant leap that reflects their desire to write.

We are proud of this anthology and what it represents. Most poets who entered the contest were not accepted to be published. The poets who are included in this book represent the best poems from our youth. These young poets took a chance and were rewarded by being featured in this anthology. Without this book, these poems would have been lost in a locker or a backpack.

We will have a feeling of success if upon reading this anthology of poetry each reader finds a poem that evokes emotion. It may be a giggle or a smile. It may be a thoughtful reflection. You might find a poem that takes you back to an earlier day when a snowfall contains magic or when a pile of leaves was an irresistible temptation. If these poems can make you feel alive and have hope in our youth, then it will be time well spent.

As we thank the poets for sharing their work, we also thank you, the reader, for allowing us to be part of your life.

Thomas Worthen, Ph.D.
Editor
Creative Communication

WRITING CONTESTS!

Enter our next POETRY contest!
Enter our next ESSAY contest!

Why should I enter?
Win prizes and get published! Each year thousands of dollars in prizes are awarded in each region and tens of thousands of dollars in prizes are awarded throughout North America. The top writers in each division receive a monetary award and a free book that includes their published poem or essay. Entries of merit are also selected to be published in our anthology.

Who may enter?
There are four divisions in the poetry contest. The poetry divisions are grades K-3, 4-6, 7-9, and 10-12. There are three divisions in the essay contest. The essay division are grades 4-6, 7-9, and 10-12.

What is needed to enter the contest?
To enter the poetry contest send in one original poem, 21 lines or less. To enter the essay contest send in one original essay, 250 words or less, on any topic. Each entry must include the student's name, grade, address, city, state, and zip code, and the student's school name and school address. Students who include their teacher's name may help the teacher qualify for a free copy of the anthology.

How do I enter?
Enter a poem online at:
www.poeticpower.com
or
Mail your poem to:
Poetry Contest
1488 North 200 West
Logan, UT 84341

Enter an essay online at:
www.studentessaycontest.com
or
Mail your essay to:
Essay Contest
1488 North 200 West
Logan, UT 84341

When is the deadline?
Poetry contest deadlines are August 14th, December 4th, and April 8th. Essay contest deadlines are July 15th, October 15th, and February 17th. You can enter each contest, however, send only one poem or essay for each contest deadline.

Are there benefits for my school?
Yes. We award $15,000 each year in grants to help with Language Arts programs. Schools qualify to apply for a grant by having a large number of entries of which over fifty percent are accepted for publication. This typically tends to be about 15 accepted entries.

Are there benefits for my teacher?
Yes. Teachers with five or more students accepted to be published receive a free anthology that includes their students' writing.

For more information please go to our website at **www.poeticpower.com**, email us at editor@poeticpower.com or call 435-713-4411.

Table of Contents

Fall 2007
Poetic Achievement
Honor Schools

* Teachers who had fifteen or more poets accepted to be published

The following schools are recognized as receiving a "Poetic Achievement Award." This award is given to schools who have a large number of entries of which over fifty percent are accepted for publication. With hundreds of schools entering our contest, only a small percent of these schools are honored with this award. The purpose of this award is to recognize schools with excellent Language Arts programs. This award qualifies these schools to receive a complimentary copy of this anthology. In addition, these schools are eligible to apply for a Creative Communication Language Arts Grant. Grants of two hundred and fifty dollars each are awarded to further develop writing in our schools.

All Saints Academy
Breese, IL
Stephanie Garcia*

Allen J. Warren Elementary School
Highland, IN
Mr. Dockery
Ms. Fleming
Ms. Guzman
Mrs. Krestel*
Sally Pagorek*

Bailly Elementary School
Chesterton, IN
Crystal Callaway
Cris Petro*

Bethel Lutheran School
Morton, IL
Renata Anderson*
Linda Moore

Chaney-Monge Jr High School
Crest Hill, IL
Wendy Mammosser*

Chrisney Elementary School
Chrisney, IN
Janet Marshall*

Christian Life Schools
Rockford, IL
Patricia Vespa*

Churubusco Elementary School
Churubusco, IN
Julie Leedy*
Dawn O'Connor

Crown Point Christian School
Saint John, IN
Mrs. Corder*

Dee Mack Intermediate School
Deer Creek, IL
Mrs. Barnhill*
Mrs. Drury*
Meghan Frerichs
Mrs. Lee*
Mrs. O'Neal

Edison Elementary School
Stickney, IL
Karen Hybl
Travis Olson*

Emmanuel-St Michael Lutheran School
Fort Wayne, IN
Connie Hoyer*

Forreston Grade School
Forreston, IL
Sharon Winterhalter*

Fox Creek Elementary School
Bloomington, IL
Nicole Henderson*

Frank H Hammond Elementary School
Munster, IN
Carol Schaap*

Gard Elementary School
Beardstown, IL
Rita Crosby
Sue DeWitt*
Tammy Ruthardt

Helfrich Park Middle School
Evansville, IN
Lynn Alford*

Highlands Elementary School
Naperville, IL
Brian Horner*

Jane Addams Elementary School
Chicago, IL
Kathleen Grannan*

Keystone Montessori School
River Forest, IL
Helen Scott*

Knox Community Middle School
Knox, IN
Mrs. K. Jerrell*

Lincoln Intermediate School
Monmouth, IL
Mrs. Hulsizer
Mrs. Smith
Mrs. Youngquist*

Meadow Lane School
Merrionette Park, IL
Mrs. Bennick*
Janice Heniff*
Mrs. Schroeder

Milltown Elementary School
Milltown, IN
Holly Barron*

Nancy Hanks Elementary School
Ferdinand, IN
Judy Lindauer*

North Knox East Elementary/Jr High School
Edwardsport, IN
Kathy Stephens*

Peoria Academy
Peoria, IL
Susan Diggle
David C. Raffel Jr.
Ali Saucier*

Perry Central Elementary School
Leopold, IN
Darlene Davis
Jamie Guillaume*
Becky Hubert
Lisa Lutgring
Angela Shelby
Francie Wagner

Pinewood Elementary School
Elkhart, IN
Carol Cantzler*

Sacred Heart Elementary School
Lombard, IL
Nancy O'Reilly*

South Middle School
Arlington Heights, IL
Sheri Meehan*

Springfield Boys and Girls Club ABC Unit
Springfield, IL
David Boggs*

St Colette School
Rolling Meadows, IL
Victoria Pepe*

St Daniel the Prophet School
Chicago, IL
K. Laski*

St Jude Catholic School
Indianapolis, IN
Suzanne Halloran*

St Matthew School
Champaign, IL
Sr. M. Margaret Gibbons
Kathleen Marietta*

St Matthias/Transfiguration School
Chicago, IL
Mr. Wiezorek*

St Peter Catholic School
Skokie, IL
Joanne Dean
Ms. Murray
Ms. Struhar

St Pius X Catholic School
Indianapolis, IN
Kathy Taber*

Stanley Clark School
South Bend, IN
Kylea Asher*
Mary Dickerson*
Doris E. Smith*

Trinity Oaks Christian Academy
Cary, IL
Debra Welch*

Trinity-St Paul Lutheran School
Worden, IL
Sheila Langendorf*

Village Elementary School
Round Lake, IL
Kim Kearby*

Walker Elementary School
Evanston, IL
Paula Maldonado
Konstantina Panagiotidis*
Freda Wood-Livingston

Warren Central Elementary School
West Lebanon, IN
Cindy Evens
JoEllen Hurt

Washington Township Elementary School
Valparaiso, IN
Beverly Zborowski*

William B Orenic Intermediate School
Plainfield, IL
Tara Kristoff*

Language Arts Grant Recipients 2007-2008

After receiving a "Poetic Achievement Award" schools are encouraged to apply for a Creative Communication Language Arts Grant. The following is a list of schools who received a two hundred and fifty dollar grant for the 2007-2008 school year.

Acadamie DaVinci, Dunedin, FL
Altamont Elementary School, Altamont, KS
Belle Valley South School, Belleville, IL
Bose Elementary School, Kenosha, WI
Brittany Hill Middle School, Blue Springs, MO
Carver Jr High School, Spartanburg, SC
Cave City Elementary School, Cave City, AR
Central Elementary School, Iron Mountain, MI
Challenger K8 School of Science and Mathematics, Spring Hill, FL
Columbus Middle School, Columbus, MT
Cypress Christian School, Houston, TX
Deer River High School, Deer River, MN
Deweyville Middle School, Deweyville, TX
Four Peaks Elementary School, Fountain Hills, AZ
Fox Chase School, Philadelphia, PA
Fox Creek High School, North Augusta, SC
Grandview Alternative School, Grandview, MO
Hillcrest Elementary School, Lawrence, KS
Holbrook School, Holden, ME
Houston Middle School, Germantown, TN
Independence High School, Elko, NV
International College Preparatory Academy, Cincinnati, OH
John Bowne High School, Flushing, NY
Lorain County Joint Vocational School, Oberlin, OH
Merritt Secondary School, Merritt, BC
Midway Covenant Christian School, Powder Springs, GA
Muir Middle School, Milford, MI
Northlake Christian School, Covington, LA
Northwood Elementary School, Hilton, NY
Place Middle School, Denver, CO
Public School 124, South Ozone Park, NY

Language Arts Grant Winners cont.

Public School 219 Kennedy King, Brooklyn, NY
Rolling Hills Elementary School, San Diego, CA
St Anthony's School, Streator, IL
St Joan Of Arc School, Library, PA
St Joseph Catholic School, York, NE
St Joseph School-Fullerton, Baltimore, MD
St Monica Elementary School, Mishawaka, IN
St Peter Celestine Catholic School, Cherry Hill, NJ
Strasburg High School, Strasburg, VA
Stratton Elementary School, Stratton, ME
Tom Thomson Public School, Burlington, ON
Tremont Elementary School, Tremont, IL
Warren Elementary School, Warren, OR
Webster Elementary School, Hazel Park, MI
West Woods Elementary School, Arvada, CO
West Woods Upper Elementary School, Farmington, CT
White Pine Middle School, Richmond, UT
Winona Elementary School, Winona, TX
Wissahickon Charter School, Philadelphia, PA
Wood County Christian School, Williamstown, WV
Wray High School, Wray, CO

Top Poem Grades 4-5-6

When Ice Crystals Fall

As I lay down on my sea blue pillow,
tiny bits of ice beat against my window.
I hear the pit-pat sound as they hit the sheer glass.
I see them, like crystals, through my open blinds.
And as millions hit the smooth surface,
they seem to form one crystal, a diamond almost.
The midnight sky resembles a bright sapphire,
combined with the blackest of pearls.
While I close my eyes, I see the crystals in my dream.
But they suddenly transform into crystal ribbon ballerinas,
dancing as they float through the sky.
They seem to move about on an even floor
under their delicate and graceful feet, wherever they go.
As the crystal ribbon ballerinas
land on windows of lucky girls throughout the city,
I can only hope I can be one of them,
and get the chance to watch them dance as beautifully on my window
as they once did, free in the midnight sky.

Ashley Gavigan, Grade 6
Westfield Community School, IL

Top Poem Grades 4-5-6

Poet Tree

I stand now by the poet tree and poems spring to mind.
The poet tree is magical and influences our kind.

It came from the great lit'rature folk. They left it here one day.
They had to hurry to their homes to keep number folk at bay.

Lit'rature folk, you see, hate math in all its forms.
The number folk strike back at them with wars of fraction storms.

The lit'rature folk now are gone but the poet tree remains.
It loves us and enriches us and ripens all our brains.

Jack Marrinson, Grade 6
Beaubien Elementary School, IL

Top Poem Grades 4-5-6

Today Is "Not" My Day!

This morning I woke up, with gum all in my hair,
As I walked into the kitchen, and gave my mom a scare.
She dropped all my waffles, sausage, and bacon too.
Splattered all with syrup, I didn't know what to do.
I finally gave up breakfast, and hurried up the stairs.
I forgot to put on my socks, but who really cares.
My shirt was on backwards. Left my sweatshirt on the bed,
My right shoe was on my hand, my pants were on my head.

I dashed into the bathroom, skidded across the floor.
With my eyes crusted shut, I ran into the door.
I quickly brushed my teeth, but got toothpaste on my shirt,
No time to change, rushed out the door. Tripped and fell in dirt.
My mom had to drive me to the next stop, because I missed the bus.
When I got to school my backpack broke, my teacher made a fuss.
At lunch I dropped my tray, food was everywhere.
It wouldn't have been so embarrassing, if everyone didn't stare.

When I got home, my hair was a mess, I was soaked from head to toe,
I took off my muddy shoes, then opened my backpack and what do you know!
My pack was totally empty, I had left my books at school,
I screamed a scream of terror, today was so not cool.

I have better days, I really must say. But who knows, maybe tomorrow will be okay.

Marissa Roper, Grade 6
Thompson Middle School, IL

Top Poem Grades 4-5-6

Happiness

Far, far above me,
beyond the cool, cozy living room in which I sit,
tiny stars twinkle in the black, velvety night sky,
a full moon glows brightly,
lamplight illuminates tiny print on the pages of my book,
my dog lies by my side, his head on my lap,
I hear the faucet gently dripping,
my dog's slow, steady breathing,
from outside I hear crickets chirping,
the sprinklers running, and the breeze rustling leaves in the trees.
I smell fresh flowers in a vase beside me,
pasta boiling on the stove,
dish soap, and through the partially opened window,
the cool, summer night air,
and wet, freshly cut grass,
I feel the pages of my book between my fingers,
and as I read on, the words carry me off to faraway lands,
painting colorful pictures in my mind's eye.
I feel my dog's soft, silky fur as I stroke his head,
and the soft armchair in which I recline.
This is love, this is peace, this is happiness.

Leigh Katherine Van Ryn, Grade 5
Stanley Clark School, IN

Top Poem Grades 4-5-6

The Season of Awakening

Spring is the time for inspirations
To blossom just as the flowers do.
A breeze blows by
Rustling those ideas
Adding more for
More buds to bloom.

Spring is the moment
For thoughts to let loose
From a winter's hibernation.
Just as the flower seeds do.
The sun shines down
Helping the seeds to grow again.

Spring is the era
For ideas to develop
Just as flower buds do.
Droplets of water sprinkle
Down with guidance
Assisting the bud
To open to the world.

Spring is the
Season of awaking.

Stephanie Wang, Grade 6
Kennedy Jr High School, IL

Top Poem Grades 4-5-6

I'm Grateful For...

I'm grateful for a lot of things
For this I surely know
But one of them is family
For we go head to toe
We never break apart and we never chip off
And even though we fight and kick
We love each other so
When we are driving in the car
And I see a girl in rags
I think of all I have
And compare it to her bags
I don't live in a cold old place
Or on the street sidewalk
But I live in a joyful place
Where people sing and talk
So like I said before
When I count my blessings high
I don't count to five or ten
But go to billions, even trillions
And I count them with a sigh.

Delaney Wilson, Grade 5
Community Christian School, IN

Mom

My tremendous mom

She has silky-golden locks
That bring out her rippling-aqua eyes
Her Polish heritage is powerful

She's magnificently-nice,
Which lets people know she is lovingly-lovable
And fantabulously funny

We talk a lot,
And also shop
Sometimes she even gets me to clean with her

When she is near, I feel safe
Like no one could ever harm me
It makes me feel gratefully-glad to have her around

Katherine Warzocha, Grade 5
Booth Tarkington Elementary School, IL

Frank the Goat

Frank the goat
Loves to wear my furry coat,
When I put him to sleep
He never makes a peep,
His favorite thing to do is bake chocolate cakes
Frank also likes to go to the bank.

Braden Foppe, Grade 6
All Saints Academy, IL

Strange Cars

There's a car that went to a bar.
There's a car that drove afar.
There's a car that fell apart.
There's a car that went to Wal Mart.
There's a car that has paint that chars.
There's a car that got stuck in tar.
There's a car that went out with a girl named Lamar.
There's a car that went to Mars.
There's a car that has Radar.

Zachary Myler, Grade 5
Perry Central Elementary School, IN

When Pigs Fly

When pigs fly it sure will be a sight.
When pigs fly that "myth" will be right!
When pigs fly it will look like a pink blob.
When pigs fly Myth Busters will have an easy job.
When pigs fly mice might think they can skydive.
When pigs fly flowers will give people high-fives.
When pigs fly salt shakers will dance with hats and canes.
When pigs fly the only type of dog will be great danes.
When pigs fly everyone on Earth will have a pet cow.
When pigs fly this poem will get on stage, and take a bow.

Erin Farley, Grade 6
Christian Life Schools, IL

I Am

I am a pretty girl who loves to have fun
I wonder what I will look like when I get older
I hear lots of people talking
I see angels sitting up on the clouds
I want to get good grades all through school
I am a pretty girl who loves to have fun

I pretend that cats and dogs can talk
I feel that everyone needs to have fun in their life
I touch the rain, the snow, and the sleet
I worry that someday they will have World War III
I cry when one of my friends, family members, or animals die
I am a pretty girl who loves to have fun

I understand that nothing is easy until you practice and practice
I say that we are all the same
I dream of being the best cheerleader ever
I try to reach my goal in life
I hope one day I will grow up and start a good family
I am a pretty girl who loves to have fun

Katie French, Grade 6
Helfrich Park Middle School, IN

The House

The house is big and fun
I can't wait to show it to everyone
It's tall and white
Oh how I want to stay all night
Pretty cabinets and such
I love it so much
A new window just for me
Looking right out at a tree
A John Deere bedroom for one little boy
And a place for a special toy
A nice new barn with 4-H calves nearby
I really want to give it a try
A big family table
To sit around to tell a story or a fable
A big white Christmas present is in store
I can't wait 'till we first open the door

Lauren Dillon, Grade 6
North Knox East Elementary/Jr High School, IN

Christmas Mess

'Twas a month before Christmas
and all through the house
we were trying our best but all we had was a mess,
decorations were laying all over the floor,
when much to our surprise someone knocked
on the door, oh no oh no!
I exclaimed, I was so excited I forgot their
names, I've been at this for hours I must
look a fright, come on in we will order pizza
for dinner tonight.

Jared Hillier, Grade 5
Benjamin Franklin Elementary School, IL

Fall

Paint dripping on to the canvas,
Yellow and orange
Red and brown
Day after day
More and more paint joins
It all goes together,
A beautiful painting.

While the wolf blows,
Little people dance
To the music
When the big performance is over,
They rest to the ground!
But their tall guardians just stand still,
Colorless.

Arts created by nature.
In the brisk, cool air.
Kevin Sun, Grade 4
Highlands Elementary School, IL

Fall

F avorite time of the year
A utumn
L eaves falling
L ovely

Matt Koszyk, Grade 6
South Middle School, IL

Sombrero

I love fiestas,
I love to cha cha,
Like many people, I'm Mexican,
I'm pretty big yet light,
I'm made of straw,
I love to dance.
Danny Scholz, Grade 6
Sacred Heart Elementary School, IL

Chloe My Dog

Chloe is my dog
she likes to play in the snow
she always gets wet
Torin Rapp, Grade 6
Bethel Lutheran School, IL

Mom

Mom, mom, mom
Funny mom
Loving mom
Respectful, caring, gentle mom
Patient, peaceful, likable mom
Last of all, best of all
My mom
Kelsey Callon, Grade 5
St Jude Catholic School, IN

Winter

Winter smells like my
mom making hot cocoa
with candy cane.

Winter sounds like bells
ringing everywhere even from my house.

Winter tastes like snowflakes
falling from the air and
landing in my mouth.

Winter feels like feet
pounding in the snow.

I see a snowman in
my front yard I must have been
gone when my brother and sister built it.
Ally Hieb, Grade 4
Fox Creek Elementary School, IL

The Statue of Liberty

The statue of liberty is big and green,
they closed the arm in 1916.
They started building in 1875,
long ago, before I was even alive.
They didn't finish until 1884,
if you walk up it, your legs will be sore.
It's 22 stories, over 300 steps,
if I were to climb it, I'd be out of breath.
Valarie Martell, Grade 5
Glen Flora Elementary School, IL

Brown Wooden Boat

I am always brown.
I am now made out of wood.
I see fish all day.
Alexis Buck, Grade 4
Rose Hamilton Elementary School, IN

Happy Halloween!!!

Ha, boo,
Did I really scare you
Let me know
To and fro
Very scary
Little Jerry
Don't cry
It's all right
If you do
Don't boo hoo!!!
Trick or treat
Smell my feet
I'm munching on some sweets
They are very special treats.
Hannah Zitko, Grade 4
Summit Elementary School, IL

Poor Man

There once was a man named Ned
He was very poor and red
He lived in a shack
He slept in a sack
He couldn't afford a bed
Logan Monson, Grade 6
Bethel Lutheran School, IL

Fashion Designing

Fashion designing is the life for me,
Colors and fabrics that I can see.

Drawing and creating a style of my own,
Stitching and flowing that is shown.

Fashion and style around the block.
Creating and sewing that is a shock!

Hair and nails polished bright,
Make the design that is right.
AshLynn Renfro, Grade 5
Coffeen Elementary School, IL

Snow

S itting in the window watching the snow
N othing to do but wait
O ther children play outside
W inter is cold and you can get frostbite
Kyle Cerven, Grade 5
St Daniel the Prophet School, IL

The Autumn of the Running River

I'm the running river
autumn has come
my body is flowing
like a nice wind
upon the ruffles of rocks
in my body
trees surround me for miles
autumn is here
more rocks beside me
I love this…
the colorful, peaceful, and beautiful
rocky hillside
I love the world in my picture.
Hannah Outcalt, Grade 6
Northwood Elementary School, IN

The Man and the Mouse

There once was a man,
Whose name was Dan.
He lived in a house,
That had a mouse.
But Dan had a plan and named him Stan.
Kyle Roxas, Grade 4
St Peter Catholic School, IL

Cousins
My family and I get out of the car.
I smell the rain on the air.
I see a house with windows of gold
From the sunset shining bright.
I see trees, guardians of the house,
Leaning in on their precious treasure.
AAH!
A cry shatters the silence as my cousins sprint towards me.
I look up.
A mirage I think.
Tears fill my eyes
As I feel warm arms enveloping my neck
And I know this can be no dream
Amanda Perugini, Grade 5
Stanley Clark School, IN

Bob Is a Slob
There once was a man named Bob
He loved to eat corn on the cob
He put butter on it
Until his friend said "quit!"
"All you do is eat like a slob!"
Andrew Sum, Grade 5
Washington Township Elementary School, IN

Cheerleading
C an't slack off; you have to do your best
H aving the time of your life
E very practice gets you closer to perfection
E very day I think about cheering
R ah, Rah! The crowd gets loud
L eading the cheers
E ven basketball players join in
A lways trying to remember everything
D oing my best no matter what
I absolutely love it!
N ever giving up
G oing to games is my favorite part.
Mackenzie Flamion, Grade 6
Perry Central Elementary School, IN

Heaven
Right behind those pearly gates
The great kingdom of Heaven awaits
With its broad streets paved with gold
Any ticket to heaven is always sold
But, the thing is, you don't have to pay
I promise you, there is another way
A way to get to God's throne
The good thing is, you don't do it alone
Look to God, He'll help you out
All you have to do is give Him a shout
I hope, by now the way to Heaven is clear
Hold Jesus in your heart, near and dear
Megan Williams, Grade 6
North Knox East Elementary/Jr High School, IN

Delicate Snowflakes
D elicate snowflakes fall with the wind,
E specially mine that's always pinned.
L ovely to my Christmas tree,
I just hope she doesn't flee.
C ause she has a name and it's Dallamay,
A wesome if my parents would let her stay.
T wo more snowflakes not far behind,
E lsie and Frannie, hopefully my parents don't mind!

S now is falling to the ground,
N ow her friends have come to town.
O nly if they could stay,
W e could play and play all day.
F irst there's one, now there's more,
L ittle snowflakes at my door.
A s if the snowflake had a wing,
K indness spreads throughout and makes us sing.
E veryone will come back next year,
S ee you soon — my friends have turned into a tear.
Megan Keith, Grade 5
Dee Mack Intermediate School, IL

Eagle
Eagle flying in the sky
Hunting for its prey
Swooping dodging everything in its way
With its bird's eye view
It can see everything
When it finds its prey
It swoops down and eats it
An eagle in the sky
I wish I could join it in the sky
Elijah Palacios, Grade 5
Benjamin Franklin Elementary School, IN

I Like Pie
I like pie with lots of whipped topping
The kind that never seems to grow old
I'd eat it all day and I'd eat it all night
Chocolate pie with lots of whipped cream
My name is Ty, and I like pie

Other foods are great
But pie is the best out of all
And topples above the rest
Many kinds are amazing
Especially, chocolate satin with cookie crust
My name is Ty, and I like pie

Pie comes in many variations
Even in numbers 3.14
159265358979323
That's not even all
My name is Ty, and I like pi(e)
Tyler Andrew, Grade 6
Concord Ox Bow Elementary School, IN

My Family

I have a mom who teaches a class
and they are learning fast
My dad who plays the bass
he calls me a nut case
I have a sister who helps me so
she liked to sing me re do
My younger sister who is funny
she takes hold of people's money
We own a dog named Gunner
he used to be such a runner
Our two cats that like to purr
One of them has lots of fur
I have a hamster named Daisy
She can be really lazy!

Jazzmin Showalter, Grade 6
Francis Granger Middle School, IL

Dead Fish

Blue and black water,
A fish is so dry on land.
It is so hot here.

Austin Roosa, Grade 4
Rose Hamilton Elementary School, IN

I Wish I Was a Star

I wish I was a star,
Shinning like gold,
In the winter,
When it is cold.

Natalie Reyes, Grade 5
Edison Elementary School, IL

Red

Red is the petal of a rose.
Red is the stripes of a flag.
Red is a cold nose.
Red is a bow in a little girl's hair.
Red.

Carrie Troncin, Grade 5
Henryville Elementary School, IN

Fall

Leaves falling
On the ground,
Children raking them
Into a towering mound
Running and jumping
Into the piles
Nothing but leaves for
Miles and miles
Orange, red,
Yellow, and brown,
The colors of fall
Decorate our town.

Ana Acevedo, Grade 4
Bailly Elementary School, IN

My Snoopy Old Cat

My snoopy old cat
whenever we turn our backs,
he always gets on the counter and gets into our food…(Arrrgh!)

My snoopy old cat
is going to get caught some day 'cause he always gets out
and goes into our neighbors backyard…(Stupid cat!)

My snoopy old cat
Drives me crazy, but I like him like that…(Aughh!)

Tommy Koranda, Grade 5
Allen J. Warren Elementary School, IN

Sweet Smell of Autumn

Mist rising off the lake,
I wake to trees on fire.
Red, gold, amber, and orange.
A cool breeze and the smell of pine, oak, aspen, and a light touch of maple syrup.
This is the smell of autumn.

Billy Bartels, Grade 6
Stanley Clark School, IN

Mercury

M ercury is a planet with
E xtreme temperatures, that can
R each up to 800F and down to -290F. There is so much heat and
C old because there is no atmosphere.
     Mercury has no water except the water frozen in craters.
     You would never want to live there,
U nless you could feed off of the 70% iron core. Mercury is named after the
R oman god of thievery, travel, and commerce. Also, can
Y ou believe that Mercury has a crater, called the Caloris Basin,
     That is 1,300 kilometers wide!

Steven Swanson, Grade 6
Pinewood Elementary School, IN

Ferocious Ferrets

F erocious but cunning.
E ats and hunts for its young.
R eally rare in the wilderness.
O utstanding animals.
C unning when traveling.
I ndiana is not its home.
O ut of sight the second you see it.
U nfriendly, only when spooked.
S ometimes small but usually medium.

F errets were descended from the polecat.
E veryone should respect, not kill it.
R eally, some animals like badgers, weasels, and stouts are related.
R unning a nest is the mom's main job.
E ven a ferret has feelings.
T hey are someone too.
S o next time you see one remember this!

Luther Rice, Grade 4
Stonegate Elementary School, IN

Now and Then

Now and then, we have so much to do.
Now and then, there is not a clue…
That we have a limit to how far we can go!
Without help, our Earth may disappear.
So help the people between now and then
That litter, pollute, and don't care when…
The Earth may disappear.
We don't know…so help everyone between now and then.
We can do so much more to save our Earth
Between now and then.

Emma Mulloy, Grade 4
Peoria Academy, IL

Mercury

M ercury is the second hottest planet in the
E ntire Solar System. Temperatures can
R each 800F. At night, it
C ould reach -290F. It is cold enough that
U nder shadowed craters ice could exist. Mercury's
R evolution is only 88 days, which means
Y ou would be a lot older on Mercury!

Colton Reeves, Grade 6
Pinewood Elementary School, IN

Miracles Happen Every Day

I think you'll all agree
that everything is not what it seems
and there's a magical world of possibilities.
Don't you find it strange
that there's a lot of snowing range?
and that every single flake is different?
From the falling of the rain
to the movement of a train
to gravity itself
electricity should be powerful.
Even wood made into your bookshelf!
Because,
flowers grow
lungs blow
OH NO!
Don't you see that
from the human body
to Hudson Bay
miracles happen every day.
I think you'll find it safe to say
miracles happen every day.

Connor Olen, Grade 5
Keystone Montessori School, IL

Beautiful Days

Roses are red, violets are blue,
I like playing in the summertime, maybe so do you?
I like school, homework is okay,
but I like to think every day is a beautiful day.

Eric Vandeloo, Grade 6
All Saints Academy, IL

Leopards

spotted, tan, black, cat
beautiful, fast animal
dangerous, creature

Lauren Wilgus, Grade 5
Washington Township Elementary School, IN

Winter

Winter, winter
Snow drifts and snow balls,
Snow ball fights and fun
Winter, winter, how beautiful it is!
Sledding down Hackleberry Hill,
Slipping and sliding, how fun it is.
Snow plowing, opening gifts on Christmas Day.
Watching kids play in the snow today.

Evan Brown, Grade 4
St Matthew School, IL

Penguin

Orange fletched faces
Embrace two petaled flowers, which unfurl to devour the air
A black jacket egg, bearing flatfoot sneakers
Waddles towards the sea
Drunken lurching, headfirst plunge
Eruption

Drowned flames twirl, around the peaked body
Under the flat white sky
Swimming along
With man's metal fire
Metal wing, feathered wing,
Twisting tempests side by side

A silver sliver flicks
Tugged toward the fish by its own mind's chain
The tempest rises, catching its prey in its winds
No longer a flower, a mountain, summit divide
Devours, ensnares

The tempest spent, magma cooled
Washes up on land
Again to struggle, again to slip
Again to reach the sea

Davis Zhang, Grade 5
Highlands Elementary School, IL

The Carnival

I am at the carnival!
I am about to go on a superb ride.
I hear all the cracks and hisses the roller coaster makes.
Seeing how fast is goes just astounds me.
I smell sweet things such as lemonade
And some less pleasant smells such as smoke.
I am so excited to go on the ride I just can't wait anymore!

Evan Todd, Grade 5
Stanley Clark School, IN

When I Am Happy

When I am happy
I feel like
A dove flying in the sky

When I am sad
I feel like a dog
Abandoned

When I am nervous
I feel like a baseball player
Waiting to hit a home run

When I am tired
I feel like a bear
Hibernating

When I am awake
I feel like a hummingbird
Full of energy

Mitchell Dunn, Grade 6
Dee Mack Intermediate School, IL

Autumn

Autumn
Restless leaves
Twisting and twirling
Ready to float down
Fall

Natalie Trail, Grade 4
Bailly Elementary School, IN

Deer Hunting

Sitting there,
Waiting, hoping
Hoping for that perfect deer
The deer you saw last week
That perfect short brown hair
The perfect antlers
That perfect venison
Then I see it,
But,
I can't shoot,
Because it's perfect!

Nathan Shaw, Grade 5
Perry Central Elementary School, IN

Autumn

Autumn leaves are falling from the sky;
As I look up, I see a rainbow of colors:
   red, orange, yellow, and brown.
I can hear the crackling leaves —
   beneath my toes.
I can taste the crispy, autumn air;
It is truly fall.

Athena Palmer, Grade 6
St Paul Elementary School, IL

Frolicking Foals

Foals run and dance
They drag you into a trance
As they jump and leap
Sneaking up without a peep

They're full of sneaky little tricks
Like a few little kicks
After this they guzzle milk
Soon their coats will feel like silk

Mariel Carozza, Grade 4
Stonegate Elementary School, IN

Winter Day

It's winter day
It's winter day
Kids play outside,
Throwing snowballs,
Building houses.
When it's cold outside,
They go inside,
Watch snow movies,
Have cocoa,
And hang out in their pajamas.
It's winter day
It's winter day

K'tyah Point du Jour, Grade 4
Lincoln Elementary School, IL

Recess and You

Recess
fun, energetic
running, jumping, yelling
balls, bars, slides, playground
playing, ending, exciting
colorful, loud
homework

Will Vavrin, Grade 4
St Matthew School, IL

In the Garden

Plow up the garden,
It's a busy time of year,
Plant a seed to grow.

Reilly Embry, Grade 4
Veale Elementary School, IN

Liberty

L ives taken away
I nnocent American lives taken
B uildings crashing down
E veryone running away
R escuers trapped in ruins
T win towers demolished
Y oung ones crying for parents

Aubrey Larkin, Grade 6
Carl Sandburg Middle School, IL

The Sun

The sun's scorching rays
Bright light, blinding my eyes, blazing
Magnificent sunsets are romantic…

Julissa Perez, Grade 6
Jane Addams Elementary School, IL

Joe the Mouse

I live in a house,
with a mouse named Joe.
I really wish he would GO!!!!!
So I told Joe he could stay,
But for only one more day.
And on that Christmas day.
The mouse named Joe wouldn't GO!!!!!

Jaynee Albers, Grade 6
All Saints Academy, IL

Likes and Dislikes

I like reading,
not biographies,
I like brownies,
not with peanut butter,
I like writing,
but no essays,
I love Webkinz,
but not typing,
I like crafts,
without such a mess,
I love animals,
but no snakes,
I like strawberries,
but not strawberry milk,
I like Flat Top Grill,
but keep away the rice,
I like winter,
but no the cold,
I love DI,
but not losing.

Valerie Pope, Grade 5
Churubusco Elementary School, IN

Winter

I get to play in the snow,
I get to slide on ice.
You get to throw snowballs,
But that's not nice.

You get cold and shiver,
Until it goes away.
The sun melts the snow
So we can play.

When it goes you will say,
"Yay for the day."

Brianna Snyder, Grade 5
Coffeen Elementary School, IL

I Like Pikachu

Pikachu is eat eat eating
His ap ap apple while he is in his tree
Wag wag wagging his tail as happily as ever.
Then he fell and I caught him.
And that's how we became friends and
That's how we got all the ba badge badges
and beat the In In Indigo Plato.

Justin Hicks, Grade 5
Gard Elementary School, IL

Flip-Flops

Winter's coming what will I do?
Guess I'll have to find a different shoe.
Flip-Flops in the heat are really neat.
Flip-Flops in the snow are dumb,
I know.
My toes would freeze…
I'd cough and sneeze…
I'll put them away for a nice spring day.

Kaitlyn Nelson, Grade 5
Benjamin Franklin Elementary School, IL

Friendship

Always by your side,
Happy to be along,
Make you laugh,
Make you cry,
Always know what's wrong

When the world seems to turn against you,
And nobody's there,
They never stop and think about not to care,
The good times you always share

You've seen each other grow,
Even though it may have never showed,
The tiny little fights you always had
That never made you mad

Your life has been shared,
With someone you love,
A someone not related,
But so close they could be,
And now you have wonderful childhood memories.

Rachel Uretzky, Grade 6
Peoria Academy, IL

Flower Girl

Velvety tan skin
Under a lace-covered dress as white as snow,
Circular halo filled with vivid roses,
Black hair without any strand out of place,
An anxious flower girl waits to drop pink daisies
Preparing for a wedding she will cherish.

Amber Furlano, Grade 6
Knox Community Middle School, IN

School Time

Math will hunt you down.
Science will experiment with your body.
Social Studies will tell George Washington
lies about you.
And recess will beat you up.
Believe in Yourself!

Mandy Peterson, Grade 4
Steele School, IL

I Can Make a Difference

I can make a difference by always giving my best.
With good, strong effort I may even surpass the rest.
I'm sure that I can pass all life's tests.
This I promise, I will do it with zest.

I can make a difference by helping my mother,
Especially with my newborn baby brother.
I can assist many others,
Just like I do for my loving mother.

I will also make a difference by truly sharing.
It's important to be tender and caring.
I can turn the volume of my radio down so it's not blaring.
I can also make a difference with the meals by preparing.

Ashley Gonzalez, Grade 5
Dee Mack Intermediate School, IL

A Silly Experience

This story might sound kind of silly,
Of my trip to Uncle Billy's.
He lives in a small house,
That can only be found,
If you stand upside down.
And when you walk onto the yard,
You'll see a bird who thinks he's a guard.
And in the bedrooms way up high,
That's were the horses lie.
And when you go down to the cellar,
You might see a dog named Old Yeller.
I'll always remember Uncle Billy.
And how his house was oh so silly!

Alyssa Kluth, Grade 4
St Matthew School, IL

America

America, America, the freest country on earth,
But was this country like this, even at its birth?
There's Columbus, Washington, Betsy Ross and more!
But who from this great country's past,
Am I really looking for?
It's not a specific person,
Or an event in America's time
It's just good ol' America,
And how she came to her prime.

Javon Goshay, Grade 5
Benjamin Franklin Elementary School, IN

Scary Teachers

pencils writing
pencils writing

doing work in our room
I hope we don't meet our doom

oh spare me teacher of our room
oh spare me teacher of our room
Noah Greenfield, Grade 5
Forreston Grade School, IL

If I Were a Cat

If I were a cat.
I would chase bees.
I would be a brat.
I would climb a tree.

If I were a cat.
I would slide down a hill.
I would chase a gnat.
I would play in a windmill.
Michael Crowley, Grade 5
Edison Elementary School, IL

Mares

Mares
Pretty, tame
Galloping, running, fun-loving
Mares are fun to ride
Horse
Shelby Morgason, Grade 6
Herrick Grade School, IL

My Dog

River
smart, funny
jumps, licks, smells
River bites a lot
beagle
Cameron Meade, Grade 4
Veale Elementary School, IN

Love, Hope, and Joy

Love is a great wonder,
Be true to love,
It is like a pot of gold
And you don't want to let go of it.

Hope is a wonderful surprise
A wonder of excitement

Joy is a great happiness
It's having a good time
And is a great amusement
Rachel Cox, Grade 6
St Patrick School, IN

Stay or Go

There is a white blanket of snow,
Outside the window shows,
There is some ice,
So you better think twice,
'Should you stay or should you go?'
Chris Millan, Grade 5
St Peter Catholic School, IL

My Brother's Work

My big brother works
at Purina and he is
really, really good.
Hunter Pruitt, Grade 4
Rose Hamilton Elementary School, IN

Cookie

Cookie
Cute, cuddly
Runs, barks, eats
Happy, Mad, Loving, Trying
Dog
Anais Zuñiga-Lopez, Grade 5
Edison Elementary School, IL

Fred

There once was a short man named Fred
He liked to eat stale bread
He ate some with mold
And so it was told
He was found dead in his shed.
Brady Robinson, Grade 5
Gard Elementary School, IL

A Tale Untold

In a forest
Laden with trees
A shadow lurks
With no unease
The evil rises
Goes throughout the land
Turning trees to rocks
And people to slaves, as dull as sand
How it happened
Nobody knew
But then a hero
Overthrew
Swords clashing
It happened fast
The end of the evil
Was here at last
So now we say
Our story ends
But truly,
It only just begins
Sonia Thosar, Grade 6
Daniel Wright Jr High School, IL

At the Ballet

On one snowy night,
When all the dancers' hearts are beating,
The crowd takes their seats
Smitten by the beauty of the scene
'Tis hard to keep steady
A canopy of red
Slowly rises and is hidden,
The music then plays
Just like that, it begins
Their grace and poise so fine
"I can't wait for my turn
For my chance to shine!"
Again and again
Until the curtain falls one last time
The dancers all bow
Roses sail through the sky
Everyone rises
Dreamers part sadly
Until the next time
At the ballet.
Katie Kennedy, Grade 5
Peter M Gombert Elementary School, IL

Basketball

I love to play basketball
on a basketball court
in the middle of the day
because I love to do it.
Hailey Horsley, Grade 6
Perry Central Elementary School, IN

Summer/Winter

Summer
Hot, humid
Swimming, diving, falling
Sunshine, heat, cold, snow
Sledding, snowboarding, snowing
Cold, windy
Winter
Wayne South, Grade 6
Herrick Grade School, IL

Chips

Hard, crisp, and full of salt,
I love them with a chocolate malt.

Eat them with your favorite lunch,
one at a time munch, munch, munch.

Put in a bag and compressed,
out of everything they're the best.

You hear a crunch here and there,
they're a great snack everywhere.
Eddie Dusik, Grade 5
St Daniel the Prophet School, IL

I Am

I am Mrs. Personality and a funny energetic girl.
I wonder if I could ever be a comedian.
I hear the screaming of the stars in the big blue sky.
I see my teachers talking on and on.
I want to be a nice, funny, but smart girl.
I am Mrs. Personality and a funny energetic girl.

I pretend to be taller than the tallest person in the world.
I feel like some tiny ant.
I touch the wind on my fingers
I worry about how long the world will last.
I cry when I think of missing my brother, Jon Teer.
I am Mrs. Personality and a funny energetic girl.

I understand that Kyleigh Paul is a great friend.
I say never give up.
I dream about being a girl football player.
I try to do better in volleyball.
I hope I achieve to go to college.
I am Mrs. Personality and a funny energetic girl.

Cherish Elizabeth Scott, Grade 6
Helfrich Park Middle School, IN

Bats

Bats are black shooting stars that fly all night.
Shooting here and swooping there every night.
Sleeping during the day and flying at night.
Shooting here and swooping there every night.

Kylie Middleton, Grade 4
Bright Elementary School, IN

Christmas

Christmas is presents.
Smelling cookies and milk.
Seeing ornaments on Christmas trees.
I hear the jingle bells on Santa's sleigh.
Santa and his deer are on my roof.
I hope he will give me lots of presents
Christmas is over and another one has just begun.
I can't wait till another one comes again.

Kirsten Chase, Grade 4
Meadow Lane School, IL

The Ocean

The Ocean is a giant home
Where schools of fishes freely roam.
She teaches lobsters all to share,
And treats the shrimp with tender care.
When the sharks begin to fight,
She makes them stay in bed all night.
She guides the clams to clean their room,
While listening to the orca's tune.
And when the sun turns out his light,
She bids them all a sweet "Goodnight!"

Mrs. May's Poetry & Calligraphy Class, Grade 5
The Learning Vine, IL

Sledding

As I haul my way up
I see buckets of snowflakes
Quietly cascading from the rooftops
Onto the white blanket
It joins the pack
Woah!! I am already at the top of the hill
As I grab onto the sled I push forward
I get a good but not great push off
Sometimes that is costly
I turn my sled right toward the ramp
I hit the ramp and my sled flies up 2 1/2 feet
As I gain control
I think I am flying as I see more snow
On the rooftops
Gently cascading
But I have to concentrate
So I don't crash
As I slow and I stop
I watch the snowflakes cascading
And dropping into the pack

Jaco Chandra, Grade 5
Walker Elementary School, IL

Dolores

Dolores, Dolores
Loved Jack Morris
She loved to see him so
And then one day
The sky turned gray
And Jack Morris did not know
Then the next day unfortunately
The church bells were ringing loud
Then Dolores soon found out
Jack Morris was not found
In the church she looked inside
To find the casket laid
And then Dolores soon found out
He was going to the grave
Two days later he was found
Alive and very safe
And then he asked everyone
"Is this one for my grave?"
"Yes it is," said everyone "Sorry for the trouble.
Maybe next time in a storm
You'll come back on the double."

Cheyenne Oseguera, Grade 6
Holy Family Catholic School, IL

People

People are nice and people are mean,
People are gentle and people are rough,
People are busy and people are not,
People have fun and some people can't,
But we are still the same.

Kyle Nixon, Grade 5
Booth Tarkington Elementary School, IL

Volleyball

Volleyball — Volleyball,
Is my sport.
I love the game,
On the court.

We love to bump,
We love to set.
We love to spike,
It over the net.

I serve the ball,
In your place.
Hoping you'll miss,
So I get an ace!!!!

Alysha Terrell, Grade 5
Dee Mack Intermediate School, IL

Silver Fox

Squinted eyes ready to attack,
Sharp teeth ready to kill,
Pointed nose used to find food,
Huge ears listening to footsteps.
Fur flowing in the wind,
Strong legs moving like lightning —
Predator fox creeping up on its prey.

Dakota Trent, Grade 6
Knox Community Middle School, IN

My Cheeses

Delicious cheeses for me.
Fresh, tasty, snacks.
Healthy cheeses for only me.

Leslie Marquez, Grade 4
Jane Addams Elementary School, IL

Teachers and Students

Teachers
pretty, teach
helping, caring, loving
board, paper, desk, pencils
funny, messy, careful
boys, girls
Students

Nia Cousins, Grade 4
Meadow Lane School, IL

Dog/Cat

Dog
Black, big
Play, dig, bark
Toy, bone, toy, mice
Play, run, sleep
Small, orange
Cat

Emily Vondras, Grade 5
Edison Elementary School, IL

The Four Seasons

The best season of the year, summer.
Once it's there, there's no such place as school.
Hot, sunny warm days tempt you to jump in your neighborhood pool. Splash!
The water feels so soothing to your skin.
When you get out of the water you hear the music of bugs buzzing in your ear.
But then from night to morn, the leaves turn green to gold.
You realize you'll have to go back to the no such place, school.
The cold autumn breeze brings chills all over your body.
Falling leaves blow softly in the breeze.
Quietly, gently, the golden leaves flow down to the ground.
The trees turn gold to bare.
The fresh blanket of snow, completely untouched,
Hear it, it's calling you to play.
It's fluffy and soft you love everything about it.
You see the snow thawing here and there, it makes you cry.
But wait you see the season of rebirth on the horizon, spring!
You remember spring is when flowers bloom.
Spring is also when you have two weeks off from school for spring break.
But be careful you may catch a bit of spring fever.
Since, spring is the season of rebirth, not just for plants but for us too.
The four seasons of the year may be the stages of your life.

Melissa Shea, Grade 6
Stanley Clark School, IN

Mars

M ars was named
A fter the Roman god of war. The two moons are not
R ound because
S cientists believe two meteorites collided and Deimos and Phobos broke off.

Nichole Besemer, Grade 6
Pinewood Elementary School, IN

The Big Hairy Monster

The big hairy monster is worse than a nightmare.
He hides in your closet and reaches for you with its big wrinkled fingers.
He is the most ugly thing you have ever seen and smelt.
If you ever get brave enough to have a peek you'll think you've seen my sister.

Brett Willing, Grade 6
Dakota Elementary School, IL

A Day at the Beach

I race through the beach!
Seagulls chasing me all the way
Flying through the beach,
I hear the waves crashing at the sandy shore,
People laughing at me,
And someone screaming at my cousins.
I look behind and see a flock of pure white seagulls chasing me,
My cousins running,
A bunch of strangers laughing at me,
And a ton of towels.
The soft white seagulls are so beautiful,
But also very loud in my ear.
This is the perfect moment for me!

Devin Murphy, Grade 5
Stanley Clark School, IN

I Am

I am a special girl I hope my dreams come true
I wonder if I will live forever
I hear the wind rustling leaves
I see my great grandma
I want to be famous
I am a special girl I hope my dreams come true

I pretend I am a movie star
I feel I can do anything
I touch my mom and dad
I worry about my mom and dad
I cry when I think of my great grandma
I am a special girl I hope my dreams come true

I understand my teacher
I say I love my mom and dad
I dream of my family
I try to do good things
I hope my mom and dad will never die
I am a special girl I hope my dreams come true

Megan Walling, Grade 6
Helfrich Park Middle School, IN

Veterans

Our nation called you veterans
And, we salute you veterans of war
Men to arms fighting for our country
Our nation calls for men like you
Supporting our belief and freedom
You, veterans supported us in wars
World War I, you fought never giving up
World War II, you fought until your last breath
Not like a coward
but like a man
Like a nation united
Lightning flashed but you fought on
Caring about others
Caring about our country
Longing for home, but still fighting
You fought with the possibility you might die
We depended on you
What would we have done without you?
Our country would have been nothing without you
Like an army you fought
How much we owe for your sacrifice

Cammille Go, Grade 5
Highlands Elementary School, IL

Horses

I wake from a soft, standing sleep
I prance through the wet, moist grass
The crisp morning air blows across my back
I watch the sun rise in the distance
Life is wonderful

Kevin Thornton, Grade 6
Sacred Heart Elementary School, IL

Soccer Ball

A soccer ball is round.
It is usually checked with
black and white pentagons.
Mia Hamm, a famous athlete, loved soccer.
Everybody should like soccer.
Do you like soccer?
I do!

Katie Slabach, Grade 4
Concord Ox Bow Elementary School, IN

An Amazing Sight

As I walked down the path
I glanced at a puddle
Crickets, looking as if they are taking a bath
All in a tight huddle
The tree's leaves dancing in the air
The waterfall crashing gently
A tree holding more than one pear
A caterpillar slithering around, oh so nicely
Many, many things here
So beautiful, gentle, or fierce
I wonder how God made it
I really, really do
Now I see a bird, a cardinal
Feeding a red worm
To its child
Curled up in the nest of twigs
The background sounds soothing and annoying
CRASSSHHHH, SSSSsssss, peck, peck, peck, chirp, chirp
Now I have to go
But I will always come back
To see this amazing show

Teresa Franks, Grade 5
St Peter Catholic School, IL

Drugs Can Destroy Dreams...

When I look at my future I see myself,
Always thinking about my health.
Making choices that keep my senses strong,
Having sense enough to know right from wrong.

Don't get me wrong I want to have fun,
To be the life of the party I'm the one.
Saying no to drugs is what I would do,
Doing drugs is bad I think you should say no too.

Paige Cottingham, Grade 5
Dee Mack Intermediate School, IL

A Day at the Beach

The beach
Enjoyable, noisy
Sunbathing, entertaining, exhausting
Relaxing under the umbrella
Lakefront

Sarah Arrigo, Grade 5
Washington Township Elementary School, IN

The World

The world
Is like a colorful bouncy ball
The world is a place to be
The world is where not to hate
The world was created by God
In seven days
For six days God worked
And on the seventh he rests
Thank God
For what He made.

Lisa Alvarado, Grade 6
Christian Life Schools, IL

Sixth Grade

Sixth grade is a roller coaster,
With many twists and turns.
Although sixth grade is fun,
You get homework by the ton.
We have a lot of classes,
And we always need hall passes.
We like to laugh and giggle,
And in our seats we wiggle.
Our teachers lay down the rules,
And you must have the proper tools.
In sixth grade,
You have it made.

Tiffany Groen, Grade 6
Crown Point Christian School, IN

Football

Life lessons
Good sportsmanship, respect
Temperament, determination, desire
Practice makes you better
A future in the NFL
Football

Tray Ottinger, Grade 6
Tri-West Middle School, IN

Dogs

Dogs are really fun!
They are really really cool
I really love them!

Skylar Kirkman, Grade 4
Rose Hamilton Elementary School, IN

Mom

Mom
Nice and friendly
Caring and loving
Thoughtful, lovable, cool and great
Sharing, working, cleaning
Fun and happy
Dad

Fernando Singh, Grade 4
Village Elementary School, IL

Rain

Rain tastes like water.
rain feels like wet beads.
rain sounds like a kitchen sink.
rain looks like clear circles.
rain smells like nothing.
I love rain!

Isabella Rossi, Grade 4
St Matthew School, IL

Sea

When we go to the sea,
The sight fills me with glee.

We see a lot of shells,
And the sea's foaming swells.

The sea is filled with wonder,
Things for us to ponder.

Some fish are just floating,
Almost like they're gloating.

As the beach says good-bye,
We walk home with a sigh.

Austin Linne, Grade 6
Perry Central Elementary School, IN

Hog

It rolls happily in mud;
it has a snout,
but it is not a pig.

Isaiah Michaels, Grade 4
Rose Hamilton Elementary School, IN

The Feelings of Me

When I am sad
I feel like a toy
That has been lost and forgotten

When I am afraid
I feel like an ant
Hiding from the rain

When I am nervous
I feel like a thief
Waiting to get caught

When I am angry
I feel like a teapot
Ready to explode

When I am shocked
I feel like a lion
Whose meat has been stolen

Joshua Ludwig, Grade 6
Dee Mack Intermediate School, IL

Nature

The sky is blue
The bird calls coo

Life goes on without a sound
round and round and round

Ooh says the owl
Moo calls the cow

Life goes on without a sound
Round and round and round

Evan Reese, Grade 6
South Middle School, IL

Grandma

Grandma, grandma, grandma
Sweet grandma
Loving grandma
Caring, thoughtful, giving grandma
Reliable, truthful, friendly grandma
Last of all, best of all
My grandma

James Brian Hayden Jr., Grade 5
St Jude Catholic School, IN

The Race of Life

On your mark, get set go!
It's the start of the race.
Everyone's in it,
I have to keep a good pace.
I can hear my heart pound,
A few laps, hurdles, and a few stumbles.
I can't give up, I'm almost there,
I can't let my chance crumble.
The finish line is in sight,
And I'm almost there.
I'm getting closer with each step,
I have no more doubt, no more fear.
I finally crossed the finish line,
Through all the pain and strife,
I was tough as iron,
I finished the race of life.

Camille Garvida, Grade 6
Christian Life Schools, IL

My Beard

My beard is growing longer
It's down to my knees.
My beard is growing longer
It's down to my feet.
My beard is growing longer
It's down to my toes.
My beard is growing longer,
I think it's time for a shave!

Maggie Monahan, Grade 4
St Matthew School, IL

Mom

The best mom that a kid could ever dream of!

Hair like chestnut with crimson highlights that glow.
Her petite height that makes her so pretty
A face so stunning that it sparkles

Always grinning and smiling
After work she does everything peacefully
She cooks and prepares food like a real chef

We like to go shopping together
Talking and calling people always works for us
We like to watch romantic movies together

When I'm by my mom I feel safe
When she is around I feel happier
I feel that she will always be there for me!
I love you mom!

Nikita Patel, Grade 5
Booth Tarkington Elementary School, IL

Winter Day

W onderful, wailing, cold weather on a wintry day.
I cicles sitting on the cars in the driveway.
N othing like hot chocolate to warm you up.
T ogether families celebrate Christmas for a time to enjoy.
E veryone gathers around the roaring fire as they open presents.
R osy red cheeks from the freezing air outside.

D azzling, beautiful, sparkly snow like a diamond on a ring.
A nd a snowy owl in a snow-filled tree.
Y ou'll love a scorching cup of hot chocolate on a winter day.

CJ Ruffing, Grade 6
Corpus Christi Elementary School, IN

Wondrous Times of the Year

A pulchritudinous jack o'lanterns glow is bright
like my face after a long exhausting winter play.
Mom's fresh ham coming out of the oven
like animals coming out of their hibernation hole.
The taste of fresh pumpkin pie melting in my mouth
like that cold winter snow melting in my hand.
Children yelling with joy at the sight of grandma and grandpa,
like a bird chirping at the sight of food in the feeders
Leaves crunching under my bare feet after a long fall play
as candy crunches in my brother's mouth inside.

Kaleb Walker, Grade 5
Churubusco Elementary School, IN

Christmas

Christmas is a time for joy
When Santa brings that favorite toy.
If you spread Christmas cheer,
He will come again this year!

Jon Nugent, Grade 5
Washington Township Elementary School, IN

Marco Island Florida

I can smell that salty sea air
My mom's picnic basket
By our towels on the beach
The seagulls singing
The waves crashing
Hear all the children splashing in the water
My brother is one of them
The sand feels so warm to the touch
Icy cold water touches my feet
This is my favorite place
Marco Island Florida

Ian Kilby, Grade 6
Dee Mack Intermediate School, IL

Anna

Anna is such a lovely sight,
When she walks, she gives such light.

And when night comes, Anna just might,
Gaze at the stars through the mist of the night.

She blows in the breeze like an elegant kite,
To Anna, everything feels right.

August Windsor, Grade 5
Forreston Grade School, IL

Putting Up the Christmas Tree

Putting up the Christmas tree
I smell the tangy pine needles
and the hard, crisp, fresh trunk.

I see lights as bright as stars,
and ornaments as shimmery as
the fresh fallen snow.

I feel the wonderfully soft,
green needles that remind me of all
the good things in life, my family and friends.

Emma R. Willhardt, Grade 5
Lincoln Intermediate School, IL

School

There's a lot to do at my favorite school
Except that there's no swimming pool!
We work and play and like to run
So school is always very fun.
Our teacher isn't so very far,
So we can see her by bus or car.
Science is fun and math is too,
Do all these things seem fun to you?
We learn a lot, spacing and all,
But will we forget that and just go to the mall?
Outside we play lots of games
Half of my class should go into fame!

Troy D'Souza, Grade 5
St Peter Catholic School, IL

Can We Help Them

Can we help them, I said one day?
Could we help them in any way?
I will hold an auction to give.
All the money they need to live.
Whoever will donate the highest bids.
Will help us feed those starving kids.
We should give all we could.
Will it help, yes it should.
Giving to them should make them smile.
It should stay for quite a while.
Then I said to myself one day.
We helped those kids in quite a way.
We gave to them, yes we did.
We gave to those starving kids.

Gabriel Iriarte, Grade 6
St Matthias/Transfiguration School, IL

Families

Families, families, families
Big families
Small families
Friendly, caring, kind families
Joking, laughing, teasing families
Last of all, best of all
My family

Annie Schrader, Grade 5
St Jude Catholic School, IN

The Best Holiday

Stockings hung on the wall,
we're eating dinner one and all.
It's time for families to gather around,
and listen to a story on the ground.
It's hectic, it's crazy, it's fun in all ways,
to get ready for each one of the holidays.
But this is no ordinary holiday,
you can go out in the snow and play.
You will never want to miss this,
because this very day is Christmas!

Sarah Morrissey, Grade 6
Holy Family Catholic School, IL

My Angel

They call him annoying,
But to me he is not.
They call him a force of evil,
But to me he is a gift from heaven itself.
They claim that he is a criminal,
But I don't care.
They mean nothing to me,
Just rumors.
All that they say,
It doesn't matter,
Because he is my angel.

Natalie Rose Lara, Grade 6
Our Lady of Guadalupe School, IL

I Am

I am a caring and humorous chick that loves chocolate.
I wonder where I will stand with life in the future.
I hear the crowd cheering my name as I finish singing at my concert.
I see fans chanting my name "Alex! Alex!"
I want everything bad in the world to change.
I am a caring and humorous chick that loves chocolate.

I pretend I am not upset, though sometimes I really am.
I feel unworthy when I beg for clothes, but some people have nothing.
I touch my best friends' hearts when I tell them how great they are.
I worry that I won't make the volleyball tryouts.
I cry when I think about my grandma that passed away.
I am a caring and humorous chick that loves chocolate.

I understand that I can't be perfect.
I say negative things that I always regret.
I dream that my parents will never die.
I try to do my best no matter how hard it may seem.
I hope that my friends and I will never separate.
I am a caring and humorous chick that loves chocolate.

Alexandra Busch, Grade 6
Helfrich Park Middle School, IN

Christmas

Chocolate chip cookies with melted fudge brownies waters in my mouth
Christmas songs staying in my ears
Noisy shuffling presents
Cold air breezing against me never letting go
The snow tapping against my porch
Whiffing up bubbling apple pie in the oven

Kayla Stucky, Grade 4
Adams Central Elementary School, IN

God

God is somebody who watches from above,
One of his greatest gifts to us is love.
When we think there is no hope, he gives us hope,
He wants us to be perfect, but to learn he makes us cope.
He gives us miraculous miracles every day,
He gives them in a church or down by the bay.
He is there when we are born,
He is there when our hearts are torn.
When we are sad he is right there,
He knows we can do it, even though we think it's too hard to bear.
He is with us when we feel like a million bucks,
He is with us when we drive semi-trucks.
God is there when we have a bad day,
We think it will ruin our lives, but he knows it will be okay.
We are all children of God,
Even if our names are Tatiana or Todd.
When it is time we will meet thee,
He will let anyone in, even if you don't have a key.
He helps us when we are apart,
He holds the world in his heart.

Ashley Mathis, Grade 6
St Bede Elementary School, IL

About Me

My hair is like strawberries on a vine.
My eyes are like brown branches on an oak tree.
My freckles are like dots on a toad's back.
My smile is like the bright sun shining down.
My heart holds joy that is as pink as a rose.
I live in a small, rural town called Memphis.
I eat cheese pizza with gooey sauce and thick, soft crust.

Hunter Price, Grade 5
Henryville Elementary School, IN

Martin Luther King

M artin Luther King was a wise man.
A t an age he was a pastor.
R ejected by skin color.
T ime passed but life was still the same.
" **I** Have a Dream" was his speech.
N ever got angry.

L ead blacks to believe in love.
U sed his life to help people.
T ough but stood tall.
H e was born January 1929.
E ven though he was hated he loved.
R easoning with rights.

K ing was assassinated on April 4th 1968 in Memphis.
I nterested in helping people.
N ever hated whites.
G raduated from Morehouse College.

Toby Combs Jr., Grade 5
Benjamin Franklin Elementary School, IN

Rainbows of Fall

Scarlet, jade, and gold
leaves are rainbows without rain.
They're the heart of Fall.

Lydia Zheng, Grade 4
Frank H Hammond Elementary School, IN

The Perfect Game

I pass the ball to Kelly
the crowd screaming wild,
I tell Kelly to give it back
she does, the fans scream louder than ever before,
I can feel the muddy grass
the salt sweat that I feel in my mouth
the hard ball is at my feet
I pick up my foot
swing it forward,
kick the ball into the net,
the announcer says,
"The Indiana Invaders U11 girls
have won the NISL Tournament again."
Now that's the perfect game!

Jasmine Stahl, Grade 5
Stanley Clark School, IN

Video Games

Video games video games, you are so fun.
Video games video games, I play good with my thumb.
Video games video games, you take away my frown.
Video games video games, you never let me down.

Kevin Campos, Grade 5
St Daniel the Prophet School, IL

Hank (A Horse That Inspired Me)

When I looked into his eyes,
all I saw was beauty.
When I looked at his face,
all I saw was love and willingness.
When he looked at me,
it was like he was saying, please take me home.
The most beautiful thing ever stared into my eyes,
and said I won't survive here much longer.
I looked back at him and said,
I won't leave you,
you're coming home with me.
I'm telling you right now,
we will be Best Friends.
— Hank

Ava Demanes, Grade 6
Peoria Academy, IL

Summer

Once green grass,
Now a dry memoir,
Bright flowers dissolve at a touch
Over-cooked?
The summer sun must like his roses well done,
And his daisies crispy.
Falling raindrops evaporate.
Bless that mud,
now turned to a hard, cracked ground, and gritty dust.
Ice cream melts if you take it outside.
My poor, dear frozen treat!
How can I escape this heat?
I have been anticipating summer all year,
But now,
I just wish winter would reappear!

Marissa M. Byers, Grade 6
Glenwood Middle School, IL

Sitting in the Jungle

Sitting in the jungle
I'm all alone
There are no noises
Not even a twitch or sound
The clouds look like cotton candy
The grass looks like seaweed
The birds chirp and chirp
Everything in the jungle makes a lot of noise
Then everything is quiet again

Alyssa Mulder, Grade 6
Dakota Elementary School, IL

Mako Shark

M ako Sharks have up to 4 babies each year, and like mammals they nurse them.

A longfin Mako Shark can be as long as 12 feet 8 inches, and as short as 7 feet.

K inds of Mako Sharks like the longfin and shortfin have the same size of upper and lower lobes.

O ut of the far end of the ocean Mako Sharks can attack humans even if there's a net. They have dagger like teeth so they can cut through any type of net. The only type of net they can't cut through is an electric net, otherwise they would die.

S hortfin and longfin Makos can swim up to 22 mph. in short bursts. Their regular speed is 5-11 mph or lower.

H abitats of the Mako Sharks are in tropical areas like the coast of Florida and the Great Barrier Reef, the most common place they are found.

A ttractive colors to the Mako Shark, are mostly white and very light grey, because when seen the Mako Shark will attack with great power. The Mako Shark will also think it is food.

R elated to the Mako Shark is the Great White Shark, and they belong to the family of Mackerel Sharks, the 2 most feared sharks.

K inds of Mako Sharks eat almost any fish like herring and squid, also bigger fish like Swordfish.

Harsh Jhaveri, Grade 4
Frank H Hammond Elementary School, IN

Toy Poodle

Eyes that glisten like clear water on a sunny day peer upward towards the sky. Touch my moist, protruding sniffer. I'm like a yapping child that never stops complaining. I wear a curly, toasty, apricot colored fur coat. Watch me scamper across the floor with grace and delicacy. Mitten-like paws protect the pads on my feet. If you love and respect me, I will lick your face. You are my master and I will treasure you forever.

Gwen Elledge, Grade 4
Walden Elementary School, IL

Nature

A small field far from any civilization.
Water laps my hand as birds twitter in the tree above me, a peaceful feeling.
An untouched landscape dotted by trees with leaves rustling, shh, shh, shh.
The shores of a small lake studded by stones like jewels on a crown as a deer bends to drink.
A perfect moment.

Elizabeth Bays, Grade 5
Stanley Clark School, IN

Jellyfish

J ellyfish have another name, zooplankton.

E nemies of jellyfish are sea turtles, birds, and some types of fish.

L ocation for jellyfish can be all over the world but they are usually found in warm tropical waters.

L ength of jellyfish can be from pea size to six feet long.

Y ellow, brown, and red are their usual colors.

F eeding for jellyfish requires tricky minds for catching food. Some jellyfish have sticky gel that helps snag passing animals. Others have a strange glow that attracts other fish.

I nstead of fins like most sea creatures such as fish have, jellyfish have stingers. Even if it is dead, its stinger can still hurt you.

S ome species of jellyfish are sea blubbers, moon jellyfish, root-mouthed jellyfish, and the lion's main.

H iding is an important part of a jellyfish's life. Its light or clear color blends in with the water, making it harder for its enemies to see it.

Vishva Maniar, Grade 4
Frank H Hammond Elementary School, IN

Venus

V enus is the hottest planet in the Solar System. This is because heat can

E nter but not exit Venus' atmosphere. Venus is the only planet besides Mercury that does

N ot have its own natural satellite. Venus is the only planet whose orbit is almost

U tterly circular. Sometimes Venus passes between us and the

S un allowing us to see it.

Michael Linley, Grade 6
Pinewood Elementary School, IN

This Is Halloween

Beware of Halloween
don't scream on Halloween
the trolls will take your soul.
The grim reaper will take your blood
and you will fall in the mud.
This is Halloween.
Beware you're in for a scare on Halloween.
Trick or treat.

Marco Alegria, Grade 4
Coal City Intermediate School, IL

Maddie

Maddie
Silly, sweet, loud, and adorable
Relative of a silly sis
Lover of her binki, blankey, and teddy
Who feels like the ruler of the house, courageous,
and as smart as Albert Einstein
Who needs her binki, ice-cream, and mommy
Who fears thunder, lightning, and cop/ambulance cars
Who gives love, joy, and happiness
Who would love to see millions of binki gift cards,
freedom of nude, and more hair
Resident of her crib
Binki Lover

Larissa Ewing, Grade 6
Helfrich Park Middle School, IN

Friends

Friends are people who help you in any way!
They are understanding people who care.
When you are in a good mood, they want to make it even better.

Friends are lots of fun.
They stand up for you when you are being bullied.
Friends are there for you when you're down.
If you don't feel like talking, friends aren't mean to you.
They are honest and true.

Monica Vandermyde, Grade 5
William B Orenic Intermediate School, IL

Sleepy Head

I am in bed.
I am a sleepy head.

Sometimes in my dreams people might attack me
and yell fight, fight, fight!
That is why I might scream in the night.

I may sleepwalk.
I may sleep talk.

When I dream things may get very very odd.
That is why before I go to bed, I pray to God.

Alec Letcher, Grade 5
St Jude Catholic School, IN

Jupiter

J upiter, a giant, rolling ball with color of
U tmost brilliance is almost the brightest thing
P ainted in our sky. A bright red raging storm
I s pushing through the clouds. A dark coldness
T raps the large planet. An
E rie silence surrounds the place. Only small movements,
R ising, falling, swirling, blowing, silence.

Jessica Murillo, Grade 6
Pinewood Elementary School, IN

Candy

Candy is great.
I had so much it made me faint.
It is so good it's hard too explain.
If there was not candy I would go insane.

Dakota Fite, Grade 5
Washington Township Elementary School, IN

Dirt Bike Dreams

Dirt flying everywhere,
Some is soaring through the air.

Radical people attempting dares,
The wind in our faces we have no cares.

Flat tracking, jaw cracking, corner turning, motocross yearning,
I start to feel my arms burning.

Holding tight, living right,
One more turn and my bike takes flight.

Throttle the gas and come back around,
Rev it up for another round.

Look ahead and watch the ground,
Get ready to fly off the next dirt mound.

Brayden Phillips, Grade 5
Dee Mack Intermediate School, IL

A Bad Day

I went to the store to buy some gum,
But then the door shut on my thumb!
Then I cried as if I would die,
But later I just had to lie!

When I went home I tried to speak.
But then I saw that my voice was weak.
So I went to the doctor to check my throat,
He said that it was covered with a heavy coat!

He gave me some cough drops to smooth my voice,
I should have gotten blueberry, I had a choice!
Then I went home to take a rest,
And oh my gosh, I had hair on my chest!

Nate Woods, Grade 6
Milltown Elementary School, IN

Through the Meadow
Jumping through the meadow
Hopping on the trees
Exploring the nature
And jumping in the leaves
Cody Yontz, Grade 5
Pleasant Lake Elementary School, IN

An Ode to My Comb
Oh, little comb,
You have so many teeth.

I'm sure you know
They are much more useful than feet.

Oh, little comb,
When I use you I won't be lazy.

I'll use you for my hair
So it won't be crazy.

Oh, little comb,
I use you every
morning, noon, and night.

Because without you,
my hair would be a fright.
Ryan Tombers, Grade 5
Allen J. Warren Elementary School, IN

Family
F orever till the end.
A ll together.
M oments together.
I n everything together no matter what.
L ove each other.
Y ou be there for them for everything.
Dacota Schaad, Grade 6
Perry Central Elementary School, IN

Ice
My mom is nice.
She'll give you ice.
If you get a shot,
Don't cry little tot.
She pays the price.
Allison Nicole Albright, Grade 4
Shoals Elementary School, IN

Homework
Homework is not much fun,
But I know it has to be done.
So this poem I write,
In hopes that I might,
Get it done tonight.
Thomas Antonacci, Grade 6
All Saints Academy, IL

Christmas
C hrist
H appy people
R oaring fire
I cicles
S ongs
T ree
M ary
A n icy time of year
S oy milk
Devin Harris, Grade 4
Warren Central Elementary School, IN

Fall
Birds are not flying,
Animals are dying.
Hibernation is here,
Animals are gone until next year.
The cold nights are here,
Make sure you cover your ears.
Mornings are frosty,
Inside I'll be toasty.
Max Evitts, Grade 4
Chrisney Elementary School, IN

Winter
WINTER is full of snow.
White drops fall from the sky
making a white blanket
that covers the town.

I see
people outside
making snowmen
Kids playing
on the white blanket of snow

As the sun fades,
They go in the house
sit in front of the warm cozy fire
waiting for Saint Nick
to come to town
and drop off the toys.

On the days of Christmas
Kids race to the tree.
Smiles fill their faces
As they open their gifts!
Taylor Ross, Grade 5
Walker Elementary School, IL

Fall
Fall winds blow today.
Leaves turn different colors in fall.
Fall is a fun time.
Mark Cooper, Grade 4
Rose Hamilton Elementary School, IN

Sledding
Nice blanket of snow,
Sledding wildly down a mountain,
Speeding over big hills!

Zooom down the mountain,
Going past other sleds fast,
No one can dodge me! Yeah!

Faster than lightning,
I hover down the mountain,
Here comes the bottom.

As I finish up,
I get off early to climb,
Let's do it again!!!
Justin Prendergast, Grade 5
Walker Elementary School, IL

I Like
I like
Pizza
But not with anchovies
Boys
But not the nerds
Math
But not the long division
Language
But not writing
Art
But not clay
Hide-and-seek
But not outside
Ice cream
But not spinach
Hanging out with friends
But not just talking
Shopping
But not having any money
Briana Modezjewski, Grade 5
Churubusco Elementary School, IN

The Tornado
They are very big,
And they are very destructive,
So get to cover.
Austin Lowery, Grade 5
St Jude Catholic School, IN

My Day in the Fog
A terrible thing is fog
It made me fall over a log
I stumbled and tripped
And then my skirt ripped
I ran and got chased by a dog
Grace Brennan, Grade 6
Bethel Lutheran School, IL

I Like…

I like school but not writing, except in Mrs. Leedy's class
I like dogs but not mean ones
I like gum but not spicy gum
I like rain but not lightning
I like cars but not show cars
I like grapes but not seeds
I like cows but not bulls
I like football but not the Colts
I like pigs but not skinny ones
I like pizza but not peppers

Lane Wolfe, Grade 5
Churubusco Elementary School, IN

I Am

I am helpful and kind
I wonder who found Earth
I hear people calling my name
I see my rabbits
I want to remodel my whole house
I am helpful and kind

I pretend to be the princess of China
I feel that my grandpa is behind me
I touch my rabbit
I worry if I can go to middle school
I cry when something that's bad happens to my family
I am helpful and kind

I understand when people are sad because
It might have happened to me before
I say that I believe in dragons
I dream of being bit by a mouse

Linh Huynh, Grade 5
Walker Elementary School, IL

Ode to My Brother

Oh, brother,
you're one funny guy.

But one time
you made me fall and cry.

Oh, brother,
you make me so happy and well

But sometimes I feel like
I just want to tell

Oh, brother,
you're so thin and tall

I know you like to play baseball
Oh, brother, you're one nice guy
So thank you so much, I love you, goodbye.

Taylor Ecsy, Grade 5
Allen J. Warren Elementary School, IN

Break Out

You see yourself in the mirror and don't like what you see
And you think why me?
You think that your life is falling apart
You feel like you have been stabbed in the heart
But suddenly you feel,
The urge to be real,
No one knows how you feel inside
Feeling like you just want to hide
Tired of pretending to be someone you're not
Like you are not good enough with what you've got
Emotions break you day after day
And suddenly your heart turns grey
You finally break out of your shell
But no one can tell
You feel as though no one cares
But with one simple glare
Everyone cared

Melanie Balanon, Grade 6
St Matthias/Transfiguration School, IL

Fall

Colors everywhere,
A rainbow just gave birth,
The fresh smell of ripe apples
cooking, juicing and baking for
apple cider and pie,
A bunch of kids jamming up
the walkway to the park taking in the fresh air

An evil goddess blows of hats and
leaves your hair like it had been
hit by a hurricane,
Folks scared by spooktacular scenes and
sitting by the window, watching
the full moon, I scarf down
scrumptious moon cakes…

Kristine Xu, Grade 4
Highlands Elementary School, IL

Pi

Pi is numerical, exciting and intelligent.
Pi is mysterious and mathematical.
Π
I like Pi it makes me feel smart,
like I am larger than myself
Π
Pi is representative of 2 mathematical functions:
The ratio of the circumference of a circle to its diameter
and division (22 divided by 7)
Pi is parity
Π
My teacher told me to write this poem
And it is over
Now goodbye

John T. Lennon, Grade 5
Keystone Montessori School, IL

Dog

My dog
Is so silly
She loves to chase the leaves
My doggie likes to bark a lot
Lilly

Alexus Pelletiere, Grade 5
Edison Elementary School, IL

Tyler

Tyler
Funny, Dependable, Hardworking, Cool
Sibling of Kyle and Rylee
Who loves skateboarding and family
Who feels like skateboarding
Who needs a board and wheels
Who gives friendship
Who fears the Boogieman
Who would like to see Tony Hawk
My village Herrick
Black

Tyler Black, Grade 6
Herrick Grade School, IL

Sweet Breeze

The wind blew softly
As I crossed the old wooden bridge
Into the wide field.

I sniffed a flower
A baby deer pranced around
There was a sweet breeze.

Audrey VanMeter, Grade 5
Henryville Elementary School, IN

A Long Fall Ago

Jumping in the leaves,
Having fun,
Run around the house,

Playing tag,
Saying hello,
Hugs and kisses,
Family is coming,

Pick some dandelions,
Make a lot of wishes,
Make it a good one,

Because before you know it,
It will just crawl up and go,
That's right,

It's gone,
It has up and ran away.

Haley Squiers, Grade 5
South Elementary School, IL

Fall Is...

Fall is fun because of all the leaves you get to rake up.
Fall is great because you get to go trick-or-treating because of Halloween.
Fall is full of colorful leaves falling from big and small trees.
Fall is wearing fluffy coats and clothes.
That is why I like having fall weather.

Colten Freeman, Grade 5
South Elementary School, IL

What the Wind Whispers

It's amazing what you hear when you listen to the wind.
You may hear secrets that winter is coming.
And that fall has somewhere else to be.
It's remarkable what you hear when you listen to the drip of the melting icicles.
You may hear that the spring is marching towards us.
And that winter has important appointments.
It's miraculous what you hear when you listen to the wolves howling at the moon.
You may hear that summer is charging at us, and spring is saying farewell.
You may hear a lot of things but that doesn't mean they're true.

Isabel Griffin, Grade 5
Walker Elementary School, IL

Birds

Birds, loving, caring and cool.
Wild birds have their own pool.
Different shapes, sizes, and colors,
The males and females work together to build a nest.
Red, white, yellow, or blue,
They are loved by you and me.
Some birds fly over the sea.
They chirp, cheep, squawk, and tweet,
That is what makes them sweet.
Their black, beady eyes so mournful,
This is what makes them hard to resist buying.
So light and graceful, tiny feet,
Soaring gracefully in the light filled, blue sky.
When they eat seeds, grain, and wheat,
They sweep me off my feet.
Soft, oval shaped feathers, little heads, beaks, feet, tails, and nails,
The characteristics of any bird.
The most loving, caring creatures on Earth.

Mary Sim, Grade 5
St Peter Catholic School, IL

Around the Christmas Tree

Around the Christmas tree lay many special gifts
Around the Christmas tree lay the special memories
Outside lie all the special wonders
Outside lies the beautiful winter spirit
Inside the kids sit and await the moment
Inside the families stay close together
By the warm Christmas fire are all cold families
By the warm Christmas fire are the everlasting memories
Around the Christmas tree I think of those who aren't as lucky as me
Around the Christmas tree I pray for all those kids out there.

Stephanie Toepfer, Grade 6
Christian Life Schools, IL

Christmas

In my bed I lay half awake,
but my ears were open so I could hear
if Santa was coming near.
I heard Santa and ran down the stairs,
and found a big bag full of toys and bears.
Then I looked up and found Santa with his red nose,
and noticed his small silver glasses were starting to show.
The he quietly said,
"Hello little child! Now please will you go back to bed?"
I said, "It is you! It is you! It is really you!"
"You are the real Santa, and it is true!"
"Ok, but you have to keep it a secret."
"If you wake anyone up, you will not be able to keep it."
I promise with a smile.
"Merry Christmas child,
God loves you!"

Charlie Fast Horse, Grade 5
St Michael School, IN

Country Rock Connection/Radio Disney

Country Rock Connection
Movie stars and teen singers
Effervescent, exhilarating
Messages of love and friendship
Radio Disney

Micaela Bartley, Grade 6
Tri-West Middle School, IN

Friends

Friends can be nice
But, some can be mean.
One day you can be friends
And the next day, they're not seen.
It's confusing
It's not fun
Sometimes you cry in the end.
Then all is forgotten
And your friends again.
After awhile you realize
It's all worth the trouble
Cause
You always have somebody that has your back
You always have someone there for you
You laugh and you cry
Which makes friends all worth the while!

Shannen Maher, Grade 6
Daniel Wright Jr High School, IL

Sacrifice?

A leaf is never lonely.
Until fall comes.
Or until someone thinks it's smart to cut down a tree for a view.
So unless your life depends on it.
Please don't cut down trees.

Adrien Soto, Grade 5
Benjamin Franklin Elementary School, IL

I Am

I am a smart girl who loves to have fun
I wonder if my grandpa will get better
I hear the crowd cheering
I see butterflies flying around me
I want to see my poppy one more time
I am a smart girl who loves to have fun

I pretend to be funny to cheer up my friends
I feel my mom's love
I touch the sky when I dream
I worry about my family
I cry because my poppy died
I am a smart girl who loves to have fun

I understand my friends more than anyone
I say never judge a book by its cover
I dream about my life passing me by
I try harder each day
I hope I make the volleyball team
I am a smart girl who loves to have fun

Savannah Sittig, Grade 6
Helfrich Park Middle School, IN

Christopher Columbus

Good old Christopher Columbus,
Sailed the world without a compass.
He stuck a flag in the ground,
And then was homeward bound.

Adriauna Silva, Grade 5
Washington Township Elementary School, IN

Shopping

Going to Hollister
Spending all daddy's money
Buying purses
Spending all daddy's money
Going to Kohl's
Spending all daddy's money
Buying expensive clothes
Spending all daddy's money
Going to Coach
Spending all daddy's money
Buying groceries
Spending all my money

Cheyennena Althoff, Grade 5
North Knox East Elementary/Jr High School, IN

Peace

Peace is like a window
Letting sunshine in
And pushing out the war so
we are out of
misery
and sadness is no more.

Jessi Rogers, Grade 5
Benjamin Franklin Elementary School, IL

Football

"Down,"
"Set,"
"Hut."
Shoulder pads cracking.
Face masks hitting.
Cleats stomping,
Fans cheering.
Ball being caught.
Whistles blowing,
Refs talking.
Sirens going off.
Coaches yelling.
That's how games are WON!

Tyler Olsen, Grade 5
Henryville Elementary School, IN

Autumn

Autumn leaves are falling
I can hear the wind calling
As it blows through the trees
My whole body is at ease

I hear the birds tweet
Their song is really neat
The breeze went all wild
Then my whole body smiled

Samantha McCarty, Grade 4
Stonegate Elementary School, IN

Fall

Fall
Is colorful
Leaves falling down
Excited holiday, sorrowful end
Autumn

Alecia Gill, Grade 4
Bailly Elementary School, IN

Aiden

Aiden is very cute
He won't keep on his boots
He makes funny faces
He don't know how to tie his laces
He has a cute little suit.

Summer Stow, Grade 5
GCMS Elementary School, IL

A Special Someone

Love is a feeling
Friends have for one another
Love can be a giant heart beating
For someone close to you
Love is a fountain
Of friendship!

Katelynn M. Newcomer, Grade 5
Lincoln Intermediate School, IL

Leaves

I watched the leaves,
They blew in the breeze.
The leaves were falling from the trees.
Now they are on my sleeves.

Matt McGrath, Grade 4
Meadow Lane School, IL

Football Player

I am a boy who likes football
I wonder if I can be a football player
I hear the crowd roaring
I see lots of people
I want to be a football player
I am a boy who likes football

I pretend to throw the football
I feel like I am getting tackled
I touch the ball to win
I worry when I get tackled
I cry when I lose
I am a boy who likes football

I understand we need practice
I say I am the best football player
I dream to play with the Bears
I hope I can play in the NFL
I try to run fast
I am a boy who likes football

D'Angelo Carter, Grade 4
Meadow Lane School, IL

My Doggies

I love my doggies
Both Jack Russell Terriers
"Lick, lick" on my face.

Playful and gentle
Soft and sweet
Licking your face
It's all so neat!

Nicholas Dunlevy, Grade 5
Henryville Elementary School, IN

Fall

Bees are stinging
Leaves are falling.
Birds are flying.
Trees are dying.
Feet are flopping.
Moms are shopping.
People are mowing.
Wind is blowing.
Animals are getting food.
People are getting in a better mood.

Samuel Bedsole, Grade 4
Chrisney Elementary School, IN

Spring Time Is Here

Flowers sprouting,
birds are counting!
How many do you have?

Children playing ball outside,
can you feel the cool crisp air?
Cold spring wind whipping at your hair.

Snow is turning into slush,
no longer makes a delightful crush.
We no longer want snowball fights!

For now the season is SPRING!
So no more hats, coats, or boots,
no more mittens, fires, or frozen roots.

New life at every bend,
spring is now in full blast!
The signs of spring have all but passed!

Emily Berryman, Grade 6
St Joseph School, IN

Halloween

H aunted house
A lways on Oct. 31st
L ots of candy
L ots of spooks
O wls frightening eyes staring at you
W olves howls frighten me
E nter, if you dare
E verything is so spooky
N ever nice, always spooky

Cheyenne Davey, Grade 4
Bailly Elementary School, IN

Mouse

In a hole,
likes cheese,
In a wall,
beside me,
below me,
searches for cheese,
under the desk,
on the floor,
into the wall,
in my room,
A mouse — a mouse

Cody Teusch, Grade 5
Churubusco Elementary School, IN

Hunting

Waiting for the buck,
Cock my gun back to shoot buck
Watching the deer die

Triston Vetter, Grade 4
Adams Central Elementary School, IN

My Loving Parents

Who brought me into this world?
Who spends money on me,
Buying clothes and candy?
No one but my loving parents.

Who teaches me?
Who spends hours of their day with me?
Who works hard to provide food and shelter for me?
Only my loving parents.

I should thank them,
I know I sometimes fuss and fight,
And take all their love for granted.
So right now I will say,
"Thank you, Mom and Dad!"

Mary Lee Mayfield, Grade 6
A Beka Academy, IN

Kelsie Hirchak

Kelsie
Honest, friendly, clean, and athletic
Daughter of Kim and Mark sibling of Kylie and Jake
Lover of basketball, my family, and animals.
Who fears bad people,
dark places, and storms.
Who feels great, awesome, and excellent.
Who'd like to see Pink, her friend who moved away,
and Hannah Montana.
Resident of Highland Indiana in the United States
and the planet is Earth.
Who needs baby sister, golden retrievers
and her own room.
Hirchak

Kelsie Hirchak, Grade 5
Allen J. Warren Elementary School, IN

The Weather

When the weather is hot, we play a lot.
When the weather is cool, we go back to school.
When the weather is freezing, skiing and skating are pleasing.
When the weather is rainy, we stay inside and go zany.

Alex Castro-Montague, Grade 4
St Matthew School, IL

Snow Fairies

I went for a walk.
On a nice winter.
I saw white fairies,
Dance my way.
Who could they be?
I asked everyone,
I could see,
Their names are Snow
Well what do you know.

Morgan Loete, Grade 5
Benjamin Franklin Elementary School, IL

Snow

flaky white diamonds
crystallized water raining
shimmering like light

Korbin Hockman, Grade 5
Washington Township Elementary School, IN

Fall

It's fall and chilly outside
A slow breeze came by.
Halloween is near and
pumpkins are by.
Leaves are turning orange
and it's beautiful outside.
Thanksgiving is on its way.
It's time to let go and feel the breeze.
Jump in a pile of leaves or rake them all up.
Do something you could never imagine.

Allie Yanello, Grade 5
William B Orenic Intermediate School, IL

Me, Me, Me

My hair
is like the flipping of a dolphin.
My eyes
are like the hazel sky.
My hands
are like a little baby's hands.
My fingernails
are as white as the white puffy clouds.
My heart
holds warm and loving feelings that are pink
as a newborn baby's face.
I live in Indiana.
I love to eat
mac and cheese and steak.

Reagan Cory, Grade 5
Henryville Elementary School, IN

Trampoline

I love to jump on my trampoline
So high I touch the sky.
I fall back down to the Earth I know,
Then spring back up again.
I get ready to jump again;
I start to bounce really slow,
'Til I get higher and higher and higher —
'Til I touch the sky!
I come back down again
With a laugh and a smile,
Then jump right off
And say goodbye.
I'll see you again,
I say really quiet.
And off I am again!

Kailee Sabin, Grade 6
Cisne Middle School, IL

How You Know It's Christmas

When bells are ringing,
their merry beats,
And carolers singing,
down the streets…

When the lights are hung on high,
casting a warm glow,
And snow is falling from the sky,
a beauty for all to know…

When people are rushing all about,
with good intentions and care,
You will know without a doubt,
that Christmas is finally here.

Justin Ferenzi, Grade 5
St Daniel the Prophet School, IL

Football Rocks!

F ootball is the best!
O h, no! We are losing!
O h! The new player throws the ball!
T ouchdown! The score is 7-14!
B ang, bang, football players collide.
A tackle is made.
L unging for the fumbled ball,
L eaping and dashing for the touchdown!

Joshua White, Grade 5
Coffeen Elementary School, IL

Sadness

Sadness is a blanket of
cold chills running down my spine,
Tears of depression fill my eyes,
The world is sad, death is sad.

Whirling winds of cold darkness,
makes me cry
Tears of wet moist sadness.

Why does it happen?

Camille E. Cseri, Grade 4
Churubusco Elementary School, IN

Books

Books are strange
Books are great
Books exist in every state
Books have adventures
Just like you
Just like friends
Books have stories too
Look inside
Tell a friend
Then read it all over again

Mikayla Spires, Grade 6
Christian Life Schools, IL

Saturn

S aturn is named after the Roman god of
A griculture, Saturnus. Its biggest moon is
T itan; its smallest is Threymer. Saturn had not been discovered
U ntil 1610, by Galileo Galilei. Each of Saturn's seven
R ings are made of ice and rock. On Saturn, there is no day or
N ight; its average temperature is -218 degrees Fahrenheit (-139 degrees Celsius).

Allison Valentijn, Grade 6
Pinewood Elementary School, IN

Football

Football, football I used to hate you.
Now I'm throwing, catching and tackling too.
The quarterback says, "go, go, go," so I'm looking for that amazing throw.
I run and run to catch the ball; all the cheerleaders are at the mall.
The quarterback fakes left and goes right, I run and run with all my might.
Someone dives at him and misses.
All the girl blew him kisses!
Some kids are playing with a hacky-sack also watching the quarterback.
The quarterback is on a dodging spree, fans gasp at his ability!
He runs and runs.
Hey look there's nuns!
He winds back, the kids drop the hacky-sack.
He launches it! Ouch! A big hit!
The football flies through the air.
A fat guy eats a pear.
The ball comes straight to me and I catch it, the 40, the 50…
TOUCHDOWN!

AJ Rowe, Grade 6
Nancy Hanks Elementary School, IN

The First Snow of Winter

You wake up on the first snow of winter,
the window frozen cold.
The fire burning leaves and rotten wood,
I know that winter has begun.
You can see your breath and feel the snowballs on your frozen fingers.
The fire goes spark, pop, spark,
the hot and creamy soup is ready to eat.
Your family sits down around the fire and you know
the winter wonderland has begun.

Maggie Hartnagel, Grade 6
Stanley Clark School, IN

Oh, My Dear Volleyball

Oh my dear volleyball,
How brave and strong you are.
In a game, you invite us to hit and try as hard as we can.
Your braveness is amazing as you fly over the net like a trapeze artist.
Oh dear volleyball you don't complain when we hit hard,
and you have faith that we wouldn't hurt you.
Oh dear volleyball it just wouldn't be the same without you.
The beach ball is too light and the basketball is too heavy.
Never think that you're not the right ball, because you are.
Thank you, volleyball.

Paola Madrigal, Grade 5
Allen J. Warren Elementary School, IN

Thanksgiving

T hankfulness
H appiness
A ll around
N ice people
K ids having fun
S weet potatoes
G iving thanks
I love Thanksgiving
V egetables
I ndoors
N ever mean people
G etting good food

Chandler Chasko, Grade 5
Washington Township Elementary School, IN

Drowned Boat

Broken, bent and shattered,
Ice cold water swirling around
A boat cold and alone.
The Titanic stays with the fish
Under the ocean blue
Covered with sand and debris.
It was said to be unsinkable
But proven wrong and
Swallowed whole by the ocean
It sailed on.
And so it stays under the water to sleep
Remembering the parties and fun.
One iceberg did it all
To the Titanic.

Brandy Smith, Grade 6
Knox Community Middle School, IN

Soccer

Soccer is the best sport of all,
Running, kicking, passing the ball.
You have to work with your team,
And a goal will happen, or so it would seem.
The game is quick so you have to think fast,
Keep your eye on the ball, don't let anyone past.
Head for the goal as fast as you can,
Kick it with the strength of a man.
In the net and you will score,
The crowd goes crazy and yells for more.

Bobby Laski, Grade 5
St Daniel the Prophet School, IL

Christmas

Christmas is cookies and has a lot of snow
It's very white and has lots of Christmas trees
It is fun because it has a lot of presents
We put ornaments on the tree and lots of lights
We sled a lot
We build big snowmen

Randy Georges, Grade 4
Meadow Lane School, IL

The Tale of Troy

With an apple a tale is told —
This is a story that is very old!
Gods and goddesses on a great stone terrace,
And it all started with one named Eris.
If you can do a queen's abduction,
You will bring one world's destruction.
If you can see a pretty queen,
If you can see her silver sheen,
You will have some mighty trouble —
All that is left is just some rubble!

Jessica Earnhardt, Grade 5
Sycamore School, IN

St. Nick

I believe in St. Nick.
He is the man.
He knows the trick.
That's why I'm his biggest fan.

Delana Arme, Grade 5
Washington Township Elementary School, IN

Halloween

Leaves under my feet, crunch!
Falling gently all over,
Covering sidewalks, driveways, streets,
Bright, beautiful colors of red, orange, and brown.

Costumes of all different sizes, colors, and styles,
Trick-or-treaters running, giggling,
Shouting, "Trick-or-treat!"
Happy as strangers drop pieces of yummy treats in their bags.

The sun is setting,
Gorgeous colors of mixed orange,
As the moon rises,
And shines on all the children.

Soon, children are yawning,
Parents pick them up,
Carry them home for a new day to begin,
Of begging and whining for their Halloween candy.

Danielle DeSalvo, Grade 6
Thomas Dooley Elementary School, IL

Nature

The trees are just starting to get back their leaves
And the Evergreens are getting even greener.
The Junipers are coming out in a month
And the Honeysuckles will wait till later.
The water splashes up on the rocks.
The wind blows through the sun setting sky.
The birds fly by after their migration.
The squirrels are coming out of the trees filled with joy
To see the beautiful blue sky

Emily Stearn, Grade 4
Near North Montessori School, IL

Recess

School is ok
except on a beautiful day
you get very giddy
the teachers sometimes take pity
go out to recess they say

Joey Jacob, Grade 6
Bethel Lutheran School, IL

White

White is the snow on my snowman's toes
White is a plain piece of paper
White is a tissue I use on my nose
White is the sky in the winter.

Kyndall Wiley, Grade 5
Henryville Elementary School, IN

Really Friendly Halloween Creatures

On Halloween, mortals
Dress up as witches,
Ghosts and goblins and
All other Halloween
Creatures because when
It started the real
Halloween creatures
Roamed only on Halloween
And on all Hallow's Eve
Because mortals thought
That they were just
Dressing up and they
Only did on Halloween so
Mortals would not be
Scared of them when
The Halloween creatures
Died out and mortals
Took over Halloween.

Melanie Lael, Grade 5
Gard Elementary School, IL

All That!

Michael is pretty cool.
Jake is kinda girlie.
After I write this poem,
I'll give Cody a swirly.

Man, I'm good looking,
Boy I'm really hot.
Poems are for girls and
I'm pretty sure I'm not.

My teacher is mean.
You know I should maybe cut this,
I can tell you one thing,
This is anything but bliss.

Dyllan Bakker, Grade 6
Crown Point Christian School, IN

Action Jaxon

Action
Lover, hyper, sweet, dirty
Relative of 9 brothers and sisters
Lover of me, people, and his kennel
Who feels energetic, loved, and hyper
Who needs love, bedtime, and outside
Who fears being alone, not getting treats,
and Aunt Jamie yelling
Who gives love, friendship,
and understandment
Who would like to see birds,
fire hydrants, and kids
Resident of my heart
Jaxon

Sarah Thomason, Grade 6
Helfrich Park Middle School, IN

Spring

Spring
It was in the air.
It was very clear and here.
Spring came very fast.
Spring

Joel Parado, Grade 4
Neil Armstrong Elementary School, IL

If I Was a Soldier

If I was a soldier,
I'd go out to war.
I'd defend my country,
For four years or more.

If I was a soldier,
I would try to end the war.
I'd fight my best.
I might even get an award.

Julian Martinez, Grade 5
Edison Elementary School, IL

Fall

A crabby cousin
Bitter, but bright
She starts young
Chilling and dull
But time passes,
And she grows older
Not dull, but smoother
More exciting with
Crumpling paper
But time passes,
With no sounds
As she fades away
And she awaits,
For the next perfect day.

Christine Rogers, Grade 4
Highlands Elementary School, IL

Every Day

Every day that we do poems
I do pretty much the same thing.
I sit in my
Chair doing nothing
Trying to think of a topic
It's just really
Hard for me to think clearly.
I do try to look for a topic.
I really do try.

Cris Flores, Grade 5
Gard Elementary School, IL

Trace

There is a girl named Trace
She likes to go every place
She walks down the halls
She trips and falls
That is the end of Trace

Olivia Erickson, Grade 6
Bethel Lutheran School, IL

The Season Summer

Summer is beautiful!
The sun shines bright.
Swings slowly glide up and down.
Kids run around in the sun.
You see all the kids playing.
Everyone is playing.
All the flowers are bloomed.
The trees gently sway.
Enjoyable and lovable.
Wonderful green grass.
The smell of mowed grass.
I love summer!

Heather Little, Grade 6
Milltown Elementary School, IN

Witch

W atch the sky
I n the dark
T ill midnight
C reepy skeletons
H aunted houses!

Chance Szubryt, Grade 4
Bailly Elementary School, IN

Cardinals/Cubs

Cardinals
Fans, red
Winning, roaring, managing
Huge crowd, small crowd
Losing, booing, pitching
Fans, blue
Cubs

Justin Barnhill, Grade 6
Dee Mack Intermediate School, IL

Days at School

School is fine
Most of the time.

When we're on the playground,
Running around…

Jumping and hopping and acting like clowns.

But when the day is over, and we get on the bus,
We laugh and talk and sometimes fuss.

When we get home and everything seems fine,
We must start our HOMEWORK
And it dulls our mind!

Jessica Patterson, Grade 6
Hawthorne Scholastic Academy, IL

Color

C reative beams of light
O pen my eyes to the natural world around me.
L ight so radiant,
O ver mountains and hills.
R eminding me of a rainbow.

Heather Maue, Grade 6
All Saints Academy, IL

Fall, Fall

Fall, fall beautiful fall
Leaves falling off the trees
All different colors I see
Rake, rake, rake all day
It is such a beautiful sight.

Halloween time is coming
Everyone is getting ready
Costumes, family, decorations galore
Everyone is excited
Fall, fall beautiful fall

Lizzy Burrs, Grade 5
William B Orenic Intermediate School, IL

Me

B asketball is one of my favorite sports
R ighteous at soccer
E ndless fun every day
N ever give up on whatever I do
D oes not skate on ice
E very day is a great day
N obody should sin

W ould always try something new
O ften I play *Guitar Hero*
O utside playing with my friends
D o you like sports?

Brenden Wood, Grade 5
Washington Township Elementary School, IN

We Sparkle Like Stars

One by one, we are placed up on the
Christmas tree.
We are shiny like mirrors,
yet sparkle like the glamorous stars.
We guard the presents until Christmas Day,
we are excited to see
joy on people's faces.
As the night ends, the light dims, then
comes to complete darkness.
We show off our beauty,
and rest for the night.

Alyssa Tolentino, Grade 5
Walker Elementary School, IL

My Pet Snowball*

I made a snowball of snow, it was as perfect as could be.
I named him little Jimmy, and he played all day with me.

Once the day was over, we went inside the house
and next to me I made him a bed,
and a small pillow to lie his head.
Then I went over to the heater,
and turned it on full blast,
And in the morning I woke up to a small mess.

Little Jimmy was gone from his bed,
and all that was left was a small puddle.

Joe Peterson, Grade 4
Lincoln Elementary School, IL
*Inspired by Shel Silverstein

Fall

I see some leaves rustling around,
and a few birds flying south.
I hear some children's feet crunching on the crispy leaves,
and some birds chirping high up in the trees.
I feel the wind blowing through my blond hair.
I know it is fall because I can smell it in the air.

Anna Nisen, Grade 4
Concord Ox Bow Elementary School, IN

An Ode to Music

Oh dear music, I love you
You make me laugh when I'm ready to cry.

When we go to parties,
without you, no one would dance.

When I'm bored, you give me something to do

When I'm sad, happy, angry,
or annoyed, you help me get through.

Oh music, that's why I love you.

Kaitlyn Hayes, Grade 5
Allen J. Warren Elementary School, IN

Miss Kitty

There was a fat cat named Miss Kitty
Her friends thought she was so very witty
She talked to the birds
Who sang a few words
And together they sounded so pretty

Chris Hairgrove, Grade 5
Bethel Lutheran School, IL

Jelly Bean

My Guinea Pig's name is Jelly Bean, or
you could call her Jelly Belly.
Her belly is big and
sometimes it feels like jelly.
If I don't clean her cage
she can even get very smelly.

She's black and tan and mostly white
and when my friends see
her they say
What a beautiful sight,

I love her so much
such a cutie,
but when she
squeaks she makes
me looney.

Shannon Grasse, Grade 6
South Middle School, IL

A Beautiful Sight

As I walk down the trail,
I begin to see my campsite.
When I get to the river,
there I see fish swimming together.
I go by the fire because it's
getting crisp outside.
As I stand, smelling the smoke,
I think how nice it would be
to sleep under the stars.
I get my sleeping bag
and pillow ready.
I lie down.
Before I know it,
I see the stars all around me.
What a beautiful sight.

Katie Penzenik, Grade 6
Stanley Clark School, IN

Friends

Friends
They play with me.
Are nice to everyone
Help me study for a test.
Are nice

Naomi Stark, Grade 4
Warren Central Elementary School, IN

Penguins

They are fat and furry
They love to jump around the Arctic Sea
I know they're just black and white but they're very colorful to me!
They waddle like a boat walking back and forth.
They slide on their little bellies into the beautiful sea
To pass the time away I'd love to watch them slide and play!
I love to watch them dive into the beautiful ocean
Penguins are the best for me!

Kira I. Damewood, Grade 5
Lincoln Intermediate School, IL

Penguins

The penguins are birds in the sky.
Even though they cannot fly.
I love penguins.
They're soft and fuzzy.
They are also so, so funny!
Penguins live in an icy land and eat a lot of fish,
as many as they wish.
They slide on their bellies into the ocean.
They're so cute and small; it would be nice to get one for myself.
The penguins are so funny.
The penguins are so sweet.
Even though they waddle on their little tiny feet.

Rachel Martin, Grade 4
Meadow Lane School, IL

The Sounds of Autumn

"Have you ever listened to the sounds of Autumn?
Have you ever just stopped and listened to the leaves blowing in the breeze?
Next time you go outside just stop ant think of the things around you.
Listen to the neighbors raking the leaves.
Listen to the kids running around, jumping, and playing in the leaves?
Think of the things you have experienced in this wonderful season.
Maybe the sounds are just the reason.
The sounds of autumn are what I love best.
What do you love best about autumn?
Next time you leave the house, stop and listen to the sounds around you.
The sounds of autumn are like the waves on the beach blowing in the breeze.
I know you will love the sounds just the way I do.
The sounds will be like in this poem I have told to you."

Sarah Stevens, Grade 6
Christian Life Schools, IL

Wondering About Bats

Have you ever wondered about bats?
How they would look in hats?
If you could use them to fly a ball?
Maybe over a fence that's nice and tall?
What would happen if you tied them to a mat?
Or if on their heads you gave them a big pat?
One thing I never wondered about, is that after you did all those things,
They would go…
SPLAT!

Lindsay Lutgring, Grade 5
Perry Central Elementary School, IN

Halloween

Halloween is so very fun
Some kids have a lot of toy guns
Some dress up as sad clowns
There is sure to be fun to go around
Some kids stay home and give out candy
Oh how that is very dandy
Some people like to decorate
Others just celebrate

Sabra Morrison, Grade 5
North Knox East Elementary/Jr High School, IN

Pigs

If you give a pig a ping pong paddle, he can beat a horse.
But if you give it two paddles, it can't beat a dwarf.

If you give a pig some pants, he will wear them with care.
But if you give it two pairs, it won't want to share.

If you send a pig to school, he will love to work.
But when he gets in 6th grade, he will really be a jerk.

When a pig plays on a sunny day, he will get real hot.
But when you get real hungry, guess who's in the pot.

Cameron Hoffman, Grade 4
Bright Elementary School, IN

Payton

Payton growls and howls
And kisses all the day
And misses the ball every time we play
He loves his dad, mom, and sister very much
And we love him back a bunch.
His tail wags a mile a minute
And his food costs us a lot of loot
Did I mention he is so cute
In the end is such a goof

Haley J. Shike, Grade 6
South Middle School, IL

Snow

Slowly falling in the sky
Coming down from way up high
So white and fluffy in the night
It is such a beautiful sight

No two snowflakes are the same
But if you find two you will get fame
I wonder how it got its name
I guess that they just named it since it came

It comes in season after fall
If there are windows you can watch them in the hall
Trying to drive to a mall
Just to go and buy a ball

Angela Wong, Grade 5
Walker Elementary School, IL

The Christmas Holiday

Christmas lights glisten on the snow covered ground,
while your heart is filled with a warm winter glow.
Visiting your family in the holiday season,
while caroling parties are singing out in the snow.
Driving down snow blanketed lanes,
with the joyful holiday cheer you will always know.

Gabrielle Spurlock, Grade 6
Batesville Middle School, IN

Houses

Do houses get tired of standing all day?
Do you think they just want to play?
Do they get tired of birds pooping on their heads?
Do they just want to marry a shed?

Jared Ross, Grade 5
Forreston Grade School, IL

Thanksgiving Day

Empty trees as empty as my wallet
on Christmas Eve.

Wind howling like a wolf
Coming for me.

Pumpkin pie as sweet as
fresh pure honey.

Excited to see my cousin
is like finding out I am never going to die.

Turkey cooking is like smelling
warm vanilla cookies.

Gage Shively, Grade 4
Churubusco Elementary School, IN

Old vs Young

Old
Wise, respectful
Helping, advising, knowing
Wrinkled, thoughtful, active, noisy
Growing, learning, playing
Happy, curious
Young

Megan Sliwinski, Grade 5
Washington Township Elementary School, IN

Football

I love seeing the field when I get thrown
I help players get touchdowns.
When I hear people cheer, it makes me happy.
I love when I soar through the air.
I hate when it's kickoff time.
My house is the football arena.
Oh no! You are going to fumble me.

Eric Galfano, Grade 6
Sacred Heart Elementary School, IL

Blowing Wind

The wind blows East and West and North and South.

It hits my face and I fly up in the air.

I see the birds soaring in the sky as the wind carries me back down.

I sit on my checkered red and white blanket eating my BLT, as ants scurry on by.

Butterflies carry a green vine up to my head and little chipmunks crawl up my spine.

They carry little purple iris flowers and tie them to the vine.

The beaver's tail slaps my leg and brings me a cape made of cloth and twine.

The animals surrounding me look into my eyes; deer, rabbits, birds, groundhogs and any other animal you can imagine.

I look back at them and sing a little song.

When all of the sudden, my hands are holding onto branches, and I am high up from the ground with my blue jean overalls and my white t-shirt.

My feet are dangling with my black high tops on.

I wasn't a queen in the forest, nor was I surrounded by animals, but earlier in the day I climbed my old oak tree as the wind took me on an adventure today!

Victoria Collins, Grade 6
Peoria Academy, IL

Looking into a Forest

Looking into a forest drains all problems away. Everything appears grander, trees seem to be as high as skyscrapers. Take a deep breath and clear your mind. It feels as if there's not a worry in the world. Look up and spy the specs of birds hovering around like shooting stars streaking across the night sky. Wind wisps around you, while whispering a calming lullaby. Squirrels dash into their tree holes as a deer ambles by proudly, with its head held high. Sunbeams glisten, forming a rainbow at a nearby waterfall, flowing into a river rushing with rapids. Listen for the sound of twigs and leaves crunching underfoot. The aroma of spruce trees drifts through the air and fills your senses with a feeling of euphoria like the first warm day of spring melting away the snow.

Seth Bornstein, Grade 4
Walden Elementary School, IL

Squirrels

S quirrels bouncing here and there looking for acorns

Q uickly before winter is here, scurrying

U p and down trees running

I n the winter weather. Even when it's

R aining, snowing or any precipitation, they always

R ocket from tree to tree. They hide their acorns

E verywhere. After winter when spring comes the squirrels get the acorns back and the

L eftover acorns give life to new trees and the

S quirrel's journey starts all over again

Aditya Mishra, Grade 4
Frank H Hammond Elementary School, IN

If I Ever

If I ever had a mansion I wouldn't have to lift a finger,

But I would have lots of bills.

If I ever get forty-eight speeding tickets, I'll go to the classes.

If I ever saw a hurting, helpless animal,

I would help it just as The Good Shepherd would help me, His hurting lamb.

If I ever heard someone say that nobody needs Jesus,

I would turn to them saying "Let me see you on that cross when you did nothing wrong,

taking the world's sin from everyone,

Dying for the people who mocked you and put you on that cross.

And then rise from the dead three days later. Then you can tell others that no one needs Jesus, after you see what He went through, He didn't have to, but He did. Even for the people who mocked and killed Him. And then to hear someone say that He shouldn't have done all these things! How could you live like that? May you be healed!!"

Rachel Stierman, Grade 6
Christian Life Schools, IL

The French Fry Alphabet

A ppetite arrived
B loated belching
C hewing cold condiments
D isgusting digesting
E ating everything
F at full with French fries
G ross globules of grease
H ot heavy heavenly
I nhaling ingesting
J ust like junk food
K etchuping
L ip licking
M outh masticating
N ot nutritious
O besilicious
P repared picture perfect of **Q** uestionable quality
R apidly regurgitated
S alty swallowing satisfied
T ummy tuck tomorrow **U** gly in underwear
V irtual venom
W aste width of walrus e **X** hibited at **Y** our **Z** oo

Jack Hirsch, Grade 6
Daniel Wright Jr High School, IL

I Am!!!

I am an Aquarius.
I wonder what it will be like in middle school.
I hear people around the world.
I see people being fair.
I want to be able to have a great year.
I am an Aquarius.

I sometimes pretend to be a singer.
I feel the wind blowing softly against my face.
I touch an imaginary wall that separates well from bad.
I worry about the people that get hurt.
I sometimes cry inside about my best friend who moved away.
I am an Aquarius.

I understand that I can't have things the way I want them to be.
I say that you can always try.
I dream about becoming a pediatrician.
I try to do my best.
I hope I do well in middle school.
I am an Aquarius.

Ajilé Jean-Baptiste Hereford, Grade 5
Walker Elementary School, IL

The Cat with a Big Hat

There once was a cat
Who had a big hat.
His mom was a witch
Who was a great snitch.
People were so scared so they bought a real bat.

Jazmin Vizcarra, Grade 5
Gard Elementary School, IL

My Horse

When I see her run,
She looks like a dove flying in the morning light.

When I watch her gallop,
She's a really lovely sight.

When she stands in a Pinto halter class,
She will stand out in the really big mass.

When she's under saddle on her longe line,
She looks so pretty she looks so very fine.

When she's outside standing in the light,
She looks so pretty and so very white.

Karisa Clark, Grade 6
Dakota Elementary School, IL

Dreamland

Dreamland is my special place
Where you can smell the fresh air
Feel the soft grass and hear the birds sing
You can see all kinds of plants, big and small
You can taste great treats
Dreamland is a place like preschool
You can sleep and have fun all day
Dreamland is a special place for you and me
Dreamland is the place to be

Tamisha Winters, Grade 4
Meadow Lane School, IL

Dear Grandpa

Hi Grandpa! Can you believe it!
YES, YES it's actually me!

I thought of you just the other day,
Did you see me? Did you hear what I had to say?

I want to cry out,
I really want to shout!

Sometimes, I lie in bed and weep,
I weep until I fall to sleep.

You really mean a lot to me,
I see you, sometimes, in my dreams.

I never knew you, but that's OK,
Because I'll love you, forever,
ANYWAY!

Love,
The granddaughter you never knew,
REBEKAH

Rebekah L.R. Morr, Grade 5
Dee Mack Intermediate School, IL

I Can Make a Difference By...

I can make a difference by,
Cleaning up the streets.
This is why I testify,
So we win major feats.

People need to stop littering,
So our kids live in peace.
We really need to clean up,
Before we live in grease.
Ryan Wood, Grade 5
Dee Mack Intermediate School, IL

Grace

I am thankful for my God,
I am thankful for my family,
I am thankful for my friends,
I am thankful for my belongings,
I am thankful for my life,
I am thankful God is like my hero.
Andre Liou, Grade 6
Christian Life Schools, IL

My Best Friend*

He sits,
Stays,
Waits,
Tongue hanging
Tail wagging
He smiles his smile
He's ready to have fun
Endless hours of fetch,
Never ending Frisbee catch,
Or some friendly tug of war
Still he'll never know
He means to me much more
Than any other friend ever could
Because he's my best friend
When I am lonely,
When I am mad,
When the world is on my shoulders
Still he understands
The way only your best friend can
You best friend
Until the End
Ashley Radee, Grade 6
Peoria Academy, IL
*Dedicated to Comet

Borneo's Proboscis Monkey

Its sunset orange hair surrounds
A blank stare gazing into space.
A small mouth munches on leaves under
An outlandish nose looking like a finger,
Borneo's proboscis monkey amuses us.
Kiersten Byerman, Grade 6
Knox Community Middle School, IN

Flowers

Colorful beauty
Scented, symbol, love
Nectar sweet as honey.
Kimberly Roche, Grade 6
Jane Addams Elementary School, IL

Monkey

Monkey on a branch
I am watching for you, see
Monkey, here I am!
Allie Mankey, Grade 4
Adams Central Elementary School, IN

Grandpa

G reat with children
R eally spoiled me
A n awesome friend
N ice as can be
D ied in May in the year 2006
P layed baseball with me
A nd loved me a lot
Shelby Steinmeyer, Grade 6
Trinity-St Paul Lutheran School, IL

Mirror

I only have a face when you look at me.
When you look at me you don't see me!
I am your reflection,
I see you!
Sneeze, so do I.
Laugh, I do too!
Sarah Clouser, Grade 6
Sacred Heart Elementary School, IL

Seasons

Leaves fluttering through the air.
Wind blowing hard through the trees
Snow is cold anywhere you go.
Hot and sweaty in the summer
When leaves flutter, they bring joy.
When wind blows, it is cool and joyful.
When it snows it is exciting
When it's hot, there is more to do.
Leaves bring lots of work.
Snow brings lots of fun.
Wind brings a joyful day.
Summer brings lots of excitement.
Todd Holeman, Grade 6
Milltown Elementary School, IN

An Emotion

Love is a feeling
Frustration and happiness
Emotions are mixed...
Desiree Arce, Grade 6
Jane Addams Elementary School, IL

Skateboarding

Driven at the speed of light
Speedy, tough, fun
Be protected for the challenge
Jeremy Villarde, Grade 6
Jane Addams Elementary School, IL

Remember Forever

Remember forever
Everything from the past
And make each memory
Last and last

Remember forever
The lives that they gave
Keep in your mind
The lives that were saved

Remember forever
The freedom we gained
Never forget
That some people were pained

Remember forever
Everything that you've seen
Always remember
What this poem means
Olivia Bertelsen, Grade 6
Dakota Elementary School, IL

My Rabbits

Rabbits are fun
Rabbits are cool
I'd like to take them both to school
I bought them some glasses
They're purple and pink
They are the coolest that's what I think
My rabbits are awesome
My rabbits are cool
So I took them both to school
My teacher yelled
My teacher shrieked
All my rabbits did was squeaked
I got kicked out
I ran to pout
So my parents took them away
Morgann Chapman, Grade 4
Veale Elementary School, IN

Fall

Fall
Shedding leaves
September, October, November
Breath taken away colors
Autumn
Nate Gowen, Grade 4
Bailly Elementary School, IN

Old and Young

Old
Wise, dilapidated
Breaking, crumbling, weathering
Ancient, old-fashioned, immature, modern
Laughing, playing, yelling
spoiled, athletic
Young

Haley Baugh, Grade 5
Washington Township Elementary School, IN

Winter

Oh, dear winter you make me feel cold and icky inside.
But still love and respect the way you love me too.
I care and love the snow you give me.
I love the way the snow hugs my feet
When I come in from school
I have a cup of cocoa,
and stand at my window and stare.
Oh, winter that is why I respect and love you.

Daja Reese, Grade 5
Allen J. Warren Elementary School, IN

A Different World

9-11, O, how your flames
grew so,
with your buildings
collapsing side by side,
to us it was quite a
sad surprise.

Madeline Carr, Grade 5
Benjamin Franklin Elementary School, IL

The Sports Kid Problem

At the game, we were down by a lot.
But when I got the ball, I took a shot.
We were close. It was all on me.
When I got the ball, I shot a three.
The crowd was loud, after we won.
My dad was proud to say, "That's my son."
This was a game I will always remember.
I will tell this story to all of my family members.

Roberto Omar Rodriguez, Grade 6
St Matthias/Transfiguration School, IL

Ode to Money

Money is soft and foldable
You can buy toys and games
They are paper and coins too
It's in 10's, 20's, and 100's, and more
It's green and makes me want to spend it
Parents, friends, and guardians give it to you
Money,
you can trade it, you can spend it, or you can save it!

Nate Brown, Grade 5
Walker Elementary School, IL

My Dear Old Faith

My best friend is Faith.
She maybe annoying, awkward, or shy.
I'm not sure.
She might know why.
I always hang out with her.
Even if she starts to pout, she is always there to cheer me up.
If she gets hurt, I try to help.
I remember the times we've had.
She never got mad.
Like the time I poured milk on her head.
Or when I spent the night and slept in her bed.
She can always make me smile.
Even if it hurts.
We met in 2nd grade and now we're great friends.

Alaina Polen, Grade 5
Allen J. Warren Elementary School, IN

What the Mirror Thinks of Me

Oh; mirror, mirror on the bathroom wall,
You are a very attractive girl that is looking into me,
But you are the most stubborn girl I have ever seen,

Your clothing style is excellent,
Your sense of humor is great with friends,
But not so much with family,

You are rude to your sisters,
Oh, and you talk a lot,
And you're as tall as a giraffe,

You are very truthful to your friends,
You are smart and always know what's going on,
And you're someone who likes to gossip frequently,

You keep secrets when it's something private,
But when it can be told you tell,
And you have a wonderful smile,

Your eyes shine like a little star,
You have a hazel dark eye color,
And your laugh is very interesting.

Miranda Ward, Grade 6
Dee Mack Intermediate School, IL

Halloween

H ave a Happy Halloween.
A ll the kids like the candy.
L ittle goblins steal candy from kids.
L ight scares away the goblins.
O wls come at night.
W itches fly out at night on their brooms.
E very boy and girl in town likes to trick or treat.
E very year on Halloween kids hide in trees.
N ight turns to day when the goblins and witches go away.

Nick Holland, Grade 6
Three Rivers School, IL

My Mom

She is sweet, kind and funny
She always has a smile
She knows when I am not happy
She knows how to cheer me up
She knows how to make me feel good
She gives me hugs and kisses
She goes to work very glad
I know that she loves me
She always tells me so
She helps me do my homework
She helps me do my cheers
She helps me do gymnastics
She even does my chores
She lets me have lots of friends over
She lets me have parties
She really is a cool mom
She is the best mom a kid could have
No one will ever replace my mom
And I am forever hers

Rachel Gwin, Grade 6
Nancy Hanks Elementary School, IN

Yellow

Yellow is the color of the sun.
Yellow is the color of happiness.
Yellow is the color of the horizon.
Yellow is the color of calico cats' eyes.
Yellow is my favorite color.
Yellow.

Kelsey Burton, Grade 5
Henryville Elementary School, IN

Drugs

Drugs are nasty,
They're not fun.
People have tried them,
But now they're done.
Please don't try them,
Oh please don't.
I know I sure won't!
Drugs can kill, injure, and hurt.
If you do them you'll end up like dirt.
You may also end up an addict,
You'll do drugs like a fanatic.
So, concludes our story,
Don't do drugs.
If you do I'll be here for a hug.

Brandon Baker, Grade 5
Dee Mack Intermediate School, IL

Apples

Apples are crunchy and sweet.
Green, yellow, red.
A good snack to eat.

Arely Estrella, Grade 4
Jane Addams Elementary School, IL

The Room of Mysteries

When Gary went to sleep at night,
He always goes without a fright!
But one day when he went to sleep,
He heard a noise, beep, beep, beep!
His mom came in the room, then gave him comfort,
They discovered it was just Gary's bird Humpert.
The next night when it was time for bed,
Gary saw a weird shadow from overhead.
His dad came rushing through the door,
To find the graceful shadow of trees,
Swaying gently in the breeze.
The night after that, when he laid down,
He saw lots of things, and heard lots of sound,
He wasn't frightened, and went to sleep,
His parents were there, and he went peacefully into slumber deep.

Angelo B. Perez, Grade 6
St Matthias/Transfiguration School, IL

The Library on Division

The doors are closed, it's not yet open, it's utterly quiet.
The doors open, people rush in, yet its still utterly quiet.
The cement building humbling all around it.
The L, riding high overhead.
The books, the people, all of them, so many different kinds.
People are all united with a common need, a need to read.
The clicks and noises from the computer beat a steady tune.

The ruffling of pages sing a very fast song.
You can tell a lot about a person from the kind of books they read.
From the historic fiction books to the fantasy I read. I can smell the
books, caught from times past, when read by another, just like me, long ago
People come to read great books and feed their imaginations.
It's good to be a person, just like that.
The doors swing shut, all the people retreat,
a day in the library's life has come to a close.

Liam Lefebvre, Grade 6
Chicago City Day School, IL

Friendship

Sticks and stones can break bones but words can shatter one's soul.
People do not notice the harsh words that they say just to be in control.

Those people that work so hard for the effort to only be torn down.
They wish for a smile only to get a hateful frown.

One person's glory is another one's pain.
Just one word can stay on the soul just like a coffee stain.

Stick up for people when they're down in the dirt.
Watch out for bullying and be alert.

You never know you might be the next person, the target.
When you walk by a helpless person just remember they won't help you,
They will never forget.

Ashleigh Graham, Grade 6
Concord Ox Bow Elementary School, IN

The Hounds

It is a quiet day, in the Fall
When all of a sudden, noise is made by all.

You look around, and you see
Something unexpected, a fallen tree.

You wonder why, that tree would fall
But then again, there is nothing at all.

You keep walking, all cozy and warm
Then that second, you think everything is out of the norm.

What you see, is a real big hound
And you think it should be kept in the pound.

You can't believe, it is as big as can be
Then you see, there isn't one there are three.

You try to run, but your feet are frozen
Then you think, it is you they have chosen.

Patrick Belczak, Grade 5
St Daniel the Prophet School, IL

Parents
Mom
Lovable, forgiving
Punishing, teaching, yelling
Caring, awkward, fair, fun
Wrestling, strict
Funny, sarcastic
Dad

Jorge Beron, Grade 5
Washington Township Elementary School, IN

I Am

I am a boy that is skilled at sports
I wonder if I will play in the NFL
I hear the crowd cheering at the game
I see another boy shoot the basketball
I am a boy that is skilled at sports

I pretend I am the best at any sport
I feel pain of the other player when he gets tackled
I touch the basketball's rough surface
I worry if we will win
I cry when we lose the championship game
I am a boy that is skilled at sports

I understand I am not the best
I say practice makes perfect
I dream of being in the NBA
I try to get better
I hope I don't have any injuries
I am a boy that is skilled at sports

Brandon Mercer, Grade 6
Helfrich Park Middle School, IN

Walter Payton #1

When I was young I helped do chores.
I really liked to clean the floors.
In high school I played football.
I really didn't want to play baseball.
Jacksonville College was the school I went to.
It was the college I knew.

Brendan Krob, Grade 4
Coal City Intermediate School, IL

Fall
Halloween.
Costumes.
Loads of candy.
Doorbells ringing.
Trick-or-treat.
Scary costumes.
Trading candy.
Long walks.
Heavy bags.
Giving candy to the poor people!

Brandon Bolek, Grade 5
William B Orenic Intermediate School, IL

My Holiday
On Christmas Eve we're baking, yummy holiday cookies,
And candies and pies, then my brother shouts, "Looky!"

We see our relatives coming with Uncle Dana as St. Nick,
They come with lots of presents, one for each to pick.

St. Nicholas sits down in a big fluffy chair,
He passes out presents each wrapped with love and care.

Every body leaves all full with Christmas food.
Then we ask to open gifts but dad is not in the mood.

We wake early in the morning to find that Santa Claus was here.
We all are very excited. Are those tracks from his reindeer?

As you can see at Christmas time we do many fun-filled things.
From frosting cookies to opening presents,
We always hear angels sing.

Emma Nicoson, Grade 6
Concord Ox Bow Elementary School, IN

Spring Is Sprouting
Squirrels coming out of hibernation
Fragrance from the flowers roams the air
The warm breeze bristling your face
Honking geese flying back from the south
Sweet tasty candy eggs
Flowers sprouting in the garden
The melting blanket of snow

Payton Feasel, Grade 4
Adams Central Elementary School, IN

Kittens

So small.
They curl into a ball

Tons of fur.
Hear them purr.

Swooshy tail.
They shred the mail.

Sharp claws.
Tiny paws.

Can be wild.
Can be mild.

So cute.
Never mute.

They take all your time.
Hope I'm never without mine.
Grace James, Grade 5
Perry Central Elementary School, IN

Chameleon

Life is a game
Of hide
And seek
They play
Both sides
Hiding from
Their foes
They blend
With their surroundings
So rarely seen
When they are
Ready to eat
They turn invisible
Sneak and…
Snatch their prey
Daily,
They turn invisible
For the game of hide and seek
Sean Davis, Grade 5
Highlands Elementary School, IL

Boys

Why do boys make so much noise?
Why are boys so smelly?
Why are boys so ugly?
Why do boys have yellow teeth?
Why are boys so messy?
Why do boys write so sloppy?
Why do boys say bad words?
Why are boys so mean?
Jennifer Plascencia, Grade 5
Edison Elementary School, IL

Music

Music is my happiness.
You sing and dance to it.
It's the highlight of my day.
Juanita Cervantes, Grade 6
Jane Addams Elementary School, IL

When I Am Sad

When I am sad,
I feel like a balloon,
That needs air.

When I am afraid,
I feel like a deer,
That caught a human's scent.

When I am nervous,
I feel like a cat,
Running from a dog.

When I am happy,
I feel like a goose,
Flying with her young.

When I am mad,
I feel like a soldier,
Furiously yelling.
Colton Clark, Grade 6
Dee Mack Intermediate School, IL

Emily

Emily G. we call her
She is such a joy
She makes me laugh until I cry
She makes my day go by
My little sister Emily is so much fun
She loves to laugh and run
Such a cute little one!
Allison Parker, Grade 6
Perry Central Elementary School, IN

Allhallows' Eve

Allhallows' Eve — the time of year
When all is gripped with ghostly fear
'Tis my very favorite season
For this one so simple reason
Look out the window and you will see
The magnificent color of the trees
Freddie Stavins, Grade 5
Countryside School, IL

Family

A sensitive bunch
Bubbly, gentle, generous
My whole life…
Karen Diaz, Grade 6
Jane Addams Elementary School, IL

Basketball

It's a fun sport to play.
Some people say no way.
I'm sure to say it's fun to play.
But you gotta do it a certain way.
Luke Roberts, Grade 5
St Michael School, IN

Fishing

Fishing is still fun.
I like fishing, it is cool.
Do you like fishing?
Jessica Ponder, Grade 4
Rose Hamilton Elementary School, IN

Friends

Friends are always caring,
loving and nice.
They are like family,
always there for you.
I love my friends.
Hillary Hubert, Grade 6
Perry Central Elementary School, IN

Go Karts

G o fast
O n the track

K arts are wicked
A erodynamics
R oads are hot
T racks are black
Jared Thomas, Grade 4
Scipio Elementary School, IN

Summer

Summer is my favorite season
It is better for a reason

It's sunny and warm
But there might be a storm

There are all kinds of sports
You might see toads with warts

So come play with me
For there's a short summer glee
Jake Webb, Grade 5
St Michael School, IN

Winter

Playing in the snow
Slide on the hills on my sled
Friends come sledding too
Brook Huntley, Grade 4
Adams Central Elementary School, IN

My Perfect Day

It's a warm summer day at the beach,
There's a cool breeze,
I can feel the warm sand beneath my feet,
The roaring waves are touching my toes,
A speedboat goes by and the cool water splashes on my face,
The water feels good on my skin,
That's my perfect day.

Madeline Fulton, Grade 5
Stanley Clark School, IN

Christmas Time

Christmas is a time for me
To spend time with my family,
I feel such a merry feeling within
My heart that beats beneath my skin.
As I trudge outside...
It is so frigid out in the snow,
Yet so warm inside my house
Beside the fire you'd never know
That outside it seems like 10 below.
When I am greeted inside...
As I come inside almost numb,
I feel a tickle to my tongue,
The flavor hops and dances and prances a lot,
My senses yelp, it's hot chocolate!
When I tread to the living room...
My Christmas tree, is smells like a forest oh so small,
But the figure before me is so tall!
When I crawl upstairs...
I hop into bed happily hoping,
That I'll have gifts for Christmas morning.

Ryan Jackson, Grade 5
Butterfield School, IL

Scared and Trapped

Two worlds.
One me.
Trapped.
Threatened by both to choose one or another.
I hate the itching, raging urge to die as I try to decide.
I don't see or hear anything.
Only feel.
I feel my heart trembling with fear.
Black.
The weight of two cinderblocks on my shoulders.
One containing one world
One the other.
The weight and pressure of the decision is too much.
I scream.
Black.
Two worlds.
One me.
Trapped.

Macy Eaves, Grade 6
Churchill Jr High School, IL

Life

Life is a wonderful thing,
So don't blink.
Life is short so move slowly.

Don't rush through life.
Because if you do,
You won't have anything to look forward to.

What will you do with your life?
Maybe 100 will come and go,
Or maybe it won't.

So take life slow.
Don't rush through life.

Luke Rumage, Grade 6
Dakota Elementary School, IL

This Circus

The always endless sounds of circus clowns:
Water squirting out of flowers.
Noses beeping with every squeeze
Jumping and laughing for the kids
In all vocabularies
Ha! Ha! Ha!
Beep! Beep!
Squirt!
Sweet hysterical chorus of language
combinations:
The crowd roars
an orchestra in a child's eyes
Assaulting my ears
The always
noise of
This Circus:
Circus music

Molly Green, Grade 4
Churubusco Elementary School, IN

Gymnastics

Walking on the balance beam up so high;
I feel like I can touch the sky.

Cartwheels and handstands may be no big deal;
But when it comes to flips and tricks,
Nervousness is all I feel.

Sometimes I feel like I'm going to fall;
Especially when I do,
The newest trick of all.

There's no doubt about it,
Gymnastics is fun;
And someday I hope,
To be the best one.

Alyssa Lepore, Grade 6
All Saints Academy, IL

Pat's Cat

There once was a boy named Pat
He loved his little cat
But one day his cat got hit
Now Pat just misses it
Because his cat went splat
Barrett Kaeb, Grade 6
Bethel Lutheran School, IL

We Are the Guardians

We are the Guardians
Who protect the dead
Our stone bodies
Lying on their corpses

We are the Guardians
And have been for centuries
The dead beneath us
So precious, so fragile

We are the Guardians
With engravings on our beds
That tells the history
Of our dead masters

We are the Guardians
Gathered in a tomb
With barely any light
The darkness looming everywhere

We are the Guardians
Ariel Halstead, Grade 6
Northwood Elementary School, IN

Guess Who?

I am an animal,
you may not know me.

I like to play in the mud
and I lay down with a big, big thud.

I'm not very sanitized
and I usually have great big blue eyes.

I can be kind and nice
and be mean like some teens.

My ancestors are like dinosaurs.

I probably weigh 2 tons,
I know it's a bunch,
I'm fast but slow,
so do you know?

WHAT AM I?
Sha Collier, Grade 6
Our Shepherd Lutheran School, IN

The Beach

When I'm at the beach,
I see sparkling water
I hear waves rolling on the shore
I feel the sunburn growing on my back
I taste sand and a cold drink
I know I'm at the beach
Alec Berndt, Grade 6
Trinity Oaks Christian Academy, IL

The Accident

Clunk, crash, bang, boom
That's how my day started out
Pain, sorrow, grief
It's all my fault, what have I done
It was going through my head
Clunk, crash, bang, boom
My six year old cousin…white as a ghost
My sister…beat red
What's going on? Are you ok?
I could tell…she wasn't
I had never felt so bad
Clunk, crash, bang, boom
My sister has two gouges in her back
It's silent except for my weeps
Sorrow got through, I was in shock
I was sitting in my room thinking…
I did this, no one else, it's all my fault
My cousin Grace is in the hospital and
My aunt calls
Grace has a broken collar bone
It's all my fault, it still rings in my ears
Ross Dilger, Grade 6
Nancy Hanks Elementary School, IN

I Am

I am a game player and a TV watcher
I wonder why the sky is blue
I hear bombs exploding
I see a meteor in the sky
I want 1 million bucks
I am a game player and a TV watcher

I pretend to do my homework
I feel scared about a meteor
I touched a skeleton it felt hard
I worry about nothing
I cry about nothing
I am a game player and a TV watcher

I understand nothing
I say that monsters aren't real
I dream about Pokemon being real
I try to fly
I hope that I will get 1 million bucks
Zachary O'Meara, Grade 5
Walker Elementary School, IL

Music

Music, Music is so fun
You can share it with everyone
Music will be there for you
When you are feeling blue
Music can be good or bad
And it might be very sad
You can play instruments
And make a pretty sound
Although you may not be good at first
I can guarantee you're not the worst
Even though you're not the best
You will always ace the test
You can start a band with friends
And the band will never end
Music can make people laugh
And make some cry
You need lessons to apply
Your music to the world
Ding, Ding there's the bell
Now I can safely say farewell
Kim Walls, Grade 6
Holy Family Catholic School, IL

School/Home

School
Challenging, long
Teaching, preaching, expanding
Family, friends, games, reading
Entertaining, loving, decorating
Cozy, fun
Home
Patrick Tracy, Grade 4
St Matthew School, IL

Christmas

Children smile with a glow,
presents wrapped with a bow.
Santa flies overhead,
while you're asleep in your bed.
So be a good boy or girl,
So Santa will not fly by in a whirl,
It's your goal,
not to get coal.
Sonia Wroblewski, Grade 5
St Daniel the Prophet School, IL

Christmas

Christmas
happy, fun
giving, eating, playing
tree, ornaments, lights, stockings
decorating, running, celebrating
best, cool
Good Friday
Jakob Bollman, Grade 4
St Matthew School, IL

Flag

F reedom of the United States
L iberty of the Americans who live here
A lways standing up for each other
G iving each other the strength to keep going

Corinne Hart, Grade 6
Carl Sandburg Middle School, IL

Fishing

Throwing the pole out there
Fish flipping in the water
Waiting for the bob to go down under the water
Fish flipping in the water
Listening to my dad snore
Fish flipping in the water
Listening to the radio
Fish flipping in the water
Finally getting a fish
Fish flipping in the water
It is so the biggest one
Fish flipping in the water
It is time to quit
Fish flipping in the water
We will be back tomorrow

Kiesha Kiser, Grade 5
North Knox East Elementary/Jr High School, IN

Fall

Fall is here, once again.
The leaves are changing colors.
It's time for colder weather to begin.

Thanksgiving Day is almost here,
so get out your turkey decorations
and make a feast in 2007 with no fear.

Friends and families are gathered around.
They love the feast, you can tell
by their very loud sound.

Leaves are falling, see them drop.
Trees are getting bare.
Please don't ever let fall stop!

Sarah Harding, Grade 5
Perry Central Elementary School, IN

About My

Why does my mom want big expensive things?
Why does my mom have to work?
Why does my mom do the dishes?
Why does my mom watch TV when she can go to the theater?
Why does my mom not like Burger King?
Why does my mom not like fire?
Why does my mom have to talk Spanish?
Why does my mom help me?

Jose Diaz, Grade 5
Edison Elementary School, IL

What's War?

It's a peace breaker.
It's a fight for freedom.
It's a heart breaker for moms who get the message
their child isn't coming home.
That's war.

Taylor Miller, Grade 6
Herrick Grade School, IL

Thanksgiving

On Thanksgiving Grandma makes a huge feast.
As soon as you go in the door your nose will soar
and when you're done you'll surely want more.
Then when you just can't eat another bite
you'll go outside to have a snowball fight.
While you're playing in the snow
you notice you lost your bow.
While you're taking a nap
your cousin will hit you with a bottle cap.
In the middle of the night
you get a scary fright.
In the morning when you're tired
you hear your dad got fired.
What a crazy Thanksgiving break.

Payton Dowell, Grade 5
Lincoln Intermediate School, IL

Dad

Dad you were always there for me
even when I spilled the tea
You set me free
Dad you were there at my one hour birth
Thanks for giving me all that's worth
Remember when we went to the game
You weren't in shame
When we suffered the pain
When we used to go to the fair
I threw up on all the rides that were there
But you didn't care
Dad you took me all around town to mow other people's grass
You even bought me the gas
But for five years we were not together
I was afraid we would not see each other ever

Alan Fentress, Grade 6
Milltown Elementary School, IN

Summer and Winter

Summer
Hot, sunny
Swimming, running, sweating
Hot, sunny, cold, dark
Throwing, sliding, sitting
Peaceful, quiet
Winter

Nick Augle, Grade 5
Washington Township Elementary School, IN

My Mom

Roses are red
Violets are blue
My mom is sweet
Her family is too.
She is always around
From day to night
Even when it's dark out
I feel all right.
She is very nice
That is a true fact
She always loves me
It is never an act.
She always tries to help,
She really likes to cook
She makes very good food
Just by looking in a book.
I wrote this poem about my mom
To show how much I love her
Now this poem is through
And I told everything to you.
Carson Banghart, Grade 4
St Matthew School, IL

Music

Music is nice,
music is soft,
music can be
rock and roll and jazz
or country.

Music can be
like a butterfly
it can also be
like a rock.

Music, music, music
I love so much
music, music, music
I love to hear it sounds
so good in my ears.

Music makes me
move it feels
so good.

Music, music, music
listen and feel.
Erika Hull, Grade 5
Gard Elementary School, IL

Radio

Musical technology
Exciting, entertaining, danceable
A spectacular sound experience!!!!!
Erika Magallanes, Grade 6
Jane Addams Elementary School, IL

Mercury

M ercury has
E xactly 88 days in one
R evolution of the sun. It
C an be as cold as
U ranus, but even colder! That's
R ight, and it can be warmer than
Y ou, but add on 700°F!
Dylan Jones, Grade 6
Pinewood Elementary School, IN

Snowball

Oh lovely snowball packed with care
A smack in the head that's unaware.
Then with freezing ice to spare
Melt and soak through underwear!
Fly straight and true, hit hard and square
This, o snowball, is my prayer.

Oh from the winter wonderland
There will be no lions of dand!
No hope of staying dry
Oh my! Oh my! Oh my!
Swiftly sailing o'er the plains
Then it goes and hits some trains.

Oh I feel no shame at all
What is hit by my lovely snowball.
And although the snow may melt
There is something to use to pelt.
Now it's summer and lots of fun
So I just use my water gun!
Mitchell Flanagin, Grade 4
St Matthew School, IL

Madison

Loving
Helpful
Loyal
Wishes to help the homeless
Dreams to stop the war
Wants to stop the pollution
Who wonders beneath the stars
Who fears the war
Who is afraid of dark
Who likes animals
Who believes in God
Who loves animals
Who loves volleyball
Who loves school
Who loves tacos
Who plans to be a veterinarian
Who plans to be a faithful wife
Who plans to live a good life
Whose final destination is heaven
Madison Aldridge, Grade 5
Forreston Grade School, IL

Werewolves

The moon was full. The
werewolves start to prowl for a
snack. They eat then change.
Joseph Collins, Grade 4
Meadow Lane School, IL

Basketball

B ank shout
A dvanced
S wish
K nell
E xtremely awesome
T ime out
B asketball rocks
A ll stars
L ay up
L eft hand shot
John Slone, Grade 5
Pleasant Lake Elementary School, IN

This Gentle Creature

As I lay my head on this gentle creature,
she feels as if her skin were silk,
I feel her warmth,

A glorious animal
black and white,
with spots that show,
she looks depressed or tired perhaps,
I should leave,

Now it's time to say good night,
as the cow drifts peacefully to sleep,
I close the barn door
and walk out into the cold, dark, night,
as I hear such silence I know,
everyone's asleep.
Sage Plunkett, Grade 6
Northwood Elementary School, IN

My Dream

Crystal blue,
sea foam green,
it is calling to me.
Many creatures within,
some are small
and some are big.
The smell of salt
and the feeling of
sand between my toes.
Rolling waves,
sun on my face.
Is this Heaven or
my own special place?
Sawyer Coons, Grade 6
Riverdale Middle School, IL

Matthew

Matthew
Awesome, sweet, cool, extreme
Brother of Stephen, Gregory, Katherine, Bernadette and James
Likes WWE, sports, and family
Who feels happy when Colts win
Who needs WWE Smackdown vs Raw 2008
Who gives love to his family
Who fears heights
Who would like to see Shawn Michaels
Who lives in a cool house
Ajamie

Matthew Ajamie, Grade 5
St Jude Catholic School, IN

Hot Summer Day

It's a hot summer day when I can lay down at the beach.
It's a hot summer day.

At the beach I reached down to catch the fish.
It's a hot summer day.

Look at that fish, can it make a wish?
It's a hot summer day.

Taylor Meents, Grade 4
Coal City Intermediate School, IL

School Is Like...

holding all those notebooks in your hand
listening to all those snapping rubber bands
and you have to carry lots of supplies
well, except for all those other guys
but sometimes school makes you want to go
out to recess to play in the snow

Malachi Spencer, Grade 5
Lincoln Intermediate School, IL

An Ode to Chad Chocolate

Hey Chad Chocolate, what's up today?
So are you feeling okay?
Hey Chad Chocolate, what's up today?
I was going to eat you but I decided to play.

Hello again, my chocolate friend,
Oh, am I feeling so fine
I want something sweet,
I want something divine.

Oh, Chad Chocolate, you are gone now,
for you are in my tummy,
And boy, was it yummy!
So goodbye to you is all I have to say,
for you have been good to me
In many, many ways!

Samantha Tedesco, Grade 5
Allen J. Warren Elementary School, IN

Holiday Memories

Happy Holidays!
Memories from the past come alive,
Bringing cheer to those far and near.
Smell the wood burning from the fireplace,
Fresh cut Christmas trees with a citrus, pine smell,
Cool, fresh air after a snowfall.
Feel the thin, smooth, paper as presents are opened,
Warm, fuzzy, mittens on my hands,
Cold, hard, glass ornaments as they are put on the tree.
Taste the sweet chocolate cocoa going down my throat,
Sweet, shocking, cleansing, taste of peppermint,
Salty, juicy, smoky, taste of ham on my plate.
Hear the sleigh bells on a horse,
Howling wind charging up my face,
Familiar tunes of the Christmas songs on the radio.
See the twinkling lights that brighten up the night,
Snowflakes dancing on your nose.
Love is flowing out of hearts,
Joy is ringing throughout the night,
Peace is settling in our minds,
Happy Holidays.

Veronica Miller, Grade 6
St Joseph School, IN

Christmas

Christmas is a time to care.
Christmas is a time to share.
Christmas is a time to celebrate Christ's birth.
Christmas is a time to spend time together.
Christmas is a time to eat.
Christmas is a time to open presents.
Christmas is a time to give presents.
Christmas is a time to play.
Christmas is a time to have fun.
Christmas is a time for joy.
And remember, Jesus is the door to Christmas.

Dalton Rydell, Grade 6
Christian Life Schools, IL

My Favorite Time of Year

Christmas is my favorite time of year,
the people all around me are filled with joy and cheer!

I love the Christmas cookies and decorations too,
Christmas trees and Christmas lights that shine in red and blue.

Families come together to celebrate this day,
each one has a tradition of doing it their way.

Nativity scenes, carolers and frost on every roof,
Santa and his sleigh and the sound of reindeer hoof.

Jesus Christ was born to us on that Christmas morning,
bringing to the earth, a savior and a king!

Taylor Kuhl, Grade 6
All Saints Academy, IL

Lions and Wolves
Lion,
Yellow, athletic
Sleep, eat, walk
Cat, feline, dog, canine
Sleep, eat, hunt
Grey, small
Wolf
Daniel Terrazas, Grade 5
Edison Elementary School, IL

Spring
Flowers blooming in the sun,
There's enough for everyone.
Pollen blowing everywhere,
In the wind and in the air.

Here comes rain plip plop plip plop,
Oh I wish the rain would stop.
All the birds sing their own song,
Their songs will go on and on.

Here is more rain watch it go,
Yes that grass is going to grow.
Once again the leaves are back,
Chlorophyll they do not lack.

The grass is lush and green,
But I must stay in and clean.
School will be getting out soon,
We will get out after noon.

I ride my bike around the block,
While Taylor plays with chalk.
The sun will set at nighttime,
It is silent like a mime.
Teresa West, Grade 6
Nancy Hanks Elementary School, IN

Outdoors
O ak trees with a honey bee,
U nbelievable sights to see.
T rees made out of wood,
D eer standing like they should.
O pen fields you just can't beat,
O ak nuts so crunchy when you eat.
R elaxation all throughout the day,
S ights to take your breath away.
Austin Lair, Grade 5
Dee Mack Intermediate School, IL

A Rose
A sign of love and friendship,
So soft, velvety, and silk,
Delicate as a dry Fall leaf.
Susanna Arias, Grade 6
Jane Addams Elementary School, IL

An Ode to Cheese
Oh, cheese of mine, you make me feel hungry when I see you.
Oh my cheese, I am comforted when my day ends
with a cheese man for my 7:30 p.m. snack.
My wonderful cheese, I love the way I can make
a cheese man and how you make my stomach full.
Oh dear cheese man, I love the way I can smash you with my fist.
I am happy with my wonderful cheese.
Thank you oh delicious cheese of mine!!
Zachary Carter, Grade 5
Allen J. Warren Elementary School, IN

Crystals
Every winter in my backyard I observe the snow crystals drifting
Fall, fall, fall into the Earth
The wind pushing them back and forth as if they were playing a game of catch
Kids watching the crystals fall on their warm hands and then melt
People packing snow crystals together
The snow flying into the air and CRACK! The snow splits back apart
Then it is carried by the wind on and on until it falls on to my winter wonderland
Bailey Hartley, Grade 5
Walker Elementary School, IL

Mercury
M ercury is the planet closest to the sun. If you
E ntered its atmosphere in the day, you would melt like hot butter. It
R eaches up to positive 800 degrees. It also
C an drop to negative 300 degrees. Some people consider Mercury to be
U gly. The
R eason for this is that it's heavily cratered. It would take 0.26
Y ears to travel to Mercury from Earth at 25,000 mph.
Joe Hannon, Grade 6
Pinewood Elementary School, IN

My Little Nightlight
My mom said I don't need a nightlight,
She said it was a little too bright.

When she took it away I was left in the dark,
I was scared because I thought I saw a big mean shark.

I told my mom and she said o.k.,
She told me she would never take my little bright nightlight away.
Mackenzie Granitz, Grade 5
Concord Ox Bow Elementary School, IN

When I'm Older
When I'm older I'll have more courage but still be afraid.
When I'm older I'll have more knowledge but not know everything.
When I'm older I'll have more experience but still leave things undone.
When I'm older I'll have more understanding from right and wrong.
When I'm older I'll be smarter but not the smartest.
When I'm older I'll be stronger but not the strongest.
When I'm older I'll be different but the same.
I hope that when I'm older I'll love God as much as I love water when I'm thirsty.
Selina Pineschi, Grade 6
Christian Life Schools, IL

Christmas Morning

Christmas morning is like a nice family get together,
present time,
getting up really early to see what Santa brought
and waking up your parents
so you can open up your presents.

Halee Rae Davis, Grade 5
Lincoln Intermediate School, IL

A Lonely Island Grows Out

A lonely island grows out
In the middle of a lake.
The sky is full of the colors of the sunset.
The lake mimics the sky, full of envy.
The island, in result, looks like it is far away.
Yellow blends together with orange.
Orange mixes with red.
Red gets together with brownish red.
Brownish red becomes friends with the dark shadows.

In the island, the trees turn off their green lights.
The island's end continues as the start of mountains.
What a sight, what a spectacular thing!
Everything is the sunset.

Edward Chang, Grade 6
Thomas Dooley Elementary School, IL

Spring

Spring is when the birds sing high in the sky.
Spring is the time flowers bloom.
Spring is when trees grow high.
Spring is me smiling!

Megan O'Lone, Grade 5
Henryville Elementary School, IN

Halloween

You might like Halloween.
But then you have a bad dream.
Monsters are in your dreams, bad it might seem.
This is Halloween.
Don't scream on Halloween.
The Reaper is mean, he gives you fright.
The wolves are stalking.
This is Halllloooowweeeen.

Jacob Weisman, Grade 4
Coal City Intermediate School, IL

Life Is Like a Bowl of Lemons

The color of a lemon is yellow, sometimes sour
But you can make it sweet with a pinch of sugar,
So you should eat it when you're mellow,
Life is like that lemon sometimes sour,
Sometimes sweet, sometimes hard, and sometimes not
But you can make it sweet with just a pinch of love,
The fruit of life is turning your lemons into lemonade

Jorge Martinez Jr., Grade 4
Keystone Montessori School, IL

I Can Make a Difference by Stopping Air Pollution

Hey you! Stop polluting air!
It is killing all the polar bears.

We can make solar powered cars.
Heck if we tried we can make one go to Mars!

If you don't stop, you will pay,
But if you do then, Hip, Hip, Hooray!

Now you know air pollution's bad
So start carpooling and be glad!

Ryan Kelley, Grade 5
Dee Mack Intermediate School, IL

Mom Loves Me

Clean your room!
Put your clothes away!
Did you do your homework?

I know mom loves me.
Even though I'm being raised right,
I still know mom hates it when we fight.

She says I'm pretty,
But she says I'm bossy too.
I know she loves me though.

Brush your hair,
And put your shoes away.
Don't forget to load your plate.

Mom loves me,
And I love Mom,
But she thinks I'm argumentative!

Mom has her likes and dislikes,
But I know she'll always love me!
I hear her yell at me but also she says, "I love you!"

Kylie Donovan, Grade 6
Dee Mack Intermediate School, IL

Christmas Flight

I want to fly so very high in the night sky,
But when I felt a breeze and it gave me a freeze.
I had to squeeze myself tight to stay warm until night.
I usually land in a cornfield where I see a lot of yield signs.
I see lots of people yelling "heel" at their dogs,
When they stop at red lights.
But when I see a boy and a girl fighting in the street,
I yell at them to come and meet me.
I saw people singing Christmas Carols.
I also saw Will Farrel with my friend Cheryl.
Then I had a Christmas party and invited my friend Marty.

Thomas Cochrane, Grade 4
St Matthew School, IL

Piano Music

The emotions of the tones will take your breath away
The welcoming sounds will soothe the soul
Embrace the wonderful moments as the music runs peacefully through your mind
The rhythm can change the energy in a room or bring back memories
When the damper pedal is forced down, I feel the vibrations rush through me like a beating drum
The craftsmanship of a grand piano is like a work of art
Each note sounds like wind chimes clanging in midair
Every key, black or white, has a place in making beautiful music

Sarah Thompson, Grade 6
Dakota Elementary School, IL

Cello

Feel the electrifying vibrations running through your body. Built from maple trees it is strong like a titanium wall. Threads of strings run across it's body. A horse-haired bow glides back and forth between the bridge and the staff to create a magical sound. Emotions flow and rush through your body. The cello is a gorgeous looking and exquisite sounding instrument.

Max Raske, Grade 4
Walden Elementary School, IL

Me and America

America is my home the honorable place to roam,
My hope is for the U.S. to always be safe it should always be an exciting place,
America also has a birthday we celebrate it like it's every day,
It's called the 4th of July, it's when the eagles really fly,
People cry with pride on America's birthday it's a very special day,
People say that, "We are the best" to themselves in a proud way,
Even though I'm an immigrant, I'm an American citizen,
When I say the pledge of allegiance I put on a grin, when I say this I am truly an American citizen,
Those words coming out of my mouth mean that I honor the U.S.A. from far, near, or any which way,
I have a feeling that America will bring people from other countries together in rain, shine or any weather,
I hope America will never suffer from slavery but rather hold our heads up high and reveal our true bravery,
It's not right, people should not fight,
But I know one thing we can fight for…liberty, we can fight with glee,
Nobody should have power over somebody else, the only power we should have is to ring the liberty bells,
So don't be mean and don't be green,
Be happy with me and America.

Sushmitha Suresh, Grade 4
Peter M Gombert Elementary School, IL

The Clash of the Monsters

The Clash of the Monsters, as you can see, is a whole bunch of monster films on TV, full of leaping lizards, giant apes, flying turtles, and mutant grapes.
Some of the best films are on the tube, films like *King Kong, Godzilla, Gammera, and Pigzilla*! In one big movie it happened, it did! King Kong fought Godzilla! It was big!
But *King Kong vs Godzilla* was sadly a disappointment, because King Kong was a guy in a costume covered in fuzz.
Gammera, the next big "G" first tried to destroy the city. But after his debut he changed his heart and save Tokyo from Barugan and his toxic dart.
They were at it again! Oh no! Not another Kong epic from Toho! Yes they made a sequel to Kong's battle with Gojira, but this time no Godzilla, but the humans captures Kong from a strange villa.
Gorgo attacked London, Rhedasouraus attacked New York, and they killed the X from outer space with a cosmic fork!
It's almost over, but you didn't see it? Don't worry good buddy because you're in luck, they're playing it again! Enough films to fill a truck!
Now you're here! You're just in time! It's starting now and ending at nine. Move over a bit! Hey, that cup is mine.
The Clash of the Monsters as you can see is a bunch of monster movies on TV, so let's make some popcorn and you can watch it with me!

Michael Edward Sherman, Grade 6
Dakota Elementary School, IL

Pigs

Pigs play in the mud
Pigs lay in the mud to keep cool on a hot day
Pigs oink at people when they walk by
Pigs eat all the time
Jacob Mueller, Grade 4
Springfield Boys and Girls Club ABC Unit, IL

The Wilderness

My mom and I were in the wild late one night,
Looking at the animals, they were a beautiful sight.
The skies were indigo and there was a pale moon above,
We were watching all the wild animals that I love.
In the darkness we saw more things than you can name,
We saw deer, bears, foxes, birds, and other wild things.

The next day we went fishing in a beautiful lake,
We saw lots of cute turtles in every size and shape.
We found a hurt rabbit that was scared as a mouse,
We decided we should help it and we found a nearby house.
The people there loved animals and they were glad to help,
The rabbit was still nervous and gave a little yelp.

They took her to the nearest vet and wrapped her in a sweater,
The vet took very good care of her until she was all better.
Jordanne Bollman, Grade 4
St Matthew School, IL

Four Seasons

Winter, spring, summer, fall,
winter is the best of all.
Spring is nice when flowers bloom,
they help take away the winter gloom.
Summer is great for swimming in the pool.
Taking a dip keeps us cool.
Fall is beautiful to watch the leaves come down,
they turn many beautiful colors all around town.
Of all, winter is my favorite season,
and I have to say Christmas is the reason.
Miranda Johnson, Grade 4
Fox Creek Elementary School, IL

The Early Christmas Tree

Beautifully decorated in crimson colored bulbs,
Towering above the children so small,
Glowing in a deep scarlet/crimson color,
Amazing to all.
With candles in the branches,
Decorated with colored leaves,
Christmas tree in fall?
I've never heard of such a thing.
Though it may seem somewhat odd,
It brings smiles to their faces,
Remembering all of the good and happy places.
MacKenzie Olson, Grade 6
West Central Middle School, IL

My Day in Horseshoes

I am a horse grazing in a pasture.
I love to eat this tasty grass.
There's a fly on my back, I flick it with my tail.
I then go back to grazing.

My owner takes me to the tack room.
She places a saddle on my back.
She mounts me and says "let's ride."
I trot to nearby woods, and then it's time to go.

I gallop past the trees, and jump over a log.
I then neigh and bob my head, because I am proud.
She brings me to a canter as I swim across a river.
We then walk home to the stables.

As I enter the stables, I see a cat.
I get scared, so I rear and buck.
She gives me an apple and puts me in my stall.
I then sneeze on her and she laughs.
This is my day in horseshoes.
Skyleigh Boehm, Grade 6
Dee Mack Intermediate School, IL

I Am

I am a silly girl that loves animals
I wonder about the future
I hear my name being announced to the crowd
I see animals and people having homes
I want my parents to be proud of me
I am a silly girl that loves animals

I pretend to score the winning goal
I feel loved when my mom wraps her arms around me
I touch everything I've always wanted
I worry about my dog's health
I cry for the people and animals that don't have homes
I am a silly girl that loves animals

I understand that no one is perfect
I say we all have imperfections
I dream that there could be no hatred in the world
I try to accept people for who they are
I hope I will never lose my friends
I am a silly girl that loves animals
Rachel Goldstein, Grade 6
Helfrich Park Middle School, IN

The Rain

When the sun goes down and the clouds appear,
the rain comes down tear to tear.
The rain comes down,
splashing on the ground,
pouring the night away,
waiting until the sun comes back today.
Yahiya Khan, Grade 4
Neil Armstrong Elementary School, IL

Surprises/Books
Surprises
Exciting, intriguing, mysterious
Running through the forest
Soaring through the sky
Looking off a mountain top
Wishing I could fly
Books
Tara Wolf, Grade 6
Tri-West Middle School, IN

Mom
Mom, Mom, Mom
Enjoyable Mom
Caring Mom
Loving, cool, funny Mom
Smart, colorful, friendly Mom
Last of all, best of all
My mom
Emma Lawrie, Grade 5
St Jude Catholic School, IN

Autumn
A mber leaves fall to the ground
U mber tones all around
T hanksgiving feast pleases the mouth
U p above geese fly south
M orning frost covers the grass
N ight time darkness comes so fast
Zoe Timmermann, Grade 6
All Saints Academy, IL

Lunchtime
Tick, tick, tick, tick
When will that bell ring!
One minute until lunchtime
I don't think I can wait!

My stomach is turning and
Making strange noises.
It's growling and yelling at me!

I'm getting a headache
I can't wait anymore!
Tick, tick, tick, tick
Why won't that stupid bell ring!

This is taking too long!
Lunch is right around the corner
I need my food right now!

Ring, ring, ring, ring
Yes! Finally!
Lunchtime is here!
Only to discover, I forgot my lunch!
Madison Parker, Grade 6
South Middle School, IL

Christmas
I see the red nose outside my window
And 7 other reindeer eating the food
I put out for them.

I taste the candy canes
In my hot chocolate.

I feel the 20 presents
That Santa left me
And my brother and sister.

I smell Santa's reindeer
On Christmas Eve.

I hear Santa saying "Ho ho ho
Merry Christmas."
Jade McGrath, Grade 4
Fox Creek Elementary School, IL

Haunted House
Skeletons in ancient coffins
Reeking dead animals
Rats making clattering noises
Running into enormous cobwebs
Gagging in the grubby air
Grimy food in the dark refrigerator
Joel Mailloux, Grade 4
Adams Central Elementary School, IN

The Fun Has Just Begun
Outside climbing trees
With friends playing with imagination.
Making new games to play,
in an open field or in trees
like it's a jungle everywhere
around you because summer
has just begun.

Wear'in baggy shorts and T-shirts
running around swinging from trees.
Jumpin' up and down driving my
brother crazy and picking on
my other one.
Tiffani L. Bell, Grade 5
Lincoln Intermediate School, IL

My Name
K ind
A mazing
L oving
E xclamatory
I ncredible
G lamorous
H ilarious
Kaleigh Wilham, Grade 5
St Jude Catholic School, IN

Fall
Fall is coming,
Color is in everything.
Birds are coming,
Birds are humming.
Leaves are crunching,
Deer are munching.
Leaves turn brown,
Then fall on the ground.
Angel Gideon, Grade 4
Chrisney Elementary School, IN

Halloween Skeleton
S pooky visitor
K nocking on doors
E ating candy
L ooking for his friends
E very friend
T aking candy from young
O n the run
N ight is a fright!
Kevin Lowery, Grade 4
Bailly Elementary School, IN

Devil
Devil
Hot fire
Angry, evil
Hairy and red, beautiful and white
Winging, singing
Fast in the clouds
Angel
Chris Ferris, Grade 4
Village Elementary School, IL

School
If you go to school
You won't be a fool
You might even get pennies
to spend at Denny's
after we go to the pool.
Kaylyn Ann Jones, Grade 4
Shoals Elementary School, IN

My Pumpkin
I once had a pumpkin,
Who liked to go dunk'in,
He has a very big smile,
And his name is Lyle.

He likes to go swimming,
When the sun is shimmering,
He hates the cold hard porch,
But he loves the hot torch,
I love my pumpkin Lyle.
Riley Kauzlaric, Grade 4
Coal City Intermediate School, IL

The Ball

It will bounce high.
It will bounce into the sky.
So high it will not touch the white clouds.

Haley Bartlett, Grade 4
Warren Central Elementary School, IN

Glasses

Glasses are pathetic even if you're not blind
so don't go to doctor Mind
He'll go get you glasses that are too wide
then he'll go get you glasses
that are too fine.
He'll go get you glasses that are too thin
Then he'll go get you glasses that are too big.
Why did my mom make me come to this place
after all he might be insane.

Hayley Keeney, Grade 5
Perry Central Elementary School, IN

Joy

Warmth flooding through your body
Sorrow and despair left behind
While a certain feeling takes its place
Accomplishment, pride, mixed into one
Worry, complications, problems forgotten
Pushed to the deepest corner of your soul
And locked away
By freedom and relief
Anger forgotten,
Swallowed up by light
Tenderness inside and out
Luck happening, tables turning
Cruelty turned around
Stomach untied, nervousness fled
Chased out by happiness
Evilness tossed out
Of your soul
Child of happiness, enemy of hatred
Caretaker of the soul

Amy Tien, Grade 5
Highlands Elementary School, IL

Mom

Her love is always true to what she always means
She is perfect in every way she may seem
Though every day I am getting older
And through the winter, it is getting colder
We always end up on that very special team

Sometimes we may fight and sometimes yell
Always after school, I hear that bell
And when I get home all I want is you to be with me
Sometimes when I am sad I love to have you make me tea
I always love you as you can tell

Jennifer Donnell, Grade 6
St Colette School, IL

Snowmobiling

Snowmobiling is fun even with no sun
It is fast and fun
Zooming over lakes hardly touching the brakes
The smell of gas when going fast
Having lots of clothes because it's so cold
Kicking up snow as you go

Brad Mugler, Grade 6
Trinity Oaks Christian Academy, IL

The Ocean

The ocean big, the ocean blue,
when you see it, it's an aquatic zoo.
The underwater reefs, the fish in the sea,
it's a great sight for both you and me.
So when you go diving, you will know,
how great fish are, and when you're done you'll say wow!

Jacob Bickel, Grade 6
Emmanuel-St Michael Lutheran School, IN

Jesus Christ

J ewish man
E ach of us loved by Him
S o many of us believe
U nited are we in His kingdom
S avior of our sins

C aring is just one of many words to describe Him
H oly in the kingdom of Heaven and on Earth
R esurrected from the dead
I n His name we pray
S ilent night when born
T ogether we will all love and worship Him

Nick Ecsy, Grade 6
Allen J. Warren Elementary School, IN

All About Me

I like turtles and pigs they rhyme with twigs
I like to try on wigs
I have a 2 story house it is sweet
And my dog Harley is weak
That is me

I have a room it is pink and pink is sweet
I love the color pink
And I have a pen it has a lot of ink
And my dad always winks
That is me

I have two sisters they are really cool
And my dogs always drool
My dad is home and he is home for good
And I like 2 wear hoods
That is me

Abigail Elaine Washburn, Grade 4
Coal City Intermediate School, IL

The Sun Is Bright

The sun is bright with all of its light
The sun is bright what a lovely sight.
The sun is warm when there is no storm.

Jacob Baxter, Grade 4
Veale Elementary School, IN

Cat

Cat
Cute and fuzzy
Eating, running, sleeping
Nice and white, mean and black
Drinking, walking, barking
Ugly and bald
Dog

Jacqueline Schmidt, Grade 4
Village Elementary School, IL

Mist

I glanced up
In the glistening sky
But never saw my reflection
In the water
When my friend saw…
A single star
Looking at the pond next to me
Still never saw my reflection
A frog leaped on a lily pad
I heard a croak and a splash
And the frog was gone like that
But it was all a dream!

Tori Smock, Grade 6
Rossville Alvin Elementary School, IL

Break the Sky with My Wings

I'm just a little bird and I'm
    learning how to fly, I'm gonna learn
to soar across the sky. But the thing
    I'm gonna do best is I'm gonna
break the sky with my wings. I'm
    gonna soar across the sky with my
two and only wings. I'm gonna fly
    across the cities. I'm gonna fly
across the towns. Then one day I'll go
    somewhere I've never been
before, I'm gonna be the one to fly
    across the earth and everywhere
I go. I'm gonna break the sky with
    my wings. I'm gonna fly across the
cities. I'm gonna fly across the towns,
    but I'm just a little bird you
know and I can't do much today
but someday my dream is to break
    the sky with my, break the sky
with my, break the sky with my wings

Madeleine Kelson, Grade 4
Near North Montessori School, IL

The Beach

When I go to the beach I see people laughing and waves crashing.
I hear seagulls screeching and water moving along the beach,
I feel shells in my hand and the salty water touching my body,
When I am at the beach I smell the salty air and the picnic food that people bring,
I taste the salty water in my mouth,
Now I know I'm at the beach.

Madison Wynsma, Grade 6
Trinity Oaks Christian Academy, IL

My Problems

Hi, I am John, also known as glasses I have a few problems
Maybe you can help or I'll just get a therapist

My owner does not care for me I yell, I scream but he just ignores me
He stares at me rudely what are you looking at?

Please answer me! Stop fogging me!
Put me away! Put me away!

Finally, it is growing dark there is no use for me now
Clunk, I am in my case not able to be stared at

Cockadoodledoo! It is morning what should I do please tell me?
I cannot stand this much longer he picked me up and dropped me

Now look at me my legs are broke I went to the hospital
Now I am telling you my problems And he is still careless with me

I am calling a therapist Hi I am Susan, what is the problem.
Well, start from the beginning John Hi, I am John, also known as glasses

Drew Shields, Grade 6
Dee Mack Intermediate School, IL

Mars

M ars is called the red planet,
A lso it is fourth from the sun, furthermore, it is the seventh largest, so it is not
R eally big. The north side of Mars is smooth because of lava flow, and the
S outh side is rugged because of mountains.

Tristen Singleton, Grade 6
Pinewood Elementary School, IN

Friends

Friends are more than people to hang out with
Friends are people who care about you
People who love to be with you
People who treat you with kindness
People who protect and stand up for you
People who make your day go incredibly faster
People who cheer you up when you're feeling blue
People who listen and tell you the truth when you need it
People who encourage you to follow your dreams
People who you can trust and tell secrets to
People who like to be with you for who you are and not for what you have
When you find those people cherish their friendship!

Natalia Guerrero, Grade 6
St John the Baptist Elementary School, IN

Snow

Crystals of ice
Float
Like wisps of lace
From the empty sky.
I glide
Across a patch of ice
And tumble
Into a sea of white.
I scoop some into my palm
And taste it.
It tastes so pure,
Like nothing Earth has seen.
As I lie in the snow
I listen
The silence is so beautiful.
I see how the snow
Makes even the bare, black trees
Look beautiful.
They say nothing is perfect, but they're wrong.

Snow is.

Caroline McCance, Grade 5
Walker Elementary School, IL

Waves…

W ashing away with the powerful tide
A gate to the ever more abyss of the ocean.
V icious cracks as the water strikes the rocks.
E verlasting joy for happy children
S o many lives have touched them

Elliott Keller, Grade 6
Concord Ox Bow Elementary School, IN

Christmas Tree

Around and around I go,
Carefully placing delicate ornaments
On the bare tree's branches
Around and around I go.

Delicate ornaments
Bursting with beautiful colors
Ruby red, emerald green, shimmering gold
Brighten the Christmas tree.

Now for the final enchantment —
Standing on the tip of my toes
I reach to the top
I place the bright yellow star.

I take a step back
To look at my creation.
I hear the tree calling
"Light me up!" it proudly announces.

Leslie Vega, Grade 5
Walker Elementary School, IL

Wind

Does wind ever get tired of blowing around?
Does it wish it could just quit?
Is it tired of blowing stuff through the air?
Does it like to blow our hair?

Anna Nowicki, Grade 5
Forreston Grade School, IL

My Perfect Moment

It is the perfect weather and the perfect moment.
I can see the sky blue waves gently crashing on my bare feet.
As I walk, I feel the cool sand between my toes.
I can smell the salty sea water.
It is this kind of day that makes me feel relaxed.
Swoosh I hear the calm wind.
I pick up a smooth seashell.
I hear a call.
It is my mother, calling to go home.
Maybe I can come back tomorrow.

Claire Migliore, Grade 5
Stanley Clark School, IN

I Am

I am creative and artistic
I wonder if I'll find out how wars start
I hear my family cheering me on
I see my mom as happy as can be for me
I want to be able to travel all around the world
I am creative and artistic

I pretend I am on *So You Think You Can Dance*
I feel happy all the time
I touch Serena Williams' tennis racket
I worry about global warming
I cry for people who lose close relatives
I am creative and artistic

I understand how people get sad
I say that I believe in most things that are possible
I dream about how my life will be
I try to be helpful
I hope that I will be a wonderful dancer
I am creative and artistic

Jenica Mullins, Grade 5
Walker Elementary School, IL

One Million Years from Now

one million years from now…
the world will be silent,
the world will be still
the sun's mighty rays will
beat down and kill,
there will no longer be you or me
for one million years from now where would the world be
"Global warming"

Marlee Jacobs, Grade 6
Daniel Wright Jr High School, IL

Stars

Stars are bright
stars are light.
When I look into your eyes,
I see stars that are bright.
And if you don't believe me,
you can see it for yourself.
And if you do,
you just might get blind.
And if you get blind,
don't blame it on me.

Caitlyn Wright, Grade 4
Glen Flora Elementary School, IL

Thanksgiving

Thanksgiving
A harvest
Turkey, pie, corn
Cranberry, relatives, leaves, candy
Holiday

Nya Lewis, Grade 4
Bailly Elementary School, IN

World War

War
Run, hit
Stabbing, shooting, killing
Vietnam, Iran, United States, Japan
Living, relaxing, singing
Harmony, free
Peace

Aaron Ludwig, Grade 5
Forreston Grade School, IL

Ode to My Guinea Pig

Butterscotch, Butterscotch,
Where are you now?
Into your castle,
Did you just plow?

You are so cute,
So nice, so tame.
Your hair is orangish,
(Hence the name.)

I love to pet you,
You are not vain.
Your hair is wild,
Like a lion's mane.

You are my pet,
You are my friend.
And I will love you,
Until the very end.

Carmen Nickels, Grade 6
St Patrick School, IN

Halloween

H alloween
A witch flies on a broom
L urking goblins and ghouls
L ooking for ghosts tonight
O wls hoot
W ind blows on this scary day
E veryone is dressed up scary
E vening comes to stay
N ight can be fun on Halloween

Terri Hayes, Grade 4
North Miami Elementary School, IN

Fall

Fall is fun
There's not as much sun
As in summer and spring
And in fall, the birds usually don't sing.

Because it is breezy,
I can fly my kite easy.
As I walk, the leaves crunch.
Then I have to go inside for lunch.

The colorful leaves are falling,
My mother is calling.
I don't want to go in,
Because then my fun will end.

Marie Speer, Grade 4
Chrisney Elementary School, IN

The World Beneath

The world beneath
so beautiful with creatures
so fascinating with creatures
so long creatures so short
so fat so skinny animals
so different from the world above
the world beneath so quiet.

Julian Shelton, Grade 5
Gard Elementary School, IL

My Aunt

It was you I cherished,
And then you perished.

I hated to watch your soul fly,
And now I'm afraid to die.

When you died,
I hated my life.

But now I see,
You watch over me.

Madison McGinnes, Grade 5
Dee Mack Intermediate School, IL

Violin

Today is the day,
That I will be cased away.
From day to day,
There will be something peaceful to play.

From what you can see,
I can play a peaceful piece.
From Susan Freier to Jim Hurley,
They are all skillful to me.

I feel stiff and cold,
Just like a board.
Nothing to do,
Besides be wooden of course.

My height is short,
But my friend is long.
Put us together,
You will get a violin duet song.

Kataryna McDonald, Grade 6
Dee Mack Intermediate School, IL

My Characteristics

C aring
L oving
A rtistic
R esponsible
K ind

Brandon Clark, Grade 5
St Jude Catholic School, IN

What My Mom Thinks About Me...

Will she ever clean her room?
Why doesn't she help enough?
She's mine and I love her!
She is excellent at soccer.
And is fun to play with.
She's mine and I love her!
She always does her homework.
And listens to me always.
She's mine and I love her!
Ky is nice to everyone,
Good or bad.
She's mine and I love her!
She thinks that she's funny.
And helps sometimes.
She's mine and I love her!
She has a positive attitude.
And very athletic in every sport.
She's mine and I love her!
I love her so much.
Good or bad.
She's mine and I love her!

Kyleigh Block, Grade 6
Dee Mack Intermediate School, IL

Frost Dragon

On a cloudy winter's day
A creature soars in the sky
As dazzling as the sun.
The creature is known as the frost dragon.

He hovers in the air
searching for kids
That will experience the magical ride
And the wonders of flying.

But when the snow is gone
And spring comes
Frost fades away till next winter comes.
He gets revived from the snow
And he will soar in the sky
Like a graceful angel
He will sparkle like snow flakes in winter.

Mikey Huynh, Grade 5
Walker Elementary School, IL

Christmas

Christmas, Christmas
hearing the sleigh rumbling against the roof
let's go downstairs and take a look.
Something's coming down the chimney, better hide in the nook.
Out comes Santa with a big book!

Presents, presents everywhere under the tree,
I hope this one is for me!
Here comes my brother, wait until he takes a look!

Cookies, cookies where did the cookies go?
And, what's that, the milk is gone too!

Thank you, thank you for the presents!
Thank you for eating the cookies and drinking the milk,
because that means you came!

Ryan Lundquist, Grade 4
Fox Creek Elementary School, IL

I Can't Think of Anything

I can't think of anything
I said to myself as my teacher looked over my shoulder
What should I write about?
I thought, and I thought till my head
Was ready to explode
I still can't think of anything
I thought it would be easy
But it isn't at all
I feel like screaming
But I might just fall
I am thinking about everything except for this
I don't know what to do
So I wrote this.

Sophie Savoie, Grade 6
St Matthias/Transfiguration School, IL

Ode to an Eraser

Oh eraser I love your shade of pink
and every time I look at you I can't seem to blink.
I'm so happy you're at the end of my pencil.
And without you I'm lost.
I'm so glad you can fix my mistakes
And I'm also glad I know where you are.

Eraser, you are my favorite tool
because without you I'd look like a fool.
Oh eraser with you I'm not afraid
because I know you're on my pencil all the day.

Brandon Haddad, Grade 5
Allen J. Warren Elementary School, IN

Shopping

I love to go shopping!
When I get there my eyes start popping.
I go buy everything in the store I buy clothes and shoes.
Then I run out of money. Now I'm broke.
I still have the stuff out of the store. Cause I bought it all.

Brianna Breidenbaugh, Grade 4
Scipio Elementary School, IN

I Am

I am a boy that likes skateboarding
I wonder if they will make hover boards
I hear one every day in the skate park
I see every one on hover boards in the park
I want to get better at skateboarding
I am a boy that likes skateboarding

I pretend I'm the best skateboarder
I feel the pain when I fall
I touch the clouds when I go high
I worry I will forget how to skateboard
I cry when I get hurt badly
I am a boy that likes skateboarding

I understand that we all fall down
I say I will get better every day
I dream all of this is true
I hope everyone will like skateboarding
I am a boy that likes skateboarding

Tyler Kirves, Grade 6
Helfrich Park Middle School, IN

Summer Fun

I hear kids screaming "school's out!!!"
I taste hamburgers.
I see creeks and trees.
I feel water running through my fingers and toes.
I smell flowers.
That's why I like summer.

Rebecca Strom, Grade 4
St Matthew School, IL

The People

Five little men,
Have a little hen.
Four little girls,
Have little curls.
Three BIG guys,
Plan an enemy's demise.
Two tall ladies,
They are both Katies.
One tiny kid,
Who knows what he did?

Ben Wellman, Grade 6
Crown Point Christian School, IN

Turtles

A turtle swims as gracefully as a fish
It's shell is as clear as a dish
It's mouth is curved like a bird's beak
But its shell can't spring a leak
On land a turtle is as slow as a snail
But a turtle doesn't get mail

Timothy Webb, Grade 4
Veale Elementary School, IN

Black

Black is night, it is not bright.
Black is the color of a hat.
Black is my favorite color.
Black is the color of my favorite shirt.
Black is the best color ever.

Jeffrey Ledbetter, Grade 5
Henryville Elementary School, IN

The Cycle of Life

Growl, growl, everywhere
Antelope there and there
It is on TV
Growl than a leap
From a huge tan heap
Soaring through the air
A cry a whimper
A mother wants to kick her
The lion finds its mark
A cry of pain
The mother takes in vain
Swift bite and no more sound
A roar of hunger
Sounding like the crack of thunder
it bent its neck
The lion took its first bite
She had put up a good fight
The lion though
More ran for the feast
Trying to make haste
They all started to eat

Arnaud Cyusa, Grade 6
St Joseph School, IN

Badger

Furry, brown, short legs, and a long body
Relative of the canine family
Lover of chew toys, treats, and going bye-bye
Who feels large, in charge, and the sheriff of the house
Who needs love, shelter, and food
Who fears the vacuum, loud noises and the rain
Who gives unconditional love, companionship, and hours of entertainment
Who would like to see more toys, more road trips and more treats
Resident of a caring family
Dog

Jordan Wharton, Grade 6
Helfrich Park Middle School, IN

Guess Who Misses You

Why did you leave us just, hanging here
With no warning you were gone
We got the news over the phone
Me and Grandma cried ourselves to sleep
After you were gone
It took me a lot of time to recoup
Even more time to realize you had passed
I wandered if it was just a nightmare
But by the time the funeral came
I realized it wasn't
It was true, that you were gone
I couldn't watch you be buried
Too scary for me to see
I was only 7 years old
Losing my grandpa — too much
Back in Indy — back home
I called Grandma every single night
To make sure she would be all right
We hoped and prayed that you would come back
But that didn't work
And that's when we knew we would never see you again Grandpa

Samantha Edwards, Grade 6
Nancy Hanks Elementary School, IN

What I Sense at a Football Game!

The first thing I hear is a tweet and a whistle, a Yes! and a No!
    and a Yeah! Yeah! Go!
And then a sudden pause and a WHOOSH! and a CRASH! and an "UMPHF!" and
    a SMASH!
But most of all...a WOW! and a BOO!
I smell sweat and dirt, grease and hot buttery popcorn...
But most of all...I can smell the meats and pizzas around me.
I taste mustard and ketchup, popcorn and hot dogs, cheese and chips...
But most of all...I taste warm, gooey, caramel apples with hot cocoa.
I feel wind and cold, sting and chill, frost and numbness...
But most of all...I feel frozen to the bone and tingly.
I see steam and seats, frosty grass and players, a football, an end zone,
    fireworks and smoke...
But most of all...I see giant raindrops and gooey puddles of mud...
That is what I sense at a football game!

John Paul Stedwill, Grade 4
Peoria Academy, IL

I Can Make a Difference By...
I can make a difference by picking up trash.
When I turn in bottles I can make some extra cash.

I can make a difference by not polluting the land.
When I don't pollute the land you will see nothing but sand.

I can make a difference by recycling trash.
When I recycle trash I can put cash in my stash.

I can make a difference by keeping my area clean.
If I keep it dirty everybody might flee.

Kaehl Murphy, Grade 5
Dee Mack Intermediate School, IL

Fridays
Fridays are the best day of the week because it's
The last day of the week.
I don't have to do my homework that night
I get to watch new shows and movies all night long.
Football games in the fall.
Hurray for Fridays!!!

Andy Aardema, Grade 6
Jerling Jr High School, IL

The Life of a Book
I am a happy book,
So please sit down and take a look.

I have many stories I like to tell,
And all who listen say they're swell.

My pictures I have are pretty sweet,
And many who peek say they're neat.

Sometimes I make you really sad,
And other times I make you glad.

My story may take you far away,
And I'll make you want to stay.

You'll never know what is coming next,
But you'll have to read me like all the rest.

Jessie Kilbride, Grade 5
Dee Mack Intermediate School, IL

The Wolverine
Eyes as black as night falling over the ocean
Nose as shiny as marbles
Teeth as sharp as razors
Whiskers as thin as needles
Fur black as night
Nails keen as daggers
People stay away from wolverines

Mikaela Carter, Grade 6
Knox Community Middle School, IN

Parties
Friends, food and fun
The dancing has just begun
Friends, food and fun
Of food there is a ton
Friends, food and fun
People leaving one by one
This party could not be outdone

Kaitlyn Ashby, Grade 6
North Knox East Elementary/Jr High School, IN

Winding Through the Mountains
Mountains, valleys, forests, lakes, and streams
Who knew it could be so beautiful
The orange color of the rocks
Make it look like Cheetos
The valleys look like heaven
Compared to the orange Cheeto-like mountains
Lakes reflect all that you can see
That makes it look twice as magnificent
As fall sets in everything is golden
After a moment I come back to reality
And I wish the Midwest was like this!

Cora Fiene, Grade 6
Dakota Elementary School, IL

Softball
I am scanty and circular.
Before a game I perch in the dust.
Whoosh! Bang!
I soar like an airplane.
The wind is striking my leather.
Thump…thump…thump I descend into the velvety grass.
A jerk of movement I'm back in the air.
Bang!
A cloud of dust arises,
No one is breathing.
Yer out!
Cheers break the silence.

Grace Miller, Grade 6
Sacred Heart Elementary School, IL

Snowballs
I woke up this morning and what did I see.
Seven inches of snow waiting for me.
I run downstairs pjs and all.
I throw on my boots and give Dad a call.
As I'm waiting I round up a snowball.
Then name it Bob.
I find a small rope and knot it to Bob and me.
As Dad comes outside looking for me.
I give Bob a toss and guess what?
He splattered all over ME!
Now I'm wet and Dad's dry and free.
Running real fast after me.

Bryce Ridener, Grade 5
Perry Central Elementary School, IN

That Poor Little Dog

That poor little dog is so old.
That poor little dog is so cold.
I glared and stared at that poor little dog
As it limped and howled.
That poor little dog feels so sad.
That poor little dog feels so bad.

Miracle Nettles, Grade 4
Neil Armstrong Elementary School, IL

Family

F amily that's there for you
A nswers questions
M akes you feel good
I deas are wanted
L oves you for you
Y ou're at home with family

Samuel Hatchel, Grade 5
Coffeen Elementary School, IL

Violet

My mother handed me a violet,
I was swept into its depths
And I was silent.
Still in awe by its beauty…
Its passion, its royalty,
I stood there for how long
I do not know,
But I do know
The Feeling!

Jerica Tan, Grade 5
Keystone Montessori School, IL

Hibernation

Winter
Sad, silence
Snoring, staying, sleeping
Snow, white, warm, awake
Enjoying, tensing, skipping
Joy, noise
Spring

Jacob Norris, Grade 5
Forreston Grade School, IL

Halloween

H owling in the night
A loud noise in the dark
L ouder and louder
L eaving the noise behind
O ut for candy
W aiting for the door
E ating candy
E ating more
N ow the night ends

Connor Royer, Grade 4
Bailly Elementary School, IN

Sports

I like sports sports sports sports
do you like sports I do.
I know lots of sports
'cause I like all sports woo hoo!
Alfonso Soriano he's my favorite star.
Brian Urlacker is going to go far.

Paul Jones, Grade 4
Coal City Intermediate School, IL

The Hungry Mice

There once were some mice,
Who ate some lice,
Then got a stomach ache.
And then eaten by a snake,
The mice didn't think he was nice.

Michael Makdah, Grade 4
St Peter Catholic School, IL

Bright as an Angel

Decorations of red
on a green Christmas tree,
sleep in the night.
Lights as bright as angels,
hang over a frosty winter.

Decorations of red
wait to start the day.
And a luminous star,
at the top of the tree,
glimmers in the night light.
Bright as an angel

Bo Bercasio, Grade 5
Walker Elementary School, IL

Fear Is Horrible

Fear is like
a bolt of lightning,
devils screaming,
spiders crawling.

Fear is as scary as
zombies at night,
an army at fight,
werewolves that bite.

Cortney Luttman, Grade 4
Churubusco Elementary School, IN

Fall

Fall
Cold breezes
Leaves falling down
Why fall is sweet
Autumn

Doug Zehner, Grade 4
Bailly Elementary School, IN

In the Morning

As the morning comes
the morning glories come out
and have such fun as
they throw the dew around and about
as they please or wish.

Jordan Ory, Grade 5
Perry Central Elementary School, IN

Dog

Did I get mail
Why don't I get to pull
the chains around their necks
I'm fluffy and very hairy
I like to run
I like to chew on stuff
The snow rocks!
People are sometimes afraid of me
but I really don't care!
Daddy is home I jump on him
If they do something wrong
why don't they get hit?

Lee Ann Brooks, Grade 6
Sacred Heart Elementary School, IL

Teachers

Teachers are great,
Teachers are fun,
Teachers are fun for everyone.

Teachers are nice,
They give you advice.
Teachers are great,
Teachers are the best people in the state.
Teachers are awesome,
they have lots of wisdom.
At the end of the year,
it will be queer
To leave your teacher until the next year.

Amy Zhou, Grade 4
Stonegate Elementary School, IN

Butler

Catching Frisbees in the air,
Running around everywhere.
Catching Frisbees is just one thing,
That my dog Butler is the king.
Running fast,
Walking slow,
Either way my dog will go.
Playing in the sprinklers,
Playing in the hose,
After doing all of this,
My dog will surely doze.

Morgan Braastad, Grade 6
Peoria Academy, IL

The Lincoln Park Lilly Pond

When I enter the Lilly Pond,
it feels as though I am stepping into a different world.
Behind me, I leave a busy street, but in front of me,
I step into a world of bewitching nature.
In the early morning,
I see the drops of dew that gracefully
wrap themselves around the leaves like pearl necklaces.
I also see the bright wildflowers that line the path.
They seem to say "hello" with their friendly faces.
A large, green pond sits in the center.
It looks like a large, magical green sheet of glass.
However, once I touch it, the spell breaks.
Ripples of water softly grow until they sink into the water
and the magic starts again.
It is almost lunchtime now;
the sun is high in the crystal blue sky.
As I say good-bye to the Lilly Pond,
I glimpse one last thing.
I look at the graceful water lilies,
silently floating there, seeming to smile.
Good-bye, Lilly Pond.

Morgan Pothast, Grade 6
Chicago City Day School, IL

The Calm Country

In the calm country,
Where I live in soothing peace,
I feel the cool easy wind,
And the soft sea of grass.

Overhead the warm sun hides,
One ray peeking out and streaming over grass,
As the birds chirp the leaves rustle,
While my dog chases the birds away.

I see the birds quickly fly away,
I hear my horse's hooves thudding,
As I turn around I see him run,
With millions of trees behind him.

As I walk to the woods I taste the cool creek,
I smell sweet pine trees,
My pets and dinner too,
As you can see I love the calm country.

Ellie Gray, Grade 6
Dee Mack Intermediate School, IL

Fall

The pumpkins are carved with big ugly faces.
The ghosts are hung in the scariest places.
In the corner of the porch is a big hairy spider,
Mom is inside drinking hot cider.
Come and see the ghost rider.
Watch out for his tiger!

Luke Nikolich, Grade 4
Chrisney Elementary School, IN

Christmastime

It's a special time of year,
It's time for decorations and
The Christmas tree,
There are cookies for you and me.

Time for ice skating, sledding, and
Snowball fights,
Many cold winter nights.

Presents under the tree,
Presents for you and me,
The giving season,
Don't you see?

For Old Saint Nick,
Cookies and milk,
Which he likes,
Since we baked them ourselves.

Snow forts, snow people, and snow pets, too,
Something from me to you,
Joy, happiness, and much, much more,
Christmas for me,
Christmas for you.

McKenzi Sidor, Grade 5
Eagle Creek Elementary School, IN

Chico

Chico
Big, black and white, silly, and energetic
Relative of a furry family
Lover of food, other dogs, and pillows
Who feels joyful, great, and tired
Who needs love, attention, and care
Who fears shots, gun shots, and losing his toy
Who gives licks, allergies, and tickles
Who would like to see a new toy, other dogs, and a big bone
Resident of my heart
My one and only true dog.

Brandi Connor, Grade 6
Helfrich Park Middle School, IN

Gingerbread Man

Gingerbread man made like a cookie but different in a way.
Lives in a house made of cookies and cakes.
Lollipops are added for you and me.
Gingerbread man wears a suit with
gumdrops as buttons and a licorice tie.
Gingerbread man bathes in milk
and sometimes chocolate milk.
Oh how I love my gingerbread man.
Crunch! crunch! yummy!
No more gingerbread man.

Zulema Contreras, Grade 5
Perry Central Elementary School, IN

Moods

Mad
Yelling, screaming,
Cry, walk away, play, laugh
Running, jumping,
Happy

Megan Nies, Grade 5
Perry Central Elementary School, IN

Christmas

Winter is a time
when family comes together.
To celebrate Jesus
in the cool winter weather.
We gather around the Christmas tree,
and open all of the presents that we see.
It is not like Halloween,
when you jump with a fright.
It is when Santa Claus makes
his famous trip through the night.

Kylie Giebelhausen, Grade 6
Central Jr High School, IL

Fuzzy Bats

Bats are black
And fuzzy.
They fly at
Night because
They can't see
In daylight.
They fly very fast.
After they are done
Flying you know
It won't be
The last.

Robby Landes, Grade 5
Gard Elementary School, IL

Master of the Snow

With ease I'm shredding
the top of the hill.
I'm having such fun
I don't mind the chill.
Grinding the rails
is my monstrous challenge.
All of my balance
I must scavenge.
My board smoothly
cuts and glides.
Off a huge jump
I can touch the sky.
Thankfully, I returned
to the slope without disaster.
Yes! I am
the ski slope master!

Joseph Brush, Grade 4
Bright Elementary School, IN

Piano

Pianos are beautiful in every way.
With smooth, creamy, crystal clear notes.
The piano is graceful with music singing out with every touch.
It's always tempting you saying, "Play me!"
It's shiny, black, and white with books overflowing on top.
Once you start playing you can't stop.
The piano loves when it is loved
and gives back when you sacrifice time and make it your passion.
Pianos are beautiful in every way!

Catherine Jacobs, Grade 6
St Joseph School, IN

A Game That Seemed to Last Forever

A person pitching me, I'm zooming toward home plate,
I try to curve my hardest, ouch I am hit,

I'm flying high over a fence, ouch, ouch,
I'm in the prickly bushes,

As someone retrieves me, oh no, I'm falling into the squishy grass,
Yet another throws me ouch, I land in the hard dirt,

Through the innings, my color is fading from white to brown,
I'm being slammed into leather gloves, squeezed so I won't fall out,

After being pinched and smacked left and right, it is the end of the inning,
The pitcher slams me to the ground, as I hear the umpire's loud whistle,

At last I am being signed, by all the players for the coach,
Now I sit in my retirement home, being looked at and admired!

Lauren Boucher, Grade 6
Dee Mack Intermediate School, IL

Candy Corn

Candy corn is sweet and chewy
But the thing I like most is the colors.
They are so pretty — the orange and yellow and white or sometimes brown.
But sometimes I wish the colors were different.
Like pink and blue and purple plus all the colors in the rainbow.
I just don't get why they have to be Halloween colors.
Maybe because they will sell better.
That is why my favorite Halloween candy is candy corn.

Ariel Wingate, Grade 5
Gard Elementary School, IL

Hot Chocolate and Winter

Hot chocolate is like a snow day.
The chocolate is for brown snow that you don't want to eat.
The marshmallows are for white snow that you want to eat.
Hot chocolate is also like the snow that falls from the sky.
The snow is like sprinkles that drop into the melted chocolate.
The hot melted chocolate is like the dirt you see after the snow melts.
When you are freezing, cold, and wet you want to go in and drink hot chocolate.
Hot chocolate is the best.

Preston Maher, Grade 6
Corpus Christi Elementary School, IN

An Ode to Rootbeer

Rootbeer, your taste is so delicious.
Your creaminess is irresistible, so nicely refreshing.

You are really good, I always wish
to see you on the shelf of my refrigerator.

Dear, dear, rootbeer, my friends love you too!
Whenever they come over, they ask if I have you.

Sweet, smooth, soda, your taste lingers on my tongue.
If it weren't for you, many meals would not be fun.

Arianna Brown, Grade 5
Allen J. Warren Elementary School, IN

Trees

The tree sways in the breeze,
As always it wants to please.

The tree has no needs,
Made and grown from a seed.

The tree gives us shade,
Sit, relax, you'll have it made.

The tree gives air to breathe,
And many, many luscious leaves.

The trunk is strong, the branches are long,
Birds in the trees sing a wonderful song.

Paul Kramer, Grade 5
St Daniel the Prophet School, IL

Wayne

I will never forget that horrible day
The day that he passed away
The hero in my life
Now gone forever
He was there for me all my life
Even the day I was born
If someone was hurt
Always the first one there and the last one to leave
Everyone could count on him
When Katrina struck
He was there to help
He loved the silent outdoors
Everything about it
Camping was one of his hobbies
He did it all the time
Most everything he did was for a good cause
He was a great man
I loved him dearly
And I still don't understand
Why he had to leave me

Abbie Jasper-Brown, Grade 6
Nancy Hanks Elementary School, IN

Oh Terrible Percy

Oh terrible Percy,
You curious little kid,
You spray our cat with a hose,
And with a shriek he ripped your clothes.

Oh terrible Percy,
You curious little kid,
You follow a bug to the street,
The town is now a mess.

The streets are blocked with burning cars,
Thick black smoke is filling the air,
choking people half to death,
With fires up to twelve feet high.

When a mob brings your child home,
Nothing can ever be good,
Carrying Percy home they shout,
"Go away Percy destroy a different town."

Oh terrible Percy,
You curious little kid,
With some matches in his room,
Oh dear God please help them.

Paul Byszewski, Grade 6
St Joseph School, IN

Dog

If I were a dog,
I'd be digging up a bone.
Sleeping on my bed,
Barking at cats and chasing them all day too.
My owner brushing my hair as smooth as possible,
Running around the backyard as if I'm an opossum

Kassandra Hernandez, Grade 5
Edison Elementary School, IL

Blind

I was blind when I didn't know Jesus.
I was blind and could not see the path I was taking.
I was blind and didn't see the people I was hurting.
I was blind and felt all alone in a dark room with no light.
I was blind but when I met Jesus I could see.
I was blind as a bat but now I see.

Anthony Sorrentino, Grade 6
Christian Life Schools, IL

A May Day

It's a very sunny day and,
I can't wait to go out and play.
I'm going to ride my bike,
and then I think I'll take a hike.
It was a wonderful day in the month of May,
a favorite day, I must say.

Melissa Matcha, Grade 5
St Daniel the Prophet School, IL

Thanksgiving Time

Thanksgiving is a time of being thankful and being with family.
Thanksgiving is filled with good times almost as good as being born again with Jesus Christ in your heart.
Thanksgiving smells like turkey, pies, and other good food.
Thanksgiving feels like a chance to say what you are thankful for.
It makes me feel like one of those times where you are sure that God is present.
Thanksgiving is a time of laughter, great memories, and maybe one on one time with God.
Thanksgiving looks like leaves are falling and fall has officially started.
To me, Thanksgiving will always be a great memory of mine.

Allyson Hooper, Grade 6
Christian Life Schools, IL

Bartimaeus vs the Golem

Imagine a night
A minotour walking through a labyrinth of holes in walls, in a British museum
Walking the demon's name is Bartimaeus walking with him is fine
We are chasing an unknown animal
I hear two things, the thump thumping of my heart
Then, the big, booming footsteps of the thing
We come to the Egyptian section another sound comes to our ears
A loud banging coming from a giant pharaoh
A dark, black cloud surrounds the creature
Bartimaeus throws a small rock into the cloud a weird cracking noise sounds
It looks around the room for Bartimaeus
Bartimaeus knocks a smaller statue onto the creature
The cloud moves aside, a blue hand shoots out from under the statue, it grabs Bartimaeus
The hand weakens him and tosses him like a tissue
When Bartimaeus is strong again, he sees a Golem
The Golem tries to kill Bartimaeus with an orange detonation it misses Bartimaeus and hits a wall
They go to the other room and the Golem tries again and hits a window
Then the cloud covers the room and the Golem hits the ceiling with another detonation
Then I put the book down. Time for school.

Quin Matthys, Grade 5
Stanley Clark School, IN

The Wild Stallion

The wild stallion stands perfectly still like a statue. Suddenly the crack of a whips sounds! Shrilling whinnies of his herd echo in his ears! His wiry mane and tail ripple through the wind as he gallops to protect his family. In the distance he sees the wranglers attacking his mares and foals! He reaches them and begins the battle. He thrashes at the wranglers using his strong legs. He nips and bucks at his enemies. Frightened, the wranglers zip away. The wild stallion has saved his beloved herd.

Mollie Heil, Grade 4
Walden Elementary School, IL

A Bird's Life

I am an elegant bird.
My eyes will tell you I'm very lonely out here soaring high above an extraordinary canyon.
I'm wearing exquisite turquoise feathers that cover me everywhere like a beautiful coat that never comes off.
I come from Arizona where I live inside and outside a breathtaking canyon.
Behind me is what I have been talking about, a very gracious canyon which I use for my home.
Sometimes I like to fly to the top of the canyon and gaze at the beautiful scenery for hours, and hours.
I long for the days when visitors stop to look and learn about this canyon I live in.
I look forward to winter, I am no longer lonely during that season because that is the time
all the birds fly south and visit me and will maybe even stay at my home all winter long.
I wish more of my family and friends would live at this canyon with me.
If they stayed for a day or two they would love everything about it.

Madison Reed, Grade 6
Churchill Jr High School, IL

Wild Life

Why do sharks have sharp teeth?
Why are cheetahs so fast?
Why do turtles walk so slow?
Why can't chickens fly?
Why are whales so big?

Why can't bats see?
Why don't snakes have legs?
Why are plankton so small?
Why do vampire bats only go out at night?
Why are giraffes so tall?

Why don't dogs meow?
Why don't cats bark?
Why can't animals talk to humans?
Why does the giant squid get so big?

Why do snakes hiss at things that walk by them?
Why do mice run so fast?
Why are dolphins the smartest animal?
Why can't ostriches fly?
Why are elephants so big?

Robert Valdez, Grade 5
Edison Elementary School, IL

Sports

The best part of the year is sports,
When you play basketball you're on the courts.
If you're in the NBA and you make a swoosh,
You just might meet President Bush!
If you score all the points in a soccer game,
You might as well get all the fame.
In football you make touchdowns,
But if you are pushed you go out of bounds.
In golf it is almost impossible to get a hole in one,
If you do you just WON!
Even though there are more sports than that,
To all of you I tip my hat.

Ethan Robert Pearl, Grade 6
Emmanuel-St Michael Lutheran School, IN

I Confess

I Confess I'm the one who gave the dog a bone.
I Confess I'm the one who played the baritone.
I Confess I'm the one who broke my backbone.
I Confess I'm the one who threw the phone.
I Confess I'm the one who dropped the ice cream cone.
I Confess I'm the one who broke the microphone.
I Confess I'm the one who is overgrown.
I Confess I'm the one who still lives at home.
I Confess I'm the one who doesn't have a telephone.
I Confess I'm the one who doesn't have a twilight zone.
I Confess I'm the one who doesn't have a tombstone.
I Confess I'm the one who got left at home.

Dalton Ransom, Grade 5
Perry Central Elementary School, IN

The Breezy Sail

Ghostly forms gliding across the sea.
Ships cutting through the mist like a knife.
Sails work hard to push the snakelike ship.
Waves are choppy.

The mist of the morning drizzles down the captain's face.
All nine sails quiver in the morning breeze.
Sails look as if they are fluffy white snow mounds.
Fishing ships slide slowly into the Yatsushiro Sea.

Airiel Kring, Grade 6
Knox Community Middle School, IN

True Friends

True friends are there for you.
They are kind and trustworthy.
They will stay by you when you are scared.
They will play all the time,
when you make play dates.
They will help you when you get hurt.
That is what a true friend is and more.

Joey Spina, Grade 5
William B Orenic Intermediate School, IL

An Ode to a Very Special Friend

Oh dear Shelby you make me laugh.
I'm happy when I see you and sad when you're not there.
You give me something to do
And someone to hang out with
We have sleepovers and tell each other funny stories.
I pick out your clothes and you pick out mine.
And now I'm sad because I have to say goodbye.

Erin Buckley, Grade 5
Allen J. Warren Elementary School, IN

The Wonders of the Sky

The sky holds many great things
Even though no one notices
The sky holds light
The sky holds night
But…What do I see way up high where the sky lies?

The sun is going to sleep 'til tomorrow says the sun.
Then…the moon awakens into the sky
"Goodnight my fellow people
I shall be watching over you
Now head to sleep.
Come stars let us shine!"

The sky holds the wonders:
Rain, sun, snow, moon, and the stars,
But…when they all look down what do they see…

A girl looking at the wonders of the sky!

Michelle Olivares, Grade 5
Walker Elementary School, IL

School

School
fun, classy
educating, thinking, playing
recess, books, pencil, chalkboard
learning, writing, working
long, quiet
Home
Taylor Hire, Grade 4
St Matthew School, IL

Halloween

H appy Halloween!
A ll boys and girls trick or treat.
L et kids get candy.
L ots of people sing a Halloween song.
O wls who-o-o at night.
W itches and ghouls put spells on you.
E verybody say HALLOWEEN!
E very day people carve pumpkins.
N obody takes just one piece of candy.
Stephanie Reed, Grade 6
Three Rivers School, IL

Drugs Destroy Dreams

It is true,
Drugs destroy dreams for you.

Do what is right.
Teach your friends not to fight.

Using drugs is definitely wrong.
Help your friends to get along.

Dare to dream and dream some more.
You will surely be successful and score.
Kenze Mitchell, Grade 5
Dee Mack Intermediate School, IL

Nature

Nature I love you.
I love the birds, too.
I like the deer.
Some I fear.
I love to hear the birds coo.
Britney Cooper, Grade 4
Shoals Elementary School, IN

Shed

There was a snake in my bed.
And in my bed it shed.
I was mad
Because it was very bad.
And because it shed I fled.
Logan Harker, Grade 4
Shoals Elementary School, IN

Scream

S creaming
C hildren
R unning
E verywhere
A voiding
M ummies
Hailey Hickey, Grade 4
Bailly Elementary School, IN

Summer Winter

Summer
Sunny, bright
Swimming, picnicking, playing
Warmth, sunshine, snowflakes, ice
Snowing, sledding, playing
Frosty, cold
Winter
Katlyn Diggs, Grade 6
Herrick Grade School, IL

My Dog Buddy

My dog Buddy is as white and curly
as the first snowfall.

To get a treat he does some tricks
like roll over, and sit, or fetch the ball.

If you give Buddy a treat
he'll be your friend.

Buddy and I may our fun never end.
Ryan Gaughan, Grade 5
St Daniel the Prophet School, IL

Football/Basketball

Football
Awesome, fun
Throwing, tackling, running
Cleats, helmet, backboard, rim
Shooting, dribbling, scoring
Difficult, interesting
Basketball
Joseph William James, Grade 6
Perry Central Elementary School, IN

Football

Football
Challenging, demanding
Coaches yelling
Opponents glaring
Fans expecting victory
Rising to high expectations
Celebration of passion
Taylor Williams, Grade 6
Tri-West Middle School, IN

Haunted Houses

Haunted houses are scary.
Some people are merry.
There's not a single light.
So there's a lot of fright.
Meet the monster Harry.
Morgan Hummel, Grade 4
St Matthew School, IL

Me, Myself, and I

I'm on a log in a clearing,
No one is around,
Sight of sky, touch of log,
Barely bearing sound.

I look around, and then I sigh.
No one is around.
I'm all alone, yes I am
Just me, myself, and I.

I'm all alone in the attic,
The mice are squeaking about.
Smell of dust, sight of trunks,
I never want to go out.

I shut the trapdoor, again I sigh,
No one is around.
I'm all alone, yes I am,
Just me, myself, and I.
Liam Maher, Grade 6
St Joseph School, IN

Bird

I hear their sweet song,
Dancing through the silver wind,
A beautiful sound.
Scott Logue, Grade 6
Dee Mack Intermediate School, IL

Love All the Same

Is this where we stand
So lonely and sad
With nothing as grand as your love?
You've taken me in
And cared for me too
Now you might already know this
But I'm still going to tell,
You'll love me all the same
Even if I yell!
If you even say
That your love is no more
I might cry out
In despair
"This world is no fair!"
Sarah Lester, Grade 4
Home School, IL

But Not

I like
Football but not when I get injured
KFC but not when it's cold
Stomp the Yard but not when they use profanity
Dogs but not when they die
Colts but not when they lose
Watch football games but not the 49ers
Money but not when you spend it
Video games but not when you lose
Playing football but not when people get in fights
Mustangs but not when they are old style
Dodge Chargers but not when they are slow
Chevy trucks but not when they crash
Camaros but not when they break down
Christmas but not when it's over
My birthday but not when it's over
Sleeping but not when you get up
Football jerseys but not when they rip
My brother but not when he annoys me
My sister but not when she is mean
My mom but not when she is cranky

Adrian Sizemore, Grade 5
Churubusco Elementary School, IN

Fall

Leaves are falling
they're changing colors
beautiful vibrant colors
red, gold, orange, and yellow
bonfires lighting against
the walls, everyone is
cuddling up by the fire
trying to get warm.
You could tell it is
fall-midwinter. You
don't want to leave
the house because it's
so cold. Fall is here
and it's getting colder.
Stay near a fire because
the cold may zap
you cold.

Lyric Griffin, Grade 5
William B Orenic Intermediate School, IL

C

Crack, smack down goes the door
    Wet sweat streaming to the floor
Gleaming sun everywhere take second for air
    Loaders, motors here and there everywhere
Rustling, hustling though the sight
Nighttime has finally arrived, the lonely men
    settle down for the night.

Gage Iles, Grade 5
North Intermediate Center of Education, IL

My Savior

My Savior keeps me warm at night.
My Savior helps me through the night.
He helps me through the dark and into the light.
My Savior is all you could ask for, He is Jesus Christ.
Jesus my Savior is my light that I walk with through my troubles.
He keeps me on track through the dark nights,
My Savior Jesus, he is ominous He foretells all dangers.
Jesus is omnipotent He is the Almighty.
He is omnipresent He is everywhere.
Jesus is omniscient He has infinite awareness.
He is the Lion of Judea that loves and cares.
Jesus is like a father that keeps his children safe.
Most of all Jesus is my friend and He always will be.

Zachary Stanphill, Grade 6
Christian Life Schools, IL

Thanksgiving

Thanksgiving is coming soon.
There is always enough food to eat.
We're going to Grandma's house at noon.
The tables are always nice and neat.

Kaitlin Dant, Grade 4
Veale Elementary School, IN

Basketball

Jerseys and Nike shoes
Nets and stands filled with fans
Sweat dripping down
Running back and forth and up and down the court
Shooting and fouling
Making new plays
Swooshing every shot
Basketball days

Raegan Lintner, Grade 6
Tri-West Middle School, IN

Moon

Pallid beauty ball of white,
Semicircle wonder in the night.
Earth's little sister, a reflective coward,
It's sunlight racism has gone sour.

Sometimes half gone and sometimes half there,
Not part of the moon can get its full reflective share.
Every day as it rotates parts vanish and are gone,
And the whole thing is ordered to turn off after dawn.

Ball of white in the well — a water illusion,
No possible way of a complete extrusion.
Sunlight plus water plus the ball of white,
Addition problem equals reflective light.

Every evening at dusk above the red line,
The beautiful moon reigns with its pallid white shine.

Matthew Wu, Grade 5
Highlands Elementary School, IL

Christmas

Fantastic
Holly
Amusing
Jolly
Loving
Gifts
Lovely
Family
Exciting
Awesome
Caring
Fabulous
Tremendous
Wonderful
Outstanding
Magnificent

Katie Ann Polhans-Vice, Grade 5
Lincoln Intermediate School, IL

Ode to My Softball

Oh, my softball
Oh, so round
I always get you
Before you hit the ground.
I love the game.
It's really not lame.
Just get your head in the game.
We hope to win again and again.
Oh, hurray we won again.

Renee Savicz, Grade 5
Allen J. Warren Elementary School, IN

Candy

Some are sweet,
Some are sour,
Sometimes I eat one per hour.

Something hard,
Something chewy,
Although something could be gooey.

Sometimes I want to burp,
Sometimes my stomach often hurts,
It makes me want to burst.

Ryan Kramer, Grade 5
St Daniel the Prophet School, IL

Mary

A girl named Mary
She had a cat named Larry
So Larry went with the balls
Then with the dolls
Then Larry saw Terry
The friend of Mary.

Michelle Barrera, Grade 5
Gard Elementary School, IL

I Like

I like the Dallas Cowboys because they are mean, more tackle football.
I like vegetables because they keep you healthy.
I like glue sticks because we can glue stuff to our paper.
I like walls so you don't fall out of a building.
I like walking because it helps build muscle.
I like cars because we get to places faster.
I like gas because it runs our cars.
I like woodpeckers because they eat bugs out of trees.
I like tents because we can camp at night.

Braden Vincent, Grade 5
Churubusco Elementary School, IN

Autumn

Autumn is feeling the crisp leaves crunching under my feet.
Autumn is seeing the beautiful colored leaves coming off the trees.
Autumn is feeling the wet grass from the frost.
Autumn is hearing the wind rustling the trees.
Autumn is my favorite season, colors all abright.

Sarah Benedix, Grade 6
Stanley Clark School, IN

The Ocean

The ocean is a simple thing just like you and me.
If you go there you will see crystal water and people bodysurfing.
When you go to the sparking water
You will hear the soothing sound of water.

When you go to the soothing sparkling ocean
It will taste like, sweet, salty, warm water.
When you go to the sparkling, soothing salty ocean,
You will feel slimy gooey kelp.

When you go to the sparkling, soothing, salty, slimy ocean,
It smells like salty misty water.
Now that is what you'll hear and see when you go to the ocean.

Sara Verda, Grade 4
Fox Creek Elementary School, IL

Soldier Field

I see sweaty players,
receivers catching the pass,
Devin Hester running from end zone to end zone.

I smell brats, burgers, and dogs cooking
the burnt, smoky fireworks
the busy bathrooms

I taste the salty popcorn
the ice cold coke going down my throat
juicy hot dogs, sour cream and onion chips, and vanilla ice cream

I hear fans yelling "I NEED TICKETS,"
the crowd booing at the refs
and roaring when the Bears get a touchdown!

Tommy Ross, Grade 6
Chicago City Day School, IL

I Can Make a Difference

I can make a difference by being your friend.
I will be with you 'til the very end.

If you are feeling lonely and blue,
I will be a friend to you.

It is great to have a friend and know that they care.
Inside jokes and giggling are memories that we can share.

Being a friend is fun,
When you are friends with everyone.

Whitney Wiegand, Grade 5
Dee Mack Intermediate School, IL

The Canoe

Inside the canoe,
On the water,
Under the stars,
Beyond the trees,
Above the fish,
Near the cabins,
Through the lily pads,
Between the swampy lakes,
Beside the dragon flies,
Toward the boat launch,
A canoe sitting there waiting for occupants.

Maura Garza, Grade 5
Churubusco Elementary School, IN

Football

Football is very fun
even though you have to run.
It is always fun to tackle
just to hear your pads crackle.
I like to lay people out
to hear the coach say, "Good job" and shout.
It is cool to hear the crowd shout
once you score a touchdown and jump about.
I like to run through the hole
just to score a touchdown and meet my goal.

Josh Orschell, Grade 5
St Michael School, IN

Fall

Fall, cold weather, cruel winds
but fall isn't always that way.
It is sometimes cold but not windy
and sometimes fall is scary.
Kids trick-or-treating
a lot and a lot of candy
Kids in costumes
everyone walking around
some people inside getting warm
but me, I'm everywhere because it's fall.

Victor X. Colon, Grade 5
William B Orenic Intermediate School, IL

Basketball

B asketball is my favorite sport.
A sleep in my bed I dream of playing basketball.
S lick is the basketball floor.
K nocking people down, they get a free shot.
E very time I play I feel as if I'm getting better.
T alent is what you need for basketball.
B asketball is a very fun sport.
A ction in the game can make you win.
L ove to watch everybody win.
L eaving is the worst part of basketball.

Kerriann Cooper, Grade 5
Coffeen Elementary School, IL

Football

F ootball is a fun sport!
O pening kickoff of the big game
O h no, there is an injure.
T o the ten, to the five, touchdown!
B all is lost and the other team gets it!
A ll the way like a freight train, touchdown!
L ong jump for a first down.
L osing is never fun

Ethan Emmons, Grade 6
Perry Central Elementary School, IN

Mouse

Can I ask, why are you leaving traps?
It's really hard to get food for my family.
I tried scurrying up the counter with no luck.
All of a sudden I heard a deafening scream.
Even though I was blinded by a light
I saw a small figure.
All I could do was squeak,
"Why are you so afraid?"
I ran back to my home. Goodnight.

Mary Nutley, Grade 6
Sacred Heart Elementary School, IL

Homework

I don't like homework, not a bit,
It makes me sad and my insides sick.
All day and night I weep and cry,
I feel like I will simply die.

Austin Wood, Grade 5
Washington Township Elementary School, IN

Salt

White grains
Adding, flavoring, shaking,
Grainy ocean flavor, mouth tingling spices
Grinding, sneezing, dashing
Brown, black
Pepper

Isabel Delia Adams, Grade 6
Perry Central Elementary School, IN

Mace

There was an angry lady named Mace.
She had an infected pimple on her face.
Every moment she got mad,
Or she got sad,
Pimples multiplied on her face.

Austin Crowe, Grade 5
Perry Central Elementary School, IN

Belief

B e yourself
be **E** ager
L ove life
use your **I** magination
give your best **E** ffort
have **F** aith in yourself

Haley Ashby, Grade 6
Tri-West Middle School, IN

Winter

So many leafless trees of fall,
in the sparkling winter snow
with its shining, sparkling trunk of glee,
upon the frozen snow
winter brings a
crystal-like
blanket of snow.

Noah Dreyer, Grade 4
Churubusco Elementary School, IN

Zebra

Snow is fluffy,
Soft,
White.
It cascades down from the heavens
In the deep dark of night

A tree is dark,
Bare,
Black,
In the winter's low sunlight.

Together,
Snow,
And trees,
Are like zebras,
Black and white
They colors fuse exquisitely.
No flaw in sight.

Bare trees and pure snow,
Belong together
Like a zebra's colors.
Black and white.

Shireen Husami, Grade 5
Walker Elementary School, IL

Love

Love is like a dove,
When it is sent from above.
You blow a kiss,
Cupid cannot miss.

On Valentine's Day,
He's hoping you will say,
"Love is great!
I cannot wait."

Kaitlin Cassatt, Grade 5
Dee Mack Intermediate School, IL

The Way a Book Opens

When a book opens
you start to read.

You make visual pictures
to make you think
of all the wonders
of the story you're reading.

Reading is my favorite thing to do
and with others too.

I can read in the hot sun,
the snowy days, and whenever
my heart desires.

Raytoria Richardson, Grade 6
Laraway School, IL

Shapes

Shapes are different
In every single way.
Ovals, octagons, rectangles and kites.

Shapes can be made
Into many different styles,
There are flat ones, round ones
And curved ones too.

Shapes that make
The simple things we see
Confusing and intricate.
Making all things beautiful
And worthwhile.

The shapes of our hands,
Shapes from the ancients and shapes
Of today.

When you think about it
The world is
One big shape.

Kendal Gee, Grade 5
Keystone Montessori School, IL

Friends

F unny
R emarkable
I ncredible
E nergetic
N eat
D ainty
S illy

Barbara E. Kratsios, Grade 5
St Jude Catholic School, IN

The Thanksgiving Monster

There goes the Thanksgiving monster.
He gives everybody a scare.
But the monster seems not to care.
In fact he stepped into my house.
He frightened the pet mouse.
The mouse ran right out of the house.
The monster giggled and gobbled.
As he juggled our Jell-O.
He ate the peas.
He didn't even say please.
He ate the whole feast.
Then he ran far east.
There goes the Thanksgiving monster.

Brandon Engelkens, Grade 6
Dakota Elementary School, IL

The Shadow

As walking
Through the dark, cold, alley
The wind whooshing through
My face
Then, right then
I noticed something strange
Through the night
The dark, evil, night
A silhouette walking
Through the bright doors
Tracking
Every step I make
Waiting till I stop
As if I was
His prey

Abbey Prilliman, Grade 6
Northwood Elementary School, IN

Ashley

A mazing
S hy
H onest
L ikable
E xciting
Y oung

Ashley Nicole Moyer, Grade 5
St Jude Catholic School, IN

The Hut!

As I walk in the fluffy snow,
I see a hut in the distance.
It is a small hut,
with smoke rising out of the chimney.
As I get closer I hear a voice singing inside.
I can now smell the apple cider
and pumpkin pie.
I can almost taste it!
I walk inside and there I see,
a little old lady singing and dancing
all around the room while she cooks.
She then stops, turns around,
and sees me, but then she says,
come in, come in there's plenty for all!
We sit down and enjoy
each other's company,
while having the delicious
pumpkin pie and apple cider.
We say our good-byes
and I am off,
as I walk in the fluffy snow.

Danielle Pasalich, Grade 6
Stanley Clark School, IN

Great Outdoors

Animals are everywhere
Starting to get their winter hair
Squirrels are gathering food
Building their homes
Hunters coming
They are making a strange noise called humming
Now hunting season is over
Spring is here
Deer are eating clover
The new people are roaming all over
Forests are filled with young
The fun has just begun

Haley Cox, Grade 6
Milltown Elementary School, IN

Just Another Dream

Red and white mushrooms sprout
All around and all about
After the rainforest rain
The leaves are coated with a dew like stain
Sugar top mountains
Statues and fountains
A bright yellow bumblebee
Landed on the neon green pear tree
As I took this peaceful walk
Through the tall tree stalks
I realized
That it's just a dream

Rachel Richardson, Grade 6
South Middle School, IL

I Am From

I am from long hours with friends and family.
I am from being with many different faces.
I am from the long and short family vacations.
I am from historical houses of St. Augustine,
And I am from the sunny beaches of Florida
And the cold streets of Chicago.
I am from the many hot days at Camp Allendale,
And the rainy days with it.
I am from the many campfires in the woods
I am from family members,
Young and old.

Morganne Belton, Grade 6
Northwood Elementary School, IN

My 3rd Grade Class

My third grade class brings back good glee,
My good ole friend is named Haley,
My third grade teacher is Miss Coop,
She often liked to sip her soup
I will miss her very much
I think of her such and such

I see her here and even there,
I'd like to see her everywhere.
Miss Coop is really nice,
At a party she had a slice (of pizza)
I will miss her very much
I think of her such and such.

Tiah Zastrow, Grade 4
Coal City Intermediate School, IL

It's Not Easy Being a Book!

No, don't
Don't, don't
Put me in there
It is cold and dark in there
Hey, what did I say?

No! That bag is dark
It stinks and it's well it's…
Ok it's just awful
No, they will crush me
Stupid, stupid textbooks

No offense but
It's not easy being me
I get stepped on
By *everyone*

The only good thing
About my life is
The library
When I am with my friends
No! Somebody just checked me out, not again!

Taylor Campbell, Grade 6
Dee Mack Intermediate School, IL

Monster Truck

A roaring monster.
Enormous crowds gather
To watch this monster.
Jumps over cars, donuts, and wheelies
Are just a few of this monster's
Tricks up its sleeve.
Storms race.
Thunder claps as they
Ready themselves.
A flash of light —
Off they go.
One storm slows its pace
Then slowly dissipates
Letting the other storm
Into the lead
Letting it win.
But these monsters
won't stay forever.
Eventually, they will sputter
To a stop,
And their lives will end.

Ethan Aquino, Grade 5
Highlands Elementary School, IL

The Red Kazoo

There once was a red kazoo
That was found in a little boy's shoe.
It was shiny and bright,
and it gleamed at night.
It sang a beautiful song,
that told right from wrong.
And played a song that sang true,
to a love that the boy once knew.

Nicholas Hernandez, Grade 5
St Daniel the Prophet School, IL

If I Was a Dog

If I was a dog,
I would play with my toys.
I would go to the pet store.
I would bite all the boys.

Brenda Diaz, Grade 5
Edison Elementary School, IL

Mystical

Fairies' wings,
Mermaids' tails;
Unicorns' horns,
Monsters' scales.

Dragons' fire,
Pixies' dust;
Elves' little shoes,
All mystical stuff.

Emily Madden, Grade 4
St Matthew School, IL

I Protest!

In war too many lives are lost — innocents die for no reason, and brave souls fall
And just for hate
Terrible hate sparked by an igniting source
Power is terrible when used wrong.
I protest
That countless should die unnecessarily
At one empowered source's whim
And that hate is living in such great numbers in one's heart
And that sometimes temptation is too strong.

Without food the body does not function, without nutrition it will not keep
And so the poor ones who must work hard and gain little will suffer
While those whose birth is rich will work less and gain more.
I protest
That while we are spoiled
Others must beg for food so that sometimes
Those who work hard gain little, and those who work less gain more
That children do not make it to adulthood
Because they die of starvation first.

I protest against those huge injustices of life separating
The poor, innocent, wealthy, and guilty
And what it does to the world.

Akanksha Shah, Grade 6
Thomas Dooley Elementary School, IL

The Beautiful Depths of Florida

Rocks jutting out like loose bricks,
A treelike structure reaching out like an octopus,
Scaly, silver fish darting around like crazed maniacs,
Beady black eyes peeking from behind coral
The dingy bottom, a playground for fish,
Exposed and wary, a wild green sea turtle haunts a Florida shoal.

Jonnie West, Grade 6
Knox Community Middle School, IN

Swinging on My White Wooden Swing

Swinging on my white wooden swing
As white as foam dancing across the blue blanket of pure liquid relief
Swinging on my white wooden swing
As I watch the waves go by
Swinging on my white wooden swing
Waiting there for the next sound of a gentle
"Crassshhh"
Swinging on my white wooden swing
While they ebb toward my feet
And I inhale the salty smell of this moist and dim place
I could wait here all day
Listening silently
Feeling gently
Watching eagerly
And smelling the ocean's aroma
But, I must go inside
And leave my white wooden swing to rest

Isabela Nanni, Grade 5
Stanley Clark School, IN

Soccer

Wind howls against your face
Well, you run faster than light itself
You kick the ball with full force
And let all your emotions drift away
The ball is like a magnet
That you stick to with your best effort
And before you know it you're by the goal
You draw your foot back with all your might
And it's as if the ball has a mind of it's own
It shoots into the goal like a rocket
And before you know what is happening
You get lifted into the air and off your feet
And feel nothing but happiness

Katherine Brady, Grade 4
Lincoln Elementary School, IL

Pickett's Charge

Into line we go.
    Muskets to right shoulder shift.
    Thousands of Rebels charging, charging.
    It seems like life is going to end. Gone.
Commands shouting, shouting, shouting.
    Drums booming, booming.
    Men yelling, yelling.
    It seems like life is so far away.
    It's not here.
Cannonballs flying and falling through the air.
    Men dying, laying on the ground.
    Feeling your gun strong and sturdy.
    I wish I was like that. But right now I'm not.
A command is given.
    Men raise their muskets.
    Another command, "Fire!"
    Rebels lives are at end.
    Lucky me. Mine's not.
We fix bayonets.
    Rebels charge. They hit our line.
    We stay sturdy. My life is not at end.

Luke Bridwell, Grade 6
Our Shepherd Lutheran School, IN

Tyler

Funny, weird, big, intelligent
Relative of a big family
Lover of Brian Urlacher, Stewie Griffin, and Wii
Who feels large, tough, and energized
Who needs Wii, computer, and TV
Who fears bleach getting taken off air, a broken
    controller, and a Wii shutdown
Who gives happiness, ideas, and parties
Who would like to see a million dollars, new games for the Wii,
    and a bigger house
Resident of Indiana
Ricketts

Alex Brust, Grade 6
Helfrich Park Middle School, IN

Nature

To people nature is how you see it.
To me, nature is beautiful.
It is a world of color; it is a miracle.
When each spring how a leaf can sprout out is a miracle.
Without nature we are nothing.
The beauty is something that many of us waste.
We are too busy to see or enjoy it.
We destroy it and never try to rebuild it.
We must try and protect wildlife and the beauty around us.
It is disappearing quickly and once it's gone,
It's gone.
Nature is important and it needs our help.

Melissa Becraft, Grade 6
Peoria Academy, IL

My Favorite Place

The taste of warm nachos and cheese is so delicious
While you eat you hear cheerleaders cheering
You smell juicy hot dogs on the grill
When you're eating you see the brand new jerseys
When watching the game you're sitting on the cold bleachers
You can smell their sweat when they play
Every once in a while you can hear bones breaking
After a play they go get a drink of water or Gatorade
You hear clacking of pads and helmets colliding
This is my favorite place because you get to hit the other team

Justis Wyman, Grade 6
Dee Mack Intermediate School, IL

Rainbow

Zzzzzzz, Zzzzzzz, Zzzzzzz
I fell asleep
I woke up on a unicorn!

I see so much!
The pretty clouds, the blue sky,
And, oh no!!!
It's the Lazy Little Leprechaun
Wearing all green, a white shirt, and his little bow tie.
He is standing next to the pot of gold!…

Yes! I defeated him!
I get to my pot of gold.
I say to myself, "I'm going to be rich!"
But then, I touch the gold,

It turns out that the gold I thought would make me rich
Would only make me hungry!
My pot of gold is actually a pot of chocolate gold.
"I went all this way to find chocolate," I said to myself.
Wait a second, I wake up…
What a wonderful dream about a rainbow.
YUM!!!

Maggie Lowenhar, Grade 5
Stanley Clark School, IN

Elk/Moose

Elk
Big, squirrel brown,
Running, grazing, jumping,
Stumpy and polite, fat and mean,
Walking, alerting, charging,
Gigantic, dark brown,
Moose
Thomas Lasher, Grade 6
Perry Central Elementary School, IN

Long Boarding

Long boarding is fun
I do it in the sun
I can go real fast
and I think it is a blast
Mitch McDonough, Grade 6
Bethel Lutheran School, IL

Shopping

So many things to do,
So many things to buy.
That's shopping!

Can't decide what to purchase,
Go back and forth on unique items.
That's shopping!

Seeing what you think will look the best,
And wondering if you will ever wear it.
That's shopping!

Wearing the clothes,
Seeing what's fabulous on you.
That's shopping!

Let's go shopping!
Emily Davis, Grade 5
Perry Central Elementary School, IN

What Is Black?

Black is the color of the night sky
when the stars do their dance.
When the moon takes a chance
to take a glaring glance,
at the planets.
Black is also the color of a black cat
when it runs past you
almost as swiftly as a bat.
That is black.
My best friend's hair
and the friendship we share
Black is a strong color,
there is nothing wrong with black.
Julie Nerwin, Grade 6
South Middle School, IL

Dog

Why can't I chew on that shoe?
I don't see a problem
Look! A squirrel! Let me out let me out!
I'll make him run right up that tree!
Not the cat again
Get away!
Rachel Leonard, Grade 6
Sacred Heart Elementary School, IL

Kickball

Kickball
Fun, fast
Pitching, kicking, stealing
Make a home run
Game
Thomas Durbin, Grade 6
Herrick Grade School, IL

My Puppy

My puppy
My puppy is sweet and kind
My puppy
He knows my mind
My puppy
He plays he sleep and loves me
My puppy
He lifts me up when I am down
My puppy
He's happy all year round
My puppy
A friend who's there for me all the time
My puppy
Puts me above his needs
My puppy
In return I give him love
My puppy
I'll love him forever
My Sabastion
Lindsey Zeiger, Grade 6
St Joseph School, IN

Care

You should care
To learn how to share

Let someone sit in a chair
To show you care

Care is cool
If you don't want to be a fool

Care can sometimes be rare
Like the blue clothes you wear
Shirin Patel, Grade 4
Summit Elementary School, IL

Earth

Earth, Earth
so full of peace.
Earth, Earth
what a wonderful place to be.
Michael McDowell, Grade 6
Helfrich Park Middle School, IN

Basketball

B right faces every game
A re keeping us very tame
S core by getting a slam dunk
K eep very aggressive
E very day we hustle
T o work with our muscles
B e aggressive
A lways impressive
L oud and proud
L oudly yelled did the crowd
Taylor Carnahan, Grade 5
Dee Mack Intermediate School, IL

The Coyote

I'm a coyote
Grey coat of fur hangs off me
Like it was glued on
Deserts of Nevada I
Howl to know I'm not alone
Angel Peterson, Grade 6
Churchill Jr High School, IL

Colts Safety Bob Sanders

a blue streak of lightning
striking like thunder
number 21
the best safety ever
he's as fast as a colt
with a long black mane
he's crazier than crazy
he's my favorite player ever
he tackles like pure pain
and hits harder than the Titans
whole entire defense
he's slamming number 86
a Titan is going down
he feels straight pain
worse than getting hit by a train
Lucio Medina, Grade 6
Northwood Elementary School, IN

Tulips

Bright colors, wonderful scents,
Pink tulips…what smiles they bring
When given to another…
Elizabeth Navarro, Grade 4
Jane Addams Elementary School, IL

Eiffel Tower

As
I
gaze up
in awe at
the iron giraffe it
sticks out wanting to be
seen as if it were a splinter in
your foot stretching thousands of
feet high inviting tourists to wander
inside an   amazing building
a beautiful prism   that is perfectly placed
in the middle   of the city
as if the city   was made for it
as I go up   things growing
smaller   and smaller
until they're   tiny specs
And the giraffe continues to stand not crushing a single soul

David Wu, Grade 5
Highlands Elementary School, IL

Volleyball

We spiked the ball over the net.
The crowd went wild,
Because it looked like no sweat.
Now I am setting,
I am low to the ground,
And getting ready for anything.
Our team served the ball.
A perfect serve, right over the net,
And the team just let the ball fall.
We served again,
But it came out of bounds.
And we knew that will happen every now and then.
We called for a time-out.
Coach said we needed to get ready,
And then we went back out.
The game went on
We were winning, 24 to 21
It took so long, I had to yawn
So far we could have won
But when I bumped the ball
The game was done.

Abby Robertson, Grade 5
Dee Mack Intermediate School, IL

Dats

Dogs
Soft, playful,
Scratching, playing, jumping,
Dachshund, Dalmatian, Persian, Siamese,
Purring, licking, sleeping,
Cuddly, kind
Cats

Ashlyn Milfs, Grade 5
Bethel Lutheran School, IL

Big Brown Eyes

There I saw her;
Looking up in her big brown, round eyes
It was like I was falling,
Down, down, down
I, the baby the quietness of the sky

Then I heard it, the sound I would always remember
Two-year-old sister,
Her mouth,
Her voice, the sound
"I love you, do you?"

It is there in my heart
Just those five words,
I am the sister of her; she is the sister of me,
We will live together as happy as can be!

Aimee Wilson-Nixa, Grade 6
St Joseph School, IN

Food

Ham, turkey, and mashed potatoes
Sandwiches, macaroni, cheeseburgers with tomatoes
Crunching, swallowing, chewing food up,
With French fries I like ketchup
Pudding, sherbet, and scrambled eggs
Fruit, meat, veggies, and chicken legs
Maybe one day you'll be in the mood
To try one of those delicious foods!

Ashlynn Marx, Grade 6
North Knox East Elementary/Jr High School, IN

Eagle

The speeding bullet whistles as it
Dives towards the sea of grass.
It swoops, just in time to
Close its claws upon the frightened creature.
Then it takes off,
Flapping its powerful
Blades, slicing the air in half.

It heads towards
The mighty flame,
High in the sky,
Then rises abruptly through the clouds,
Searching for its nestlings,
Snuggled close together.

After a tiring journey going back and forth,
The golden chariot snaps the neck
Of one final creature,
Then ascends towards the heavens,
And crashes through the solid barrier of pearl white bricks,
Listening for the waiting chirps of little nestlings,
And watching the clouds burst into flame as the sun slowly set.

Kireem Nam, Grade 5
Highlands Elementary School, IL

School

School is so gloomy.
School is so stale.
Whenever I show up there,
I'm always looking pale.

I may not pass fourth grade,
There's so much work to do,
Math is my least favorite subject,
It's probably yours too.

If I had a wish,
I would wish there'd be no school,
And you know what that would be
That would be so cool.
Madeline McMahon, Grade 4
St Matthew School, IL

Wonderful Country

I look at our flag
And I feel so sad
But happy, cause they fought
Fought just for us!
And our lives hold many things
Our memories will never forget
What those people did
For our wonderful country
I live in!
Felicia Campbell, Grade 6
Chaney-Monge Jr High School, IL

Snow

Icy cold
Shining very brightly
Falling fast from Earth
Blizzards
Jordyn Byrd, Grade 6
Perry Central Elementary School, IN

Seasons!

In spring the flowers grow,
Grass turns green and we mow.
Summer is lots of fun,
I play all day in the sun.
The leaves turn colors in the fall,
We rake them up and jump in them all.
In the winter it will snow,
But how much, no one knows!
Noah Seaford, Grade 4
Chrisney Elementary School, IN

Mom

Sometimes you are cool.
You take good care of me.
I love you a lot.
Arin Hupp, Grade 4
Scipio Elementary School, IN

Winter

Feeling the chilly breeze whiz on by.
Knowing it is the last day of fall.
Then on my back, water trickles down. It burns.
Then a snowflake falls down from the sky.
Then another falls. Soon the sky is white with snow.
Then BOOM!
A snowball hits me from behind.
It makes me open up all my senses.
My nose smells wet leaves.
I hear snow crunching but it is not coming from my own feet.
I start to get the feeling that someone is watching me.
I hear a snowball coming. It's darting sound is unforgettable.
It makes me duck and it misses by a hair.
I taste water in my mouth from all the snow.
I run inside and then, I see my mom.
Laughing away like a pack of hyenas. Instantly I know it was her.
She must have just got back from feeding the horse.
I go downstairs, where I feel the warmth.
Then I feel very relaxed. I fall asleep
Dreaming of summer and the warmth.

Taylor Hieber, Grade 6
Stanley Clark School, IN

When I'm a Grandpa

When I'm a grandpa I'm going skydiving with my grandchild
When I'm a grandpa I'm going to spoil my grandchildren
When I'm a grandpa I'm going to dress like a teen just with wider pants
When I'm a grandpa I'm going to a lot of theme parks with Advil
When I'm a grandpa I'm going to jump out of a plane with special medication
Tyler Mains, Grade 6
Christian Life Schools, IL

Jupiter

J upiter is larger than
U ranus. You could
P ut more than 1,300 Earths
I nside of Jupiter. Jupiter is made of ninety percent hydrogen and
T en percent helium. It takes ten
E arth hours for Jupiter to do a full
R otation.

Kyllee Miller, Grade 6
Pinewood Elementary School, IN

Who Is She?

Who is she to me?
Is she my friend?
I cannot decide because she is hard to understand.
Who is she to me?
I cannot tell because she is into things like death and blood.
Who is she to me?
I know she watches TV day and night and sometimes even wants to fight.
Who is she to me?
Is she my friend?
That is a question that will never end.

Maureen Kesterson-Yates, Grade 6
Rousseau McClellan IPS School 91, IN

The Beach Unknown

There is a place on an island unknown
Where the seagulls cry and the waves rumble

A place where you can touch the hot sand
And you can feel the cool water

A beach where you can smell the salty air
And you can sense the freshly squeezed pineapple

You see the light shining in the trees
Through the open spots between the leaves

You see dolphins and crabs wading through the water
The dolphins' fins waving and the crabs' shells gleaming

There is a place on an island unknown
Where the seagulls cry and the waves rumble

Samantha Vique, Grade 6
Dee Mack Intermediate School, IL

Winter Ice

Ice storm, ice storm go away so we can go out and play.
All snowy and all icy for it may be winter ice.
Branches and trees fall from all the weight.
That's how you know that you're in the winter gate.

Samantha Nelson, Grade 4
Tallula Elementary School, IL

What Is Pink?

What is pink?
A rose is pink by its fountain brink.
What is yellow?
A pear is yellow.
All rich, ripe and mellow.
What is green?
Grass is green with small flowers between.
What is orange?
Why an orange
Always an orange.

Savanah Hay, Grade 5
Gard Elementary School, IL

An Ode to Football

My Football

I thank you football for letting me play catch with you.
When I am angry or sad,
"I just go outside and throw you.

Or just being able to go out for a pass," to catch you and
score a touchdown "or recovering you in a
fumble" or catch you in an interception.

I thank you.

Brandon Chong, Grade 5
Allen J. Warren Elementary School, IN

Gumdrops

Gumdrops, lollipops, candy canes too!
that's what comes to mind when I think of you!
Gumdrops are sweet, candy canes too!
that's what comes to mind when I think of you!
thinking of you; how sweet you are!
Am I sweet to you?

Katie Matkovich, Grade 6
Riverdale Elementary School, IL

Peace in the Fall

Beautiful birds sing with their colorful fall feathers
sitting there in the trees
with the orange, red, yellow, brown, and green leaves
lying there on the grass,
the smell of nature filling the air,
the sound of birds chirping, the wind chimes swaying,
just so peaceful

Daniel Goodman, Grade 5
Stanley Clark School, IN

Charging Cat

Sadly, I hear a small chattering sound
That seems to be all around.
It's squeaking so loud in this room,
I know he's peaking
I'll find him soon.
Tip tip toe I know he'll show.
He might be down low, under the bed.
"Yes! Yes!" that's what I said.
I know you're here "come out! come out!"
I said to him, "Don't make me shout!"
"Uh Oh." There he is, his claws out,
and has a wig. "HUH!?"
"Ok! Ok! I give up!", I say.
It's over I'm done for.
"Oh well, I'll be ok!"

Daisey I. Ramirez, Grade 5
Lincoln Intermediate School, IL

Reef

Harried fish make the scene,
Flying and floating, swimming and flipping.
Constantly searching for foodstuffs
In the salty, penetrating blue.
Only to look stark, put out in the dark.
Against a reef.
Iridescent and sparkling.
Royal reds and magenta pinks,
Deep blues and soothing greens,
The colorful monarchs of this majestic world.
Corals, standing tall,
Are, the mighty monarchs of this majestic world.
Corals, standing tall.

John DeBuysser, Grade 6
Stanley Clark School, IN

Belmont Harbor

Sun rises and dawn pays a visit. The instructors come to do their job.
We arrive shouting with glee. We're going sailing!
The instructor tells us what to do, rig our boats, listen up, or even be quiet.
The breeze picks up. We can feel it on our faces.
The wind streaming by, whistling in our ears.
The flags start to flutter. We all put our boats in the water.
Looking forward to the day ahead, we sail out together as a group to the lake.
This is where we separate.
The more advanced sailors head out to the lake while the less experienced stay in the harbor.
We sail, learning what to do and learning how to do it. Oh dear!

We must go in otherwise we'll be late for lunch! We all sail in as fast as we can.
After that we go to the barge to have lunch.
Lunch is an hour of talking, messing around, and having fun.
As for the food, it is hardly edible. I even got food poisoning once.
It's 12:45 and it's time for foosball! We all gather around to see who is playing,
Sometimes making bets other times just watching.

It's now time to go back out to the water. We shuffle our way to our boats.
Out to the lake we go. We sail and drill ourselves. We keep learning new things.
It is almost sunset, time to go in. All of us derig our boats,
Waiting ever so patiently for the parents to arrive. They take us home.
Sun is on the horizon. Dusk comes to call. Night falls on Belmont Harbor.

Michael Andrew Duncan, Grade 6
Chicago City Day School, IL

Manta Rays

M anta Rays live in the sunlight zone of the Atlantic Ocean.
A tlantic Manta Rays are 22 feet across. They are the largest of the Manta Rays.
N o spine on their tail but other rays, like sting rays, do have spines.
T he Manta Ray is like a giant flying carpet because it is so large.
A plankton or small fish is a great meal for a Manta Ray. They open their mouths and suck the fish into their mouths.

R ays like these leap out of the water and fall back with a loud smack.
A Manta Ray can weigh up to 3,000 pounds.
Y ou know Manta Rays have 300 rows of teeth in their mouths which are good for eating.
S ome Manta Rays are dark brown to black on the top and mostly white on the bottom.

Steven Nowaczyk, Grade 4
Frank H Hammond Elementary School, IN

Eduardo

My little brother was a twin.
He was only 9 days old and too young to die.
But God thought it was his time.
You see he had trouble breathing on his own and had a machine.
They took the machine off one day and he breathed on his own for 3 days.
We were all so proud of him.
But God didn't want him to suffer so he went up to heaven.
We all knew it was best for him even though we wanted him to live.
You see he no longer suffers.
I hope he is happy in heaven and watching over me.
I wish he had the chance to see what I see.
He would be three years old now and I would be showing him how to play basketball,
But instead he is happy in heaven with God and hopefully sees what I see but in a more special place.

Alyssa Estrada, Grade 6
St John the Baptist Elementary School, IN

Feeding My Goats

When I bring a pail of grain to the gate
They all look up and just can't wait
When their heads go down their tails go up
I give them water with a cup
When they get done eating, I give them some hay
And it all starts all over the very next day

Samantha Huston, Grade 6
Dakota Elementary School, IL

Snowman

S nowflakes are falling,
N o one is calling.
O ver the ground is a blanket of snow,
W indows are frosted and there is nowhere to go.
M aking hot chocolate we'll do,
A nd a warm fire, too.
N estling in a blanket on a cold winter day,

Sun is setting and this is nature's winter way.

Zach Austin, Grade 5
Dee Mack Intermediate School, IL

I'm From

I'm from…a small town,
Not much known on a map.
Summers of bike rides,
Dives and cannonballs into a pool.
Race day parties, and
Heather's golf seasons.
I'm from…Jeff, Deanna, Brent, and Dwayne,
Our New Year's Eve parties.
I'm from…an old cat named Stray,
And her seven kittens.
Our five year old dog,
As yellow as a sunrise.
I'm from….my loving family,
That is my world,
And that's where I'm from.

Danielle Warthen, Grade 6
Northwood Elementary School, IN

But Not

I like
Food but not when it is hot
Football but not when my team loses
Mom but not when she is mad
Dad but not when he is hollering at me
Brothers but not when they are mean
Colts but not when they lose
Books but not fiction
Monkeys but not when they bite
Mrs. O'Connor but not when she is giving "Snip-Its"
Bike but not when I wreck

Dakota McGuire, Grade 5
Churubusco Elementary School, IN

Almost Spring

I can see a bubbly stream
Against a wallpaper of blue,
And a carpet of green.
Chirping birds sing lullabies to their newborn babies
"Chirp Chirp"
As they bring food
And nourishment.
I can hear the rustle of the wind,
Like whispers of children.
My bare feet move across the cold water
And smooth stones at the bottom of the stream.
I feel the sharp pine needles
As I brush against bushes,
Moving on my way.
The snow-covered mountains are right ahead of me.
Their beauty is amazing.
I can smell the perfumed scent of flowers,
And they guide me through the unknown forest.
I am almost there.

Indiana Cote, Grade 5
Stanley Clark School, IN

The Three-Pointer

We were ready for the B-Ball game
When that horrible team came
We were just shooting around
But then it sounded like a pound

They strutted in all might
Ready for the big fighting
Everybody took the court
Wearing our baggy shorts

We started off taking the lead
But they had a dirty deed
They were fouling away
But we decided to fight and stay

It was 64 to 60
Then we came good and ready
1 minute left in the quarter
The seconds clocked down shorter

I had the ball at the three pointer
Then I shot the ball from the corner
When the ball swished through the basket
It was cool and fantastic

Devon Merder, Grade 6
Nancy Hanks Elementary School, IN

Birds

I hear birds singing
They fly so high in the sky
They are so pretty

Wyant C. Held, Grade 5
North Knox East Elementary/Jr High School, IN

Winter

Winter is here.
Winter is near.
The snow is all around.
The snow is on the ground.

The trees are covered with snow.
When the wind blows,
The snow falls on ME and I go,
Play in the snow.

Delanie Kwiecinski, Grade 5
St Peter Catholic School, IL

Dead Winter

Winter, winter...
How cold you make me.

Cold winds blow,
deep drifts of icy white snow.
A brisk breeze
always makes me want to sneeze.
So dark, bleak and gray
makes me wish for a warm sunny day.
No leaves on the trees.
No flowers on the plants.

The lovely colors long gone...
Why does winter have to feel so long?

Cameron McGraw, Grade 6
South Middle School, IL

Ashley

A rtistic
S hy
H elpful
L oves Swimming
E ntirely honest
Y oung

Ashley Dye, Grade 5
Forreston Grade School, IL

Best Friend

Best friend
Lean, exotic, lovable
Greeting me with a wagging tail
Trusting me with her head in my lap
My dog, Brittany

Sylvia Willis, Grade 6
Tri-West Middle School, IN

Slithering Cobras

Slithering in grass
Munching on delicious mice
Too full for movement

Brittney Hughes, Grade 4
Rose Hamilton Elementary School, IN

Christmas

Christmas is a joy.
Lots of kids get a toy.
When your Christmas is fun,
You don't want it done.
If you are bad,
You will be sad.
When you meet Santa Claus,
You will have a pause.
When Santa puts a present under a tree,
Then he will flee.
If your holiday is the best,
It will stand out from the rest.

Eric Mielke, Grade 4
Summit Elementary School, IL

Black Cat

I had a black cat
That was fat like a rat
Who ran in the store
And got knocked out from the door!

Erin Morris, Grade 5
Gard Elementary School, IL

The Candy Store

My mom is the Dove's chocolate,
Sweet not dark.

My brother is the Pay-Day
Always nutty.

My sister is the War-Head
Always mean.

I am the Sour Punch Straws
Sour and sweet.

My dad is the store
Protecting us!

Elaine Horn, Grade 4
Churubusco Elementary School, IN

My Family

My family is the best of all,
We always laugh and have a ball.

I never, ever have to fear,
When I know they are near.

I really do love them dearly,
And I know they see me clearly.

Mommy, daddy, and brothers too,
All that's left to say is I love you.

Emily Green, Grade 5
St Jude Catholic School, IN

Playing Video Games

Exploring the obstacles
Random, challenging, problematic
I like to enjoy these moments!

Michael Saldana, Grade 6
Jane Addams Elementary School, IL

Christmas Night Rocks!!!

Christmas is so great.
Santa has to stay up late.
He delivers presents to Rome.
To my cousins to my home.
Santa works real hard.
We should sent him a post card.
He knows when you're awake.
So do not try to fake.
If you find a reindeer.
You should yell big cheer.
Santa is going to take a nap.

Tyler Perez, Grade 4
Summit Elementary School, IL

Ally

A very awesome girl
L ittle, but mighty
L ikes to play tennis
Y our friend

Allyson Crouch, Grade 5
St Jude Catholic School, IN

Turkey

Turkey is fun to eat
It's full of delicious white meat
With delicious pumpkin pie
I hope you don't lie
When friends and family can meet.

Samantha Blair, Grade 5
Gard Elementary School, IL

The Dog and the Cat

There was a dog
That saw a cat.
It was afraid of the cat.
The dog chased the cat
All over the house.
The dog was sleeping
On the floor.
The cat scratched the dog
They chased each other
Around the house again.
The dog barked —
The cat ran fast into the
Door and its name
Is Cookoo now.

Drew Patrick, Grade 5
Gard Elementary School, IL

Wind

Wind is like a person walking in the sky,
Its job is to carry whispers from person to person,
It always knows where to go and what to do,
It moves with a smooth, gentle sway,
When you open and close a door it slips in,
Wind is always there like a best friend.

Tyler Meyer, Grade 6
Trinity Oaks Christian Academy, IL

Tacos

Filled with meat, lettuce, tomatoes and cheese.
Tacos are a food that is sure to please.
Tortillas soft or crunchy, it matters not.
They taste good, as long as they're hot.
I like grandma's tacos; they're good for sure.
They're addictive; there is just no cure.
Can you tell from this little rhyme?
I could eat tacos all the time.
I like tacos.

Josh Roeckenhaus, Grade 6
All Saints Academy, IL

The Divine Birth and His Effect Upon the World

In early spring Gabriel sounded his horn
To the Virgin Mary the Son of God would be born.
Jesus was born on Christmas Day
New Year's wasn't so far away.
While They were rejected every day
All Joseph said was, "Pray to the Lord, pray."

Of all kings these three had Faith
Followed the Star to an open gate
And also Hope brought them through
The dreadful road that God's Will drew.
In the end Charity led them to find
The Savior Who loved and died for mankind.
That one day in sanctifying grace we would be
With our Heavenly Father for all eternity.

Chris Orange, Grade 6
Our Lady Immaculate Academy, IL

My Birthday

It's my birthday and I'm a year older.
It's not in summer, it's not in spring, so it's colder.
My friends and I eat pizza and cake until our bellies are stuffed.
Then we get our pillows until they are nice and fluffed.
We play games until someone is tired of losing.
We tell ghost stories until someone starts snoozing.
You may think it's over but don't get flustered.
It's not over till someone gets a face full of mustard.
The sun begins to rise.
Then we open our eyes.
Time to say goodbye because the end is near.
See you next year.

Alexis Glenn, Grade 4
Summit Elementary School, IL

Grandpa, Forever Loved

He passed on, on a tragic day,
Now he keeps close eye on me in the sunny rays.

We miss you, mom and I,
When she thinks of you I can tell she wants to cry.

I never got to meet you,
And that's what makes me blue.

They say you're in a better place,
But I just wish you could be here face to face.

I read your obituary the other night,
As sad as it is, I know it will be all right.

Robert James Lowrey is my grandpa, forever,
And he will be forever loved.

Jordan Larsen, Grade 5
Dee Mack Intermediate School, IL

Football

F un sport that can be taken away
O nly sport that you really get broken bones
O nly sport that you can't take it easy or you get creamed
T ight end that can sneak a touchdown
B all that looks like a foot and can be thrown a long way
A sport that can be painful if you don't want to play
L ong gone for a touchdown
L ong practices that really pay off

Larsan Waddell, Grade 5
Lincoln Intermediate School, IL

Winter

Winter is awesome, snow falling and all.
Snowmen being built, snowballs being thrown.
Laughing kids all around, parents playing, holy cow!
It's an awesome sight to see.
The snow is out there for you and me.
So let's go out and have some fun.
For soon this great season will be gone.

Michael Behrensmeyer, Grade 4
St Matthew School, IL

Drugs Will Destroy Dreams…

I'd like to be a vet,
And take care of all those pets.
But if I do drugs, I will cream all my dreams,
It's not as easy as it seems.

Drugs can make you lazy,
They will also make you go crazy.
They might make you sad,
They sometimes make people mad.

Kerestyn Ludwig, Grade 5
Dee Mack Intermediate School, IL

Goldfish

Small fish
Swift in the pond
Flying through the water
Zooming everywhere out of sight
Goldfish
Kenan Cheatwood, Grade 4
Warren Central Elementary School, IN

The Dog Who Ate Like a Hog

There once was a dog
Who ate like a hog
He had no hair
And he did not share
But he always slept in a log.
Maddie Fox, Grade 5
Gard Elementary School, IL

Witches

Witches are scary
Cast spells, secret potions, ugly
Flying on their brooms!
Natalie Moya, Grade 4
Jane Addams Elementary School, IL

The Seasons

All the seasons,
are beautiful,
All are joyful and energetic
Winter
can be cold and cruel
but the snow, the happiness
makes it all wonderful
Fall
feels very warm hearted to me
When you walk and hear
the crunch of the leaves
Spring
is nature healing itself
getting ready
Summer
is hot
All of nature comes out
This is when children play
School goes away and we relax
But overall,
Winter is my favorite season.
Carly Johnson, Grade 4
Keystone Montessori School, IL

Snowball

You throw the snowball at a person
That person says nooooooooooooooooo
Then boom, bam, wack
You are knocked out
David McCray, Grade 5
Walker Elementary School, IL

Teachers

Sometimes teachers go mad when you don't bring in your homework
or you did not finish it.
Some teachers are mean.
Some just act like themselves, old and cranky.
Some are nice.
That is how teachers are.

Jose Martinez, Grade 5
Perry Central Elementary School, IN

The Season Tree

As my big, yellow bus took me home,
I smelled mac and cheese, my favorite food.
I wiped off the fog on the dirty window.
I saw Bourbon Street.
There was a big and beautiful tree behind it.
The clouds hid in the tree and made it look full with white snow.
I wanted to rush home to play in the
cold, beautiful, white fluffy snow with my friends.
As we passed the tree, I remembered it was autumn
and it was not snowing at all.
I was sad until I realized that autumn meant I could go home
and get rakes and friends and family too,
and we could make a huge pile of leaves to jump in again and again.
That's just what we did!
Samantha Rose Presco, Grade 4
Meadow Lane School, IL

My Awesome Class

Mrs. Buchanan is a doll, in her class, we have a ball.
Drake is one of my friends, and when he moves, that won't end.
Brady is shooting for the sky, and his voice is very high.
Tyler is the class clown, he turns your frown upside down.
Kyra may be very small, but she likes to shop at big malls.
Emily has curly blonde hair, you would know her anywhere.
Katlyn is a caring kid, and her heart is very big.
Thomas is new to us, but we try not to make a big fuss.
Alicia is my best friend, we will be friends till the end.
Taylor is the sheriff's kid, I liked him ONCE, yes I did.
Shelby likes to smile, for you she'll go the extra mile.
Dylan loves to play kickball, he loves to play it in the fall.
When it comes to Wayne I have a hunch, I think his favorite time is lunch.
Everyone in my class has a part, they all have a place in my heart.
Maria Brown, Grade 6
Herrick Grade School, IL

Venus

V enus is known as
E arth's sister planet. It is
N amed after the Roman goddess of beauty and love
    At first people thought it might have life on it
U ntil they found out that the atmosphere was made of carbon dioxide,
    And even though it was the
S econd planet from the sun, it was the hottest planet in the solar system
    with temperatures of 900 degrees F.

Anya Stucky, Grade 6
Pinewood Elementary School, IN

My Sister

My sister is so mean,
she always yells go clean.
If you don't do what she wants,
she yells "you little brat you're trying to get out of work."
My sister can be a real jerk.
She acts like she's perfect in town,
and just leaves me to drown.
She yells, she screams, she kicks and she throws.
She doesn't let anything flow.
Oh yeah, did I tell you she has a unibrow!!
When I talk she gives me an evil eye.
She makes me want to lay down and cry!!
She always makes me do the dishes
every day I make a lot wishes
that one day she will disappear.
I wish I could kick her in her rear.
When I'm around her I am full of fear,
she always screams in my ear.
My sister is so mean I call her a
mean, lean, screaming machine.

Sarah Sagebiel, Grade 5
Perry Central Elementary School, IN

There Lives a Woman Down That Street

There lives a woman down that street,
I said trick-or-treat, and she gave me a beet.
She started laughing and slammed the door,
I guess I'm not trick-or-treating there anymore.

There lives a woman down that street,
I said hello, and she gave out a big bellow.
I gave out a little squeak of fear,
And as fast as can be she disappeared,
And thank goodness did not reappear.

There lives a woman down that street,
It was close to Christmas,
So I got her a mini Christmas tree.
She looked pretty disturbed,
So I left before she did something absurd.

There lives a woman down that street,
Who came knocking on *my door*,
She gave me a heart shaped box,
And didn't say a word.

Anaiis Rabiela, Grade 5
St Daniel the Prophet School, IL

George Washington

George Washington lived a long time ago
However, most people do not know,
That when he was young, about ten or eleven,
He chopped down Dad's tree, made him shout to high heaven.

Seth Hostetler, Grade 6
Bethel Lutheran School, IL

Christmas

Christmas is here;
It's that time of year.
Everybody's wrapping gifts,
And lots of snow is in drifts.
Holiday movies are playing,
People are in churches praying.
Stores are crammed;
Traffic is jammed.
Visiting relatives from far away,
Thank the Lord for the Christmas holiday.

Emily Anderson, Grade 6
Crown Point Christian School, IN

Being Drug Free

I don't know about you, but I'm going to be Drug Free.
If I don't, I will hurt my body.
Being drug free means I can be me.
I choose to "Just say No!"
Because for me, that's the only way to go!
There may be times that people ask you, "Here, try some!"
Your answer should always be, "No, that's dumb!"
There are many types of drugs in the world,
But every time you come across them, keep walking.
The effects that happen to your body, can be quite shocking!
If you continue to do drugs, your life will become dim.
Drugs are a race that you can never win!
Drugs don't care if you are young or old, rich or poor,
When drugs come knocking, shut the door!
Drugs don't care who you are.
If you do drugs, you won't go far!
So set some goals, stay in school!
Your true friends will think that's cool!
The lesson to be learned today,
Is to "Stay away from drugs!" Ok?!

Taylor Ryder, Grade 4
Peter M Gombert Elementary School, IL

Popcorn

Popcorn
Salty, buttery
Popping, crunching, melting
Delicious, yellow, everyday snack
Treat

Heather Burton, Grade 5
Washington Township Elementary School, IN

Leaves

I rake leaves into a bunch
Then I jump in with a great big crunch
All the colorful leaves fly up in the air
When they come down they land in my hair
I wiggle and giggle and roll all around. So…
I rake leaves into a bunch
And then I jump in with a great big crunch

Hannah Harshbarger, Grade 6
Dakota Elementary School, IL

My Love Is in You

The high winds are high
The low winds are low

I think of you all of the time
Whenever I play in the snow

I want you to play with me
Wherever I go

Now we fell apart from each other
Because I had to comfort another

I want to make you happy
But you let me go

I find you very kind
Because I love you so

I will care for you all of the time
If you love me so

My destiny is my goal
That is why I love you so
Emma Turbyville, Grade 6
St Matthias/Transfiguration School, IL

The Ups and Downs of Life

I love my teachers but, not school
I love softball but, not losing
I love reading but, not research
I love chapstick but, not lipstick
I love lime green but, not sweet pickles
I love ice cream but, not strawberry
I love camping but, not dirt
I love summer but, not the heat
I love being unique but, not weird
I love honey but, not bees
    Life has ups and downs but,
    The good things over rule the bad.
Kennedy Sade, Grade 5
Churubusco Elementary School, IN

Popcorn

I am popcorn,
Fluffy and white.
A great taste sensation,
In every bite.

Butter, garlic salt, and parmesan cheese,
Careful, not too much please.

Everybody likes me,
Definitely at the movie.
Wyatt Stedman, Grade 5
Dee Mack Intermediate School, IL

Global Warming

Ice melting
Ice breaking
Thinning, no ice lands
What can I do?
What can we do?
It's coming
after me and you!
It will affect our lives
and our generations, too.

Will it ever end?
Global warming…
Elyzandra Freitas, Grade 4
Lincoln Elementary School, IL

Nightmare

My sadness
is an inescapable
box closing in on me
like I said inescapable.

My sadness is in
my heart my weary
weary heart trapped
in my weary weary heart.

But happiness is filling
me with joy.

No more pain grandma
No more pain!
Kaylee Leeuw, Grade 4
Churubusco Elementary School, IN

Winter

W hite snow
I gloos
N ever ending fun
T oys
E ternal joy
R udolph
Matthew Garatoni, Grade 6
Stanley Clark School, IN

Fall

Fall is fun,
Even when there is not much sun.
Birds are singing,
When church bells are ringing.
Fall has music in the air,
So beware…
Fall is a time to be lazy,
Maybe even a little crazy.
Brandon Allison, Grade 4
Chrisney Elementary School, IN

Monkeys and Tigers

Monkey
Black, white
Swing, climb, fast
Ape, chimp, cat, feline
Speed, eat, sleep
Black, orange
Tiger
Alex Martinez Jr., Grade 5
Edison Elementary School, IL

Autumn

Autumn
Thanksgiving Day
Leaves falling everywhere
Every day is really cold
Fall
Lexi Justak, Grade 4
Bailly Elementary School, IN

Winter

Snow is like a white blanket.
All the leaves are fresh off the trees.
I hear the wind blowing
It sounds like a ghost.
I feel the cold snow tickle my toes.
All the animal tracks in the snow.
Patrick Yergler, Grade 6
Stanley Clark School, IN

Cake

Cake
Squishy, puffy
Cold, soft, messy
Big or small
Ice cream island
Claire Cordoba, Grade 6
Bethel Lutheran School, IL

Baseball

We all have bats.
We all wear hats.
There are four bases.
We all have races.
We all have our own dugouts.
I hope I don't strike out.
Bailey Niblett, Grade 4
Chrisney Elementary School, IN

Toot!

Saxophone, percussion,
    clarinet and flute
I didn't say trumpet
because all it does is toot!
Aileana Rawlins, Grade 5
Gard Elementary School, IL

Snow

The falling snow is silent,
The falling snow is peaceful,
When you wake up the big hills are covered with snow,
So we can have some fun sledding,
In the silent, peaceful snow.

Grace Y. Carlson, Grade 5
Benjamin Franklin Elementary School, IL

Vivid Image

The forest bright brown, green, and gold leaves
blowing against each other.
The water washing the banks
as a sapphire shining
The sky as blue crayon that was just used
and moving slowly
Flowers as bright as the sun
and whispering in the wind as it blows.
The house is floating on a lifeless raft.
The house as white as snow, shutters as caramel candy
moving back and forth in the silent wind.
The sun shines above in the sky and will fade for nightfall.

Becca Maves, Grade 6
Dakota Elementary School, IL

Chocolate Bar

C hocolate lovers
H ot melted chocolate in your mouth
O h so good
C old chocolate
O h so chocolatey
L ove chocolate
A lmonds make it crunchy
T astes like cocoa
E at it forever

B est candy ever
A candy bar lasts forever
R esistance not possible!

Dalia Raya, Grade 5
Benjamin Franklin Elementary School, IN

The Muskie

If I could make just one wish,
It would be to catch a three-foot fish.
I would sit on the pier and there I would wait,
For the giant Muskie to take my bait.
It may take an hour, or two, or even a day,
For the Muskie to come and decide to play.
Give it a jerk, give it a tug,
Until I catch that great big lug.
Be patient and then he takes the hook,
I land him and say that's one for the book.
My day is complete my Muskie is tall,
Come home and relax, it's a fish for the wall.

Jack Laski, Grade 5
St Daniel the Prophet School, IL

I'd Rather

I'd rather spread my wings
And fly like a bird,
Than be kept in a cage
And never be heard.

Like a house pet I'd rather be lapping my water
Than like a desert animal,
Every day getting hotter.

I'd rather jump like a frog
Or hop like a toad,
Than like a piece of grass,
Every day be gone and be mowed.

Like a cheetah I'd rather
Jump and attack my meal,
Than like a raccoon in the trash can
Eating a rotting banana peel.

Like anyone else I'd rather be,
Without anyone stepping or picking on me.

Alexa Bates, Grade 5
Allen J. Warren Elementary School, IN

Wrong Life

My life to me seems like a struggle.
I feel like a girl struck in a bubble
Having a hard time between reality and fiction,
Asking the Lord what is my mission.
All these distractions are what blurs my vision.
Too many problems running through my head.
It fells like a head-on collision.

My life is so fast, I guess I'm stuck in the fast lane.
I'm sick of losing while others gain.
Why am I the one who has to feel pain
While others reach fortune and fame?
I'm stuck in this so called "LIFE,"
But to me it's all a big game.
I have one last chance in this game,
And I'm in the final stage.
The outcome of this battle
Will be the words that are written on my final page.

Karen Rivera, Grade 6
Our Lady of Guadalupe School, IL

Uranus

U ranus is named after the Greek deity that
R uled the Heavens.
A s of today, Uranus is tilted, and its rings are
N ot across, but up and down.
U ranus is
S everely cold. Its average temperature is -319 degrees F.

Joanna Dixon, Grade 6
Pinewood Elementary School, IN

Wolf

Such a mysterious creature
Calm, swift, silent
A fearsome predator!

Angela Trevino, Grade 6
Jane Addams Elementary School, IL

The Light

Even in the lightest light,
there is dark.

The kind of dark that,
makes you mad.

The kind of dark that,
makes you sad.

But even in the darkest dark,
there is light.

The kind of light that
makes you want to jump for joy.

The kind of light that,
saves you from the dark.

Elijah Smith, Grade 6
Perry Central Elementary School, IN

Brother

Brother
Amusing, destructive
Giggling, investigating, grabbing
In his own universe
Highlight of my life

Jordan Parrish, Grade 6
Tri-West Middle School, IN

1, 2, 3's ABC's

I learned my ABC's and
1, 2, 3's in class and I'm having a blast.
I'm going to learn and take turns.
I'm going to learn A to Z
and I'm going to have a mystery.
I am going to learn my 1, 2, 3's
and I'm going to
take a quiz till 3.

Shawndell Adaway, Grade 5
North Miami Elementary School, IN

Troy

There once was a little boy
And his name was Troy.
He was mad
Because I was bad
So I gave him a toy.

Ashley Phillips, Grade 4
Shoals Elementary School, IN

Racing at Full Speed

As I'm racing down the backstretch
I hear a loud crash I try to get through
I flip and turn down the backstretch
I catch on fire and get impounded

I am very broken and sad
I get repaired and get new stickers and spoilers
I race at 200 mph again
I'm very happy

I get dizzy real easy because all I do is go around in circles all day
I'm driven by the best Dale Earnhardt
I win every race
I hate getting bumped but then there would be no competition

I finally retire
I'm put in the hall of fame
Everybody stops and stares
They think I'm amazing

Cody Wheat, Grade 6
Dee Mack Intermediate School, IL

Snow, Perfect Snow

Snow, beautiful snow. It drifts down like a shower of crystal stars.
Snow, icy cold snow. It makes you shiver in delight and wonderment.
Snow, brilliant snow. It melts on your tongue like the spring breaking through winter.
Snow, unique snow. People are like snowflakes. No two are exactly alike.
Snow, serene snow. It's like an angel always there quietly watching over you.
Snow, wonderful snow. It numbs your fingers and turns your lips blue.
Snow, glistening snow. You shimmer like a thousand diamonds of the purest form.

Snow, perfect snow.

Abbey Jester, Grade 6
Corpus Christi Elementary School, IN

Jupiter

J upiter is the king of all planets. Even that is an
U nderstatement. It is 90
P ercent hydrogen and 10 percent helium. It
I s named after
T he king of all gods and goddesses, Zeus. Plus
E ven if you could land on it you would be swept away by the Great
R ed Spot, a neverending storm!

Austin Miller, Grade 6
Pinewood Elementary School, IN

Thanksgiving

Thanksgiving is a time to give thanks to God.
Thanksgiving is a time so spend time with your family
Thanksgiving is a time of peace and love.
Thanksgiving is a time of giving.
Thanksgiving is a time of caring for others not yourself.
Thanksgiving is a time to sit down as your tummy are growling like a lion.
Thanksgiving is a time for enjoying having no school work.

Lindsay Palmer, Grade 6
Christian Life Schools, IL

A Winter with My Special Dog

My cow just moos like a normal cows song
But my dog meows and I don't know what's wrong
But he is my special dog
I can't just throw him in the fog

I took him to Van Gogh
But all he did was painted
I took him to the vet
But oh my gosh he fainted
But he is my special dog
I can't just throw him in the fog

I took him to a guy that plows
But all he did was bought some sows
I took him to Coal City Intermediate School
But my chemistry teacher said, "That is so cool."
But he is my special dog
I just can't throw him in the fog

He does not go to Dr. Lee
But when we snuggle it's him and me

Tori Knutson, Grade 4
Coal City Intermediate School, IL

Oceans

The crushing waves fall upon the light.
The sparkle of the sun makes the ocean look so bright.
The wind rustling falls from the sky to deep inside.
The ocean opens up to get some bright life.

Danielle Vasiliev, Grade 6
Daniel Wright Jr High School, IL

I Am

I am an energetic girl who loves to have fun
I wonder if dogs can understand me
I hear in the future my children calling me mommy
I see the world a better place
I want a puppy for my dog to play with
I am an energetic girl who loves to have fun

I pretend I am a veterinarian
I feel that all animals should be treated with respect
I touch the animals that need help
I worry about the men and women in Iraq
I cry when I think about my grandpa
I am an energetic girl who loves to have fun

I understand that people aren't perfect
I say follow your dreams
I dream I am a vet
I try to help people in need
I hope I will make it to college to be a vet
I am an energetic girl who loves to have fun

Danielle Thomas, Grade 6
Helfrich Park Middle School, IN

Orbit

As I walk through the gates at Six Flags,
I see the "doorway to death" opening...
I ask, "How fast does this ride go?"
The man says, "You don't want to know"
I sit in this wobbly seat
Clutching my mother's hand and gripping the rusted handlebar

The ride creaks
AW!
It's starting!
B A M!
My hair is flying into my mom's face
My stomach lurching in every possible direction
Around, around I feel myself go
Finally feeling my head jerk to a wild halt.

Tess Caras, Grade 6
Chicago City Day School, IL

Beach

Sunny day, bright afternoon
playing volleyball, 97 degrees, buying food
Swimming at the beach.

Jose Diaz, Grade 6
Jane Addams Elementary School, IL

Corvette

There once was a boy named Brett.
He wants to buy a stylish Corvette.
When he tells his mom she screams.
She says "In your dreams."
This is something Brett will never forget.

Brett Neumann, Grade 5
Washington Township Elementary School, IN

The Italian Alps

Steep cliffs at the edge of life
Jagged rocky hills tumbling toward death
Void of all life, nobody to save.
Rotting trees being eaten by worms
Points of history written into the walls
A place where all is gone, but not forgotten.

Zachery Carlson, Grade 6
Knox Community Middle School, IN

Halloween

H atchets are scary on Halloween.
A pples and pumpkins are abundant.
L aughter is common on Halloween.
L ittle garden gnomes look alive on Halloween.
O h my! Monsters up ahead!
W eird Costumes!
E at as much candy as you can.
E verything is alive on Halloween!
N ight is so scary on Halloween, isn't it?

Matthew Szymel, Grade 6
Three Rivers School, IL

I Am a Baseball

Here I am
On a musty old rack
Covered with dust and filth
Wait, I see a light

Hey, how'd I get here?
Don't throw me, whoa
I'm moving really fast
The wind in my face feels great

Hey, what are you doing with that bat
Mercy, mercy, please don't
THWACK
Oh, that's going to leave a mark

Whoa, how high am I
I feel like a bird
Hey look, the crowd is cheering
Aaaggghhh now I'm falling

Person, look out
Thank goodness you caught me
Hey, where are we going?
Stop writing on me, I don't need a tattoo
Brock Lockenour, Grade 6
Dee Mack Intermediate School, IL

Football Season

F avorite sport
O n every TV
O n every Sunday
T he halfback runs with the
B all and destroys
A ll the
L inebackers by
L aying them out

S o they can make a touchdown
E very time they get the ball
A nd when they get the touchdown
S afties get mad
O n every Sunday and
N ot everyone is happy
Tyler Klein, Grade 4
Stonegate Elementary School, IN

Brothers

Thoughtful brothers
Funny brothers
Handy, loving, joyful brothers
Coolest, athletic, kind brothers
Last of all, best of all
My brother
Shannon McCarthy, Grade 5
St Jude Catholic School, IN

Sadness Is...

Sadness is like the ice floating in water.
or

The cold snow in a freezing snow storm.
or

The darkness in the night.

Sadness can be any one of these
or
All of these

You choose.
Matthew Cox, Grade 4
Keystone Montessori School, IL

My Football Is an Airplane

My football is an airplane
flying high in the air,
zooming fast and
quick. My football
flies so high I
can't see it
anymore. My
football is an
airplane.
Christian Andis, Grade 4
Veale Elementary School, IN

Rain Forest

Hot steamy forest
Vibrant beautiful colors
Crazy animals
Ashlyn Miller, Grade 4
Adams Central Elementary School, IN

My Bunny

He kisses
He nibbles
He bites
And he loves to be held
He nibbles on carrots
He gnaws on clovers
He will chew the leash and try to get free
He is cute when he makes
His fur fluffy and soft.
Olivia Carroll, Grade 6
Milltown Elementary School, IN

Coyote

A wild coyote
Enormous amount of fur
Wanders the desert
Katee Lingafelter, Grade 6
Churchill Jr High School, IL

I'm the Boss Today

I'm the boss today,
I'll do whatever you say.
I'll clean your room,
and let the flowers bloom,
but you will have to pay.
Rosa Garcia, Grade 5
Glen Flora Elementary School, IL

Candy

Candy
sweet, sour
eating, chewing, biting
chocolate, gummies, skittles, m&m's
melting, licking, tasting
big, small
vegetable
Virginia Disch, Grade 4
St Matthew School, IL

The World

The world is big.
The world is round.
The world has people.
The world has sound.
The world is green.
The world is brown.
The world is great, in many ways.
If you take a moment to look, you'll see
all the things the world is to me!
Josey Robertson, Grade 5
Allen J. Warren Elementary School, IN

Brothers

Brothers are,
Crazy,
Awesome,
Bothering,
Bugs,
Cries,
Kicks,
Screams,
Mean,
Horrible,
Humorous,
Fantastic,
Joyful,
Jolly,
Cheerful,
Kind,
Gracious,
Clever,
Sharp,
Wise.
James A. Rogers, Grade 5
Lincoln Intermediate School, IL

Fall

F alling chestnut leaves.
A pple pies always sticky and delicious
L ove them so!
L et people be joyful because it's Fall!
S carlet leaves blanket the ground too.

F amily time is now!
U litmately having dinner with the family.
N obody knows what winter will bring!

Chris Wolak, Grade 4
Frank H Hammond Elementary School, IN

Taffy Apples

Gooey, tangy
crunching, chewing, savoring
loving the stickiness
Granny Smith

Julie Chael, Grade 4
Frank H Hammond Elementary School, IN

Scooby

I have a dog named Scooby,
He wags and shakes his head.

He walks around with pity for
The wrong that he has done.

He wakes up in the morning
Yawns and stretches.

And comes into my room and
Jumps into my arms.

I wake up in a shock ready to
Hit someone.

And say "Oh, it's just you, I
Thought you were a robber."

He gives me kisses, and I give
Him breakfast.

Kaitlyn Black, Grade 6
Emmanuel-St Michael Lutheran School, IN

My Christmas Day

C ocoa warms me up
H ears us opening presents
R eading the Christmas cards
I love Christmas
S mell of pine trees
T eam up and play games
M y family wakes up early
A white blanket covers the land
S it around the tree and admire the beautiful lights

Destiny Mizell, Grade 4
Fox Creek Elementary School, IL

Friends

Friends are there for you.
They are there when you're sad,
when you're hurt, and when you're stuck.
They help you when you need a place to stay.
They always accept you and respect you.
Friends are there for you.
Friends always help.

Cody K. Dye, Grade 5
William B Orenic Intermediate School, IL

A Fall Night

As I take a sip of the warm hot chocolate
It slips down my throat,
While the fireplace warms my heart.

Outside the leaves gently float down,
As the outside of green grass and trees,
Now disappear under a layer of crunchy leaves

The music in the background
Relaxes and soothes,
My stressed mind.

My dog greets me with a welcome pant.
He smiles and licks my hand,
As I turn the page of the book.

My fireplace slowly dies down,
As I know it is time for me to sleep.
I climb into bed with a happy smile.

I wake up in the morning,
As if last night
Was all a wonderful dream.

Abby Winters, Grade 6
Thomas Dooley Elementary School, IL

Good Day, Bad Day

I wonder why the sun's not out today
Everyone is happy, there is no blue,
It's spring I tell you, we're in the month of May,
How nice, I just learned how to tie my shoe.
It may be that I just don't understand,
where's the key to open the sunlight's gate?
I'd rather be there then on this cloud land.
One thing I know, I will investigate,
I come to see, weathermen can be wrong,
So I thought, it won't hurt me to forgive,
I came to the door, and it went ding-dong,
Then I pinched myself to see if I live,
I was awake, I went to bed to lay,
Oh!, it's Monday, figured why it's this way.

Carolina Figueroa, Grade 5
Booth Tarkington Elementary School, IL

Caring

When you share,
You can get care.
And when you get care,
You can share.
All of your friends might say,
Give him care and share.
Then you always share and care.

Lionel Watson, Grade 4
Summit Elementary School, IL

My Best Friends

My first best friend is Mandy,
she is crazy but she comes in handy.
My other best friend is Freddy,
he is so ready and very steady.
My third best friend is Emily,
she is nice and oh so friendly.
My other best friend is Miley,
she is always so smiley.
My last best friend is Lissandra,
She is so ra, ra, ra
It's hard to have friends,
and that's enough for me.

Cinthia Patricio, Grade 5
Glen Flora Elementary School, IL

Happy Birthday

Presents wrapped in colorful bows
Balloons rising in rows
Confetti everywhere
Tons of joy in the air
Friends coming to stay
"Happy Birthday!" they all say
It's time to bake
A 10 layer cake
Happy Birthday

Hadley Smithhisler, Grade 4
Stonegate Elementary School, IN

Fall

Scarecrows watch like
A guard in a jail

Ham fills my nose like
A winter's cold

Pumpkin pie with whipped cream like
Ice cream on a hot summer day

Leaves crunch like
Candy in a mouth

Leaves feel like
Candy wrappers that are empty

Devon Zeigler, Grade 5
Churubusco Elementary School, IN

Butterfly Fish

B lack stripes on the Butterfly Fish's eyes also helps protect them.
U p to 4 inches can a Butterfly Fish jump out of the water and into the air.
T he Angel Fish and the Butterfly Fish are related.
T he Butterfly Fish live in the Coral Reef near Australia.
E very Butterfly Fish eats coral, coral polyps, and other invertebrates.
R ound and flat is the shape of the Butterfly Fish.
F ins on the Butterfly Fish are called dorsal fins.
L ength of the Butterfly Fish is 5 to 9 inches.
Y ellow, blue, orange, and other colors are shades of the Butterfly Fish.

F rom the front, they're too thin to be noticed.
I t is a diurnal species: active during the day, and sleeping at night.
S hape of the Butterfly Fish is best adapted for swimming in tight spaces.
H abitats of Butterfly Fish are usually at reefs.

Dara Medina, Grade 4
Frank H Hammond Elementary School, IN

Friends

Friends are always willing to listen and help,
no matter the problem, your friends will be there without a doubt.
Friends like you for who you are,
they are there for you near or far,
Friends are kind, caring, and fun,
they like to play, dance, and sometimes run,
Friends know all about you, your secrets and feelings,
Friends can be your greatest healing.

Cadence Niccum, Grade 5
William B Orenic Intermediate School, IL

Neptune

N othing is unusual about this gas giant that is the
E ighth planet from the sun. Neptune is named after the Roman god of the
     sea or the Greek god
P oseidon. It is the neighbor of the "no longer a planet" Pluto and Uranus which
     pulls Neptune on its orbit. Neptune, like Jupiter has
T he great dark spot which is a raging storm blowing across Neptune and
U nder it are smaller storms.
N one as big as the great dark spot,
E ven all of them combined!

Kiley Warlick, Grade 6
Pinewood Elementary School, IN

Ode to a Wild Horse

Standing tall under a shady apple tree, he whinnies
like a lone trumpet playing taps.

Gracefully trotting over to greet the rest of his herd, the rhythmic
beat of his hooves pound on the ground attracting a beautiful mare.

He approaches his lady and they amble towards the pond.
The reflection of a setting sun sparkles on the rippling, shallow waves.

The gentle glimmer in the mare's dark eyes display a portrait of her
in the stallion's light eyes, creating a connection between them.

Alexandra Seitz, Grade 4
Walden Elementary School, IL

Ding Dong!

Whoosh, yikes, ooooo
All sounds of Halloween
Creak, swoosh, wind blowing
Makes me feel so keen
Trees and houses stand black in the distance
People stirring up and down the streets
Ringgg! went the doorbell and I opened the door
To see a face as black as coal
I ran away like a little girl
To find it was only my imagination
That gave me this tingling sensation
That I had seen a ghost

Reid Meier, Grade 6
Dakota Elementary School, IL

I Am

I am short but crazy at sports.
I wonder who I will be when I am a grownup.
I hear voices in my mind.
I see myself the king of the world.
I want to get a 4.0 on my report card.
I am short but crazy at sports.

I pretend I'm God's best friend.
I feel poor people should get treated better.
I touch the stars at night.
I worry if I'll make it in college.
I cry when my family or friends die.
I am short but crazy at sports.

I understand why people are mean.
I say you can follow your dreams.
I dream I cannot do anything.
I try to be awesome in school.
I hope to be a pro football player.
I am short but crazy at sports.

Preston Wells, Grade 6
Helfrich Park Middle School, IN

Thanksgiving

T hankful for turkey
H appy Thanksgiving
A mish butter
N o cookies till after dinner
K indness or I'm kicked out
S tuffing is the best
G ood turkey
I mpressive green beans
V ery special
I nvited every time
N ever full
G reat mashed potatoes

David Stover, Grade 5
Washington Township Elementary School, IN

Sunset

sunset in the sky
with half an orange sphere
shooting rays of flames

Tiffany Wang, Grade 4
Frank H Hammond Elementary School, IN

Winter Time

The first snow falls on my eyelashes,
And clutches to my fingertips;
Hot cocoa burns my lips in the morning;
The mailbox is frozen shut;
Slippery icicles hang from the roof;
That smell of warm cookies sails to my nose;
The blankets of snow are like fluffy
clouds glimmering bright;
Scarves and hats are everywhere
adding color to the white world;
I can see my breath in the cold air;
Flowers wilt and trees are almost nothing;
Animals are sound asleep in their burrows;
Sheets of ice cover the ground;
The sounds of birds in the morning have faded away;
Water freezes in the air when spilled;
The pond is no longer blue but white;
The fire warms my red fingertips and toes;
When the world changes,
It's winter time.

Emily Sun, Grade 4
Butterfield School, IL

Christmas

C hristmas is the best time of year
H appy people all around
R unning, falling in the snow
I cing cakes for the family
S inging all the Christmas songs
T ime to meet new family
M aking cookies oh so sweet
A mazing presents to receive
S kating on the newly frozen Christmas ice

Rosa Schwartz, Grade 6
Perry Central Elementary School, IN

Halloween

Stinky smoke makes me sneeze
Ghosts glide across your porch
Creep, creep and then
BOO!
People plopping candy in your bucket
Doorbells ringing from all over the place
Mask, make up and anything you want
Screams from all the haunted houses
A lot of people saying, "Happy Halloween!"

Jenessa Smedley, Grade 4
Adams Central Elementary School, IN

Spring

In the spring you see leaves blowing and blowing across the yards. The leaves blow in the wind. The leaves are colorful. The leaves are joyful to jump in. You can jump in them that is really fun and they are soft. You can jump in them when you get a big enough pile. It smells brisk and cold. It smells like hot chocolate.

Casey Prewitt, Grade 4
Fox Creek Elementary School, IL

The Reappearing Friend*

The friend I once never had is standing right in front of me, I was really glad, that you believed in me.
When I feel down, you come over and talk to me, I used to always have a frown, because everyone laughed at me.
You're a great friend, that's all I have to say, I wish this friendship will never end, I'll always come to you and say,
I love you like a sis, is that okay?

Katelynn Drake, Grade 6
Rossville Alvin Elementary School, IL
*Dedicated to Jacki (my bffl)

My Little Cousin

I remember when my little cousin spent the night for her first time and really liked it.
I remember when I'm bored, I ride my bike up to her house.
I remember she drives me crazy sometimes but I don't care.
I remember when she was little and I saw her so much I think she thought I was her dad.
She's like a sister to me.

Nolan Nordenberg, Grade 6
Christian Life Schools, IL

The First Teddy Bear

The first teddy bear wears small, beady eyes, and a velvety nose. The stuffed bear's mouth has a tiny, unhappy frown that sags for all to see. The teddy's fur, brown, droopy ringlets, match his frown. Around his neck a red bow resembles a line of honey that the real bear cub wore around his neck. Even if the sad bear is silent, we love him to this very day because Theodore Roosevelt brought him to life for us to play with!

Alana Hirsch, Grade 4
Walden Elementary School, IL

Catamaran

Listen to the wind whispering like a willow tree while blowing in the breeze on an open field.
Water softly taps against pontoons like a rain shower.
The scent of ocean spray fills the air like a bouquet of flowers.
Taste the salty air burn your tongue like tears rolling down your face and into your mouth.
Slowly bobbing up and down like a log of driftwood being swept downstream.

Henry Aufderheide, Grade 4
Walden Elementary School, IL

Wild Coyote

I'm a wild coyote.
My eyes will tell you that I'm very alert and on the lookout.
I'm wearing a thin layer of short gray fur that bristles when I feel danger coming like a
patch of dry prickly grass.
I come from a large cave where my family lives.
Where I was born and lived till I was old enough to be on my own.
Besides me is a pointy stick that a tourist must have left behind which I use for warding
off other animals and maybe some people.
Sometimes I like to run and play with other coyotes.
I long for the days when the weather will cool down at least a bit.
I look forward to the rain.
I wish I could find a better cooler, safer place to live.

Mara Yelm, Grade 6
Churchill Jr High School, IL

First Day of School

S melling markers and erasers.
C rayons.
H earing my teacher tell me new things.
Staying **O** ut of trouble.
W **O** ndering what my lunch will be.
L ooking for friends.

Zach Hall, Grade 4
Fox Creek Elementary School, IL

The Wall

There once was a man named Paul,
Who sat on top of a wall,
Got too close to the edge,
Fell into the hedge,
And won't be found 'til fall.

Daniel Hurley, Grade 5
Washington Township Elementary School, IN

Busco vs Triton

The	Language Combination
always	light coming up from
endless	darkness
cheering around	a band
from highschoolers	of drums
in a circle	and
yelling getting louder	trumpets
people	blasting
running and jumping	my ear drums
on the bleachers	with
in all vocabularies of	the
yelling	always
booing	noise of
yelping	the crowd
hot sweaty	football music.

Josh Howk, Grade 4
Churubusco Elementary School, IN

Penguin

Penguin
Fuzzy, adorable
Squeaking, cuddling, warming
Penguins are so cute!
Bird

Aubrey Draves, Grade 5
Washington Township Elementary School, IN

Halloween

Halloween
It's scary great and fun
The scariest when there's no sun
The candy is good the candy is great
Just hope you're not too late and you don't get anything fake
I am scared I just might get fat
And I'm just worried that they will laugh

Joey Thomas, Grade 5
North Knox East Elementary/Jr High School, IN

Snow

The snow falls softly to the ground.
Quietly, silently drifting down.
Crystal snowflakes fall at night.
Making everything more beautiful and bright.
As if God had raised His hand fulfilling another part of His plan.

Kaitlyn Judkins, Grade 6
Emmanuel-St Michael Lutheran School, IN

Lemon Pie

As I walked in the bakery
My back started to tingle.
My mouth started to go dry.
I knew what had happened
Lemon pie that's what.
The smell was so strong.
You could smell it a mile away.
I could not swallow.
It's like I can taste it.
Then the man came out.
The pie looked so good I could not resist,
So I asked "Can I have just a bit?"

Sarah C. Dwyer, Grade 5
Lincoln Intermediate School, IL

Sounds

There are so many sounds all around,
WE can even hear them upside down.

Some are sweet, like a baby cooing.
But some are so rude, like a rowdy crowd booing.

Some sounds are loud, like a cymbal gong.
Some are nice, like a beautiful song.

The sweetest sound I know, it's true, is when
God whispers I love you!!

Brittany A. Wing, Grade 6
Christian Life Schools, IL

Lunch Hour

The lunch bell rings — it's time to play.
I go in the field to play football, two-hand touch.
I wish recess could be all day!
I get lots of grass stains, my mom hates so much.
The whistle sounds, time to eat.
Peanut butter sandwich and crackers,
I can't wait for dessert, bon appetite!
I eat my treat yum, it's stackers.
Playing with my friends is so much fun.
Lunch and recess, my favorite time of day!
I especially love to play under the bright sun.
Please, oh, please don't ever go away!

Ashley Whitefield, Grade 5
J W Riley Elementary School, IL

Secrets

Will and won't, truth be told.
Secrets kept, the secrets of old.
This dream of mine, I will behold
To the teller of tales, oh so bold.

Kylie Fife, Grade 6
Tri-West Middle School, IN

Will It End

Why are people sad?
Why are people crying?
Did someone die?
Did someone go missing?
There are some who hunger.
There are some who kill.
How do these things happen
no one knows
Will these things ever end
no one knows

People hope and dream
for these things to end.
People work and try
for these things to end.
It will end eventually
END

If we keep hoping and working.

Erik Guevara, Grade 6
Keystone Montessori School, IL

Thanksgiving

Thanksgiving
Turkey, cranberries,
Decorate for Thanksgiving
And just have fun
Leaves

Krisdeana Rich, Grade 4
Bailly Elementary School, IN

Snow

In the winter snow falls down,
You can even make a snowman clown,
Snow, Snow everywhere,
Jumping around without a care.

Wanting to play,
A joyful Christmas way,
We build snowballs and throw them,
Maybe sometimes we can't control them.

Snow tastes good,
Hot Chocolate warms you up,
You should have a big cup!

Ryan Woods, Grade 5
St Daniel the Prophet School, IL

Horses

Click, clack, click, clack,
Eat hay and apples all day,
Run, jump, a big kick, and a stomp
Nay, nay, nay, phrrrrrrrrrrr!
Now back to munch, munch, munch!

Danielle Banet, Grade 5
Henryville Elementary School, IN

My Sister

My sister's name is Kari,
She sings like a canary
She's very smart
Has a big heart
And always acts like Mary

My sister is not the best jock
But Kari sure knows how to rock
She likes to cook and bake
Cookies are things we make
They'll burn if we don't watch the clock

My sister likes to read
And helps us when in need
Volunteers her time
Doesn't charge a dime
My sister does good deeds

I miss her now that she's at school
But when I visit it's so cool
At Christmas time she will come home
I really hope she likes this poem
If she likes it she sure does rule

Derek J. Tell, Grade 6
St Colette School, IL

Up on the Block

I have stretched
My arms,
My legs,
My whole body.
I hop on the block.
As I breathe the cold,
Cool,
Air,
Butterflies become my stomach.
The cool air gives me goose bumps,
As I wait to start.
The official stays,
"Take your mark"
"Go"
Splash!
All of the swimmers are in the water.
The race has begun.

Emily Beach, Grade 5
Stanley Clark School, IN

Time

Day
Fresh, radiant
Walking, glowing, living
Resting, darkening, blackened
Sky, sun, moon, stars
Eerie, gloomy
Night

Max Barkalow, Grade 5
Forreston Grade School, IL

The Willow Tree

Oh, weeping willow
Why do you cry so often?
I love your dark shade.

Arial Oilar, Grade 4
Warren Central Elementary School, IN

Perfect Moment

Aunt baking,
waves splashing,
fish jumping,
and dogs barking,
oh what a wonderful day to play,
'til night when crabs,
come out of their holes,
and only then do I go to bed.

John Lochmandy, Grade 5
Stanley Clark School, IN

My Dog Arby

I have a Pit Bull
He likes to nibble.

I like to take him for a walk
Bark, Bark, Bark is his talk.

Arby is his name
Fetch the toy is his favorite game.

He gets bigger and bigger
But I love him the same.

Alexandria Griffin, Grade 5
St Daniel the Prophet School, IL

Mary

That night
My dog
Didn't come home
I was dreading the truth
And when my mom
Came in I knew
My dog wasn't coming back
Ever again.

Loraina Trujillo, Grade 5
Gard Elementary School, IL

Birds

Birds love to fly in the air,
they love to fly without a care.
They do not know about the dangers of the land,
they think the air is just grand.
But if a cat is walking, and spots a bird you see,
the bird will not be happy, but the cat will get all snappy!

Sarah Rosenberg, Grade 6
South Middle School, IL

Pumpkins

Pumpkins are round
Pumpkins are orange
Pumpkins are funny like me
Pumpkins have orange stuff — inside!
The seeds are good to eat when you bake them
Pumpkins are round
Pumpkins are orange
Pumpkins are needed — just like me.

Macy Gibbeny, Grade 5
Pleasant Lake Elementary School, IN

Fall

Leaves,
Falling gently off the trees,
Crisp in the bright sunlight,
Deer moving slowly through the woods,
Staring back at me,
Bringing their heads back to the grass,
Leaves scattered on the ground,
Analyzing the creases on a brown leaf,
Picking leaves up,
Putting them into a pile,
A leaf pile full of colors,
Red, orange, green, yellow and brown,
Running fast toward the pile of leaves,
Lying back, sinking my head into the leaves,
Staring at the sky,
Smiling wide and happily,
Getting up to a standing position,
Walking to the door,
Taking off my shoes and jacket,
Excitedly waiting for tomorrow to come.

Brielle Forler, Grade 6
Nancy Hanks Elementary School, IN

The Greatest Christmas

Misty white breath floating in the air
Being excited for huge presents
People singing beautiful Christmas carols
Soft chocolaty cookies steaming in the oven
Mouth watering while waiting
The changing colorful lights on the Christmas trees

Kyle Hill, Grade 4
Adams Central Elementary School, IN

Winter

The first day of December
is when all the fun starts.
Snowflakes are dancing across the sky
and the once green ground becomes frosted fluff.
The sweet smell of pine tree in my house
and the taste of Egg Nog has me hungry
I can feel the warm crackling fire
and the cool winter mist.
Christmas carols can be heard,
at every corner,
and bright Christmas lights
are strung along houses.
Children anxiously await in their beds
as Christmas Eve turns to Christmas morning
Stockings filled with toys and treats
while the tree is piled with presents.
Winter months go by
The last snowflakes fall
bright flowers appear
Winter is over
and spring is here!

Kaitlin McKernan, Grade 5
Butterfield School, IL

The Life of a Kite

I am a kite; a great big triangular kite
With many colors, oh, so bright.
Colors which include red, yellow, green, and white.
It feels ever quite right to be so light.
To my string they cling tight.
They tie me to their big, shiny ring.
And as they sing, sing, sing, it makes me feel like a king.
It would never work to have a fear of the height
If you wanted to be like me…a flying kite.

Megan Welsh, Grade 5
Dee Mack Intermediate School, IL

Winter

cold and crunchy snow
long icicles on the house
red noses with colds

Kristi Hotter, Grade 5
Washington Township Elementary School, IN

Snowball

Whoosh!
There it goes drifting and sailing into the freezing air.
It is clear until you reach the center.
The ball of freezing winter rain sparkles in the air.
CRACK!
Slams across someone's face like a bird running into a window.
The person hit by the ball is as frozen as a popsicle.
Teeth chattering.
The effect of a snowball.

Andrew Nummy, Grade 5
Walker Elementary School, IL

Pepper Is My Dog

Pepper is my dog.
She hops like a frog.

She is black
And eats Scooby snacks.

She likes to play in the snow.
Even when we say "NO."

We know Pepper won't run away.
Because she listens when we say "STAY."

Pepper is cuddly and fine.
She is all mine.

I love Pepper.
She loves me.
She's as silly.
As can be!!!

Katie Zale, Grade 5
St. Daniel the Prophet School, IL

The Ocean

The indigo ocean.
Salty, enormous, bright
A swimming place

Briana Robles, Grade 4
Jane Addams Elementary School, IL

Clouds

As I watch the clouds fly by
So pretty in the sky
Flying with such power
Looking like a flower
As I lie here in the grass
I watch the clouds pass.

Madi Kelly, Grade 6
St Patrick School, IN

The Sunset

The sunset with so many colors,
Brings me to so many wonders.
With the reds, pinks, and blues,
How it got that way I haven't a clue.

I look out my window every night,
Just to see that wonderful sight.
That sun setting so low,
Make a beautiful glow.

The sunset with so many colors,
Brings me to so many wonders.
I wish I knew how it makes that glow,
Sadly I will never know.

Morgan Rich, Grade 5
Dee-Mack Intermediate School, IL

Uranus

U ranus is
R eally Cold. Its
A tmosphere is 83% hydrogen, 15% helium, and 2% methane. So
N o human can live on its surface. But,
U ranus doesn't really have a
S urface. It is really just a freezing sea under its gas filled sky.

Marta Kloess, Grade 6
Pinewood Elementary School, IN

Life as a Kong

Ah, life as a Kong, sitting on a shelf at PetSmart,
Hey, hey, hey! Come on and buy me, if only I had a home.

There's a boy, buy me, yes! He bought me! I have a home!
NO, NO, NO! Not the plastic bag! I *hate* being carried around!

We're home! Oh, no the dog is happy! NO, I *do not* want to be flung around!
Hey, this is kind of *fuuuunn*! Offf, you're done like that?

Oh, he went and got the boy, yes! We're going outside,
Oh, no he's gonna throw me! Wow! I feel like a plane!

Offf, the ground is really hard, why do we have to do it again?
Hey, the dog caught me this time! Inside we go!

Tug o' war time, hey, don't stretch me that far!
I'm gonna snap! Finally, they stopped.

I'm really hurting bad, ouch, don't step on me,
Playtime — again, I wish I was back at PetSmart.

Brock Emery, Grade 6
Dee Mack Intermediate School, IL

Mars

M ars was named after the god of war
A res, because of its
R ed color. Mars is red because of iron oxide in the atmosphere.
    Some of the weather on Mars includes
S nowfall, dust devils (really big dust storms) and avalanches.

Michael McQueen, Grade 6
Pinewood Elementary School, IN

Ode to Jake

Jake is a guinea pig.
Jake was like a pumpkin with a white smile on his face.
Jake was so kind, but be careful he bit!
His nose was like an FBI sniffer. He found chocolate everywhere.
When you hugged Jake he would cuddle up and sleep in your arm.
His fur was like a puffy cloud.
His cage was a dream home.
It was red and toasty.
Jake made squeaky noises.
I feel sad because Jake died.
Jake is my guinea pig.

Diana Nguyen, Grade 5
Walker Elementary School, IL

My Brother and Me

I am a girl with three brothers
I wonder if they can be nice to me
I hear them wrestle
I see my brothers going to Hamlin School
I want them to take me to Hamlin again
I am a girl with three brothers

I pretend to watch TV when I'm playing Xbox 360
I feel my brothers when we wrestle
I touch my bed when my brothers push me
I worry if we get hurt
I cry when my brothers hurt me
I am a girl with three brothers

I understand that my brothers are nice
I say my big brother Darrick is the nicest
I dream that my brothers will be nice
I try to be really nice to them
I hope when I get older they will still be nice
I am a girl with three brothers

Ashlyn Longoria, Grade 4
Meadow Lane School, IL

Friends

I love my friends.
They are great.
Friends care and friends are always there.
They love you and you love them.
I love my friends.

Hannah Harpenau, Grade 6
Perry Central Elementary School, IN

World: Part I

Our world is dying,
Ending,
Finishing painfully.
We will die too
If we don't do something
Do you want to die?
Help me.
Help you.
Help everybody else.
Plant trees.
Stop and smell the roses.
And ask yourself,
Do I really want to be cast into oblivion?
Do I really want to become unknown, lost history?
Or...
Do I want to survive?
Yes.
Yes, you should want to live.
You should want to experience life to the fullest.
So...help me cure Mother Nature. But hurry.
She is dying, and time is running out.

Eunice Shek, Grade 6
Kennedy Jr High School, IL

Pretty Flower

I want to grow a pretty flower,
It might take a day, it might take an hour.

A dahlia, a rose,
I hold them by my nose.

They smell good and they should.

It all starts when I put in a seed,
And give it water and soil to feed.

Yes I give it lots of water and soil,
And when it is done growing
I will be knowing
To put it in wrapping or foil.

I give it as a present,
A lovely gift.
It all starts as a seedling grows very swift.

Now you can grow a pretty flower,
It might take a day, it might take an hour.

Mia Connery, Grade 4
Eugene Field Elementary School, IL

An Ode to Gatorade

Oh gatorade, oh gatorade how I love your taste.
You give me energy, and I go above my pace.

You help me play good football.
And get ready for the day.

You help me stay outside longer so
I can play and play and play.

Without you I wouldn't live another day.

Matt Markovich, Grade 5
Allen J. Warren Elementary School, IN

Best Friends

My friends are always there for me.
When we're together we're as happy as can be.
My friends are nice.
My friends are witty.
My friends all love little kitties.
My friends can be very funny.
My friends are very sweet just like honey.
We go shopping together and we share secrets forever.
My friends are a blessing to me,
our friendship will last till eternity.

I love my friends!

Danielle Hofsteadter, Grade 5
William B Orenic Intermediate School, IL

My Love for You

My love for you
is like the sky
with dreams that soar
and hopes that fly
my feelings for you
are like a sweet tart
it tastes so sweet
but breaks my heart
Especially when I love you so
you spin my head
when you look straight in my eyes
I will not lie
but I love you

Seth Fell, Grade 6
Milltown Elementary School, IN

Leaves

Leaves
Falling leaves
Rake, pile, jump!
We also have…break!
Fall

Sariah Brimberry, Grade 4
Bailly Elementary School, IN

Grandparents' House

Sitting on a quiet street
next to a bunch of oak trees
and great neighbors
there is a wonderful house.
With granite front steps,
and delicately crafted windows,
it's great.
It has seen many Thanksgivings,
reunions and
parties.

Now, it's being sold.
My grandparents are moving.
I am going to the house
for one last Christmas.
One last party.
One last everything.
For my family
And the house
This is a sad goodbye.

Peter Regan, Grade 5
Walker Elementary School, IL

Lizards

Three little lizards
crawled deep into the sandbar;
then I watched them move.

Harley Jackson, Grade 4
Rose Hamilton Elementary School, IN

Nature

Nature is a beautiful thing,
Watch all the birds sing.

One part of nature is trees,
And flowers are helped by bees.

There are a lot of fruits and plants,
Fruit is really liked, by ants!

Take care of nature every day,
And it will be here to stay.

Cameron Papandria, Grade 5
St Jude Catholic School, IN

Stalking Wolf

Sprinting as fast as lightning
With the grass just a blur
Fur as soft as cotton,
Beady eyes blacker than night
Seeking for his prey
The endangered wolf prepares
To pounce on his dinner.

Evan Scherf, Grade 6
Knox Community Middle School, IN

Band

cool, fun
drum, flute, saxophone
loud, pretty, musical, movement
Cameron likes to play bass drum

Kendall Mitchko, Grade 4
Veale Elementary School, IN

Seasons

Spring flowers bloom with glee.
The tulips say hello to me.
When spring has sprung away,
A new season enters to play.

Summer's hot and toasty days,
Makes your cares all go away.
When that season has blown away.
A new season enters to play.

Fall leaves for jumping in.
Makes you never want to end.
But when fall is covered in snow,
Winter soon begins to grow.

Winter ways are so much fun.
Snowmen brighten everyone.
When the snow melts again,
Spring has finally sprung again.

Amanda Morris, Grade 6
Milltown Elementary School, IN

My Cousin Sierra

Sierra is so sweet,
She can eat lots of treats,

She likes to stay with me,
And we act like a bee,

Her hair is pretty and blonde,
And she has a big yawn,

And when she's with her mom,
She likes to play with Tom,

But when it's time for bed,
She likes to hide her head.

Kayla Mosley, Grade 6
Perry Central Elementary School, IN

Girl/Boy

Girl
Adorable, functional
Polishing, organizing, skipping
Beautiful, womanly, rowdy, sour
Running, jumping, catching
Ignorant, lazy
Boy

Kaitlyn Cleary, Grade 6
Dee Mack Intermediate School, IL

Woodland

Woodland
Lively, active
Birds flying all around
Beautiful animals at work
Peaceful

William Pratt, Grade 5
Bethel Lutheran School, IL

Fall

Fall is here,
Too bad summer isn't near.
Summer is done,
It has been fun.
Dad is going to take me hunting
To get the big one,
It is going to be fun.
The leaves will crunch,
The deer will munch.
The babies will be born
And eat the corn.
We will make piles of leaves
Then with massive heaves,
We will count to ten
Then jump in!

Owen Ninke, Grade 4
Chrisney Elementary School, IN

Fall

Pumpkins and bright colored leaves
those are a few of my favorite fall things.
Families and friends all by your side
waiting for you to open the big surprise.
It is a wonderful puppy licking your face,
smiling so happy and picking up the pace.
Fall is a beautiful and wonderful time
we should enjoy it while we have a fresh lime.

Grace Hipskind, Grade 6
St Pius X Catholic School, IN

Jon Joseph James McGee

Jon Joseph James McGee,
Always tried to be the best he could be.
He tried to shoot a basketball
He could not shoot a three at all.
He tried to catch a baseball
But he just simply let it fall.
He tried to score a soccer goal
But he just hit a mole in his hole.
He tried to score a touchdown
But all he did was fall to the ground.
He tried to hit a tennis ball
But all he did was watch it fall.
He tried to bowl a strike
But he let it go and it hit my friend, Mike.
He tried to hit a hockey puck
But even there went down his luck.
Lacking the talent to play sports you see
Jon Joseph James McGee,
Became the best he could be as a referee.

Jonathan Cline, Grade 5
St Daniel the Prophet School, IL

Honey I Love…

I love to do things with my friends,
go out and have a great time with them
I love to cook, I love the look of my mom's face
when I show her what I've cooked for her
Honey I love…
I love watching movies,
I love to find out what happens next
I love sleeping in, and feeling great and not cranky
Honey I love…
I love shopping,
I love going to the mall and
getting new clothes to wear to school
Honey I don't love…
I don't love the snow
Honey I love…
I love to play a round of golf with my mom
Honey I love…

Keegan Joyce, Grade 5
Walker Elementary School, IL

Molly the Puppy

My puppy's name is Molly,
She is very jolly.

She is white and black.
I'll teach her to roll on her back.

Molly has a big bark,
But she is scared of the dark.

On December 2nd she was 11 months old,
She is bright and very bold.

When she goes for a walk her leash is not on,
She won't run away because we share a great bond.

Joe Powell, Grade 5
St Daniel the Prophet School, IL

The Sun Is…

The sun is a big, bright, yellow,
balloon in the sky.
It is a big ball of fire.
In the solar system, it is like a huge fireball,
from a dragon's fire.
The sun is as hot as,
flaming hot cheeto's that you eat.

Christine Marie Elliott, Grade 5
Lincoln Intermediate School, IL

The Ocean's Sunset Calms

The waves crashing talking to me
makes me smile with glee
the ocean's sunset calms.

The ocean's sunset on the water
reminds me of how I'm a daughter
the ocean's sunset calms.

The sunset on the ocean glistens
in a certain way that really makes me start to listen
the ocean's sunset calms.

The cool sand on my palms
the ocean's sunset calms.

The calm winds toss my hair
as I start to look everywhere
the ocean's sunset calms.

The water's wind whistling on the shells
make them start to sound like bells
the ocean's sunset calms.

I lay down and I frown as I realize…
the ocean's sunset is gone.

Hannah Hamlin, Grade 6
Our Shepherd Lutheran School, IN

Basketball

The Earth is a basketball,
if you take it to the pool and drop it,
that's what makes a flood.
If you launch it straight in the air,
you've got a tornado.
When it hits the backboard,
watch out, it's an earthquake.
Don't leave it out in a storm,
if you do, you'll scream
"The sky is falling, the sky is falling."

Connor Lynch, Grade 4
Bright Elementary School, IN

Oh Summer

Oh summer, Oh summer
I can't wait for you.
If you don't come it will be a bummer.
Oh summer, Oh summer
you are so cool.
I love the way you get me
out of school
Oh summer, Oh summer
You are so hot,
I feel like
I'm in a boiling pot.
Oh summer, Oh summer
I feel like a fool.
Because I wrote this
on the first day of school

Zachary Sims, Grade 5
St Daniel the Prophet School, IL

A Song of Life

Music notes are in my head
Eighths, wholes, halves
The song of life in my heart...

Alexis Sierra, Grade 6
Jane Addams Elementary School, IL

Fall

Fall is a fun time of the year
Baseball ends, football begins
In stadiums people cheer
I am happy when we win

Leaves fall off the trees
They turn colors like yellow and red
I enjoy the cool breeze
Add a blanket for my bed

There are tricks and treats on Halloween
Hunters are looking for deer
So many great costumes are seen
Fall is a fun time of the year

Colton Bogich, Grade 4
Bailly Elementary School, IN

Drugs Destroy Dreams

I wanted to be a big rock star,
But my dream was ruined when I went to the bar.
I wanted to be a vet,
But when I did drugs I couldn't even help one pet.
My dream was to be a physician,
But drugs and alcohol put me in the mission.
My dream was to be a movie star.
That dream was ruined when drugs made me crash my car.
When I was growing up I wanted to be an artist,
But drugs made me not the smartest.
I wished one day to settle down and have a family and home,
But my dream was smashed when drugs made me wander and roam.
I dreamed of one day bow hunting and killing a monster buck,
But my dream was destroyed by drugs, and so was my luck.
I dream to one day to have a good paying job.
Hopefully, I can stay away from gang type mobs.
My advice to every girl and boy,
Live your life and fill it with joy.

Adam Payne, Grade 5
Dee Mack Intermediate School, IL

Night Cycle

Now dusk has arrived,
The sky is alive,
With glimmering stars,
So bright you can see Mars,
A shooting star passing by is like a car driving in the sky.

The moon has descended,
The sun has attended,
This wonderful day,
You have to stay,
And watch the way the sun will decay.

The sun is setting on the ocean bay,
Now that you're here, I hope you don't go away,
The sky is a big painting,
So beautiful no one is complaining,
Come over here, lay down with me, and enjoy this, magnificent day.

Once again dusk has fallen,
And the moon is a'callin,
In the night,
It's a wondrous sight,
So quiet you can hear creatures crawling.

Jenna Fogel and Anna Kitchen, Grade 5
Towne Meadow Elementary School, IN

Mars

M ars has two moons named Phobos and Deimos. Mars is named
A fter the Roman god of War, Mars. The
R otation is 24 hours, 37 minutes, and 23 seconds. It is the fourth planet away
from the
S un.

Olivia Wallar, Grade 6
Pinewood Elementary School, IN

Raven

I am very **R** espectful, responsible, and reliable.
I am very **A** wesome too.
I am really **V** aluable and vicious.
    I'm **E** xcellent at art, I'm also elegant, and eligible.
    I'm very **N** aughty but nice.

Raven Boyd, Grade 6
Helfrich Park Middle School, IN

Mysterious Chestnut Horse

The wind screams in my face
But I can still feel the pace
His heat is never tamed
As I reach for his mane
I feel like I'm flying
As I'm in the sky
When we start to speed up
We are being splashed with mud
I hear quiet voices
I felt his breath starting to quicken
I squeeze with all my might
As we are running away
I feel a little rambunctious
We do a tight turn right and left
I lose control and let go
And I fall with a loud bang
I see him come to a halt
He whinnies and snorts as he comes over
His long mane and pretty frame make him look untouchable
I get on again and we started to canter faster
Now we are in a gallop and I know this is the best moment ever

Carly Leonard, Grade 6
Daniel Wright Jr High School, IL

Christmas

C hristmas is fun.
H ave a happy Christmas.
R eindeer drive Santa every where.
I get a lot of presents on Christmas.
S anta has hardworking elves.
T oday is Christmas.
M ovie theaters on Christmas hand out presents.
A ll the reindeer are on your roof on Christmas.
S anta brings you presents.

Katie Loveall, Grade 4
Warren Central Elementary School, IN

Sisters

S is for sisters who make me mad
I is for invisibility, I wish I had
S is for superpowers, oh how I wish I had
T is for tape of mine which my sister wishes she had
E is for earplugs which is what my mom wears when we fight
R is for riot which my sisters make
S is for sisters who feel better now

Quentin Johnston, Grade 4
Warren Central Elementary School, IN

A Search for Warmth

Winter has come
filling the world with coldness.

Trees start to lose their hair,
one by one, then two by two.
Every single day, an old piece cascades to the ground.
Once the last hair cascades off,
it knows that winter has come.

The worst thing about winter
is when snow flakes dance their way down
onto the trees' branches.
There the shivering tree lies waiting for summer to come,
in search for warmth.

Winter has come
filling the world with coldness.

Megan Forby, Grade 5
Walker Elementary School, IL

Snow

Crystaling joy
Fantastic bunches of fun
Snowmen coming alive with joy
White, cold, fluffy, fun
Snowballs fly like a dime in a sky
Igloos getting built for Frosty the snowman
Children playing in the snow
If you want to have fun just play in the snow

Zach Ruley, Grade 5
Walker Elementary School, IL

But Not

I like
Skateboarding
But not the bruises
BMXing
But not crashing
Football
But not losing
Philly Eagles
But not the cruddy offensive line
09 Camaro
But not the ones that change colors in the sun
General Lee
But not when it gets dents
TV
But not the commercials
Playing XBox
But not when I die
07 Mustang
But not when they catch on fire

Cole Tinney, Grade 5
Churubusco Elementary School, IN

Bubbles

Bubbles
Fly very high
Soar big and in the blue sky
Look like a star in the moonlight
Shiny
Borden Kennedy, Grade 4
Warren Central Elementary School, IN

Winter Joy

I step outside to a winter wonderland
A place I can escape to
A place with crystals that glisten
A place where there's a circus in the sky
I hear the wind singing a song
So soft and gentle it tickles my bones
I feel the snow on my dark red cheeks
I taste the joy of winter on my tongue
It melts in a flash
Too fast to be seen
I pick up some snow so wet and cold
I smell the damp gloves on my hands
Winter joy is here
But the bell rings
And we'll have to wait till next year
Lina Velcheva, Grade 5
Walker Elementary School, IL

October

Jumping in bright pools of leaves
Trees bare, lean, vivid colors
Icicles will soon hang off the limbs.
Tyler Bohacik, Grade 6
Jane Addams Elementary School, IL

Winter

warm chocolate
drink runs
down my
throat as the
snow pats the
window panes
I sit inside
sip
sip
sip
munching on
sugar cookies
as the wind
fades away
I stuff it
all in my
mouth and
go play
Trevor Batchelder, Grade 5
Pleasant Lake Elementary School, IN

The Beach at Night

Soft, smooth sand between my toes
The cool, salty ocean air blows

Where is my sister
I must have missed her

On the beach, with a kitten in her lap
We find her wearing her cowgirl cap

Hear the waves crashing ashore
I look at the moon more and more

Lilies, shoes, and shells so bright
They seem to glow under the moonlight

If you guessed right
My color is *white*
Taylor Sanzotta, Grade 6
Dee Mack Intermediate School, IL

Emme Lou

E mme is a puppy.
M aking fun is her game.
M y puppy is sweet and nice, too.
E mme is the best puppy.

L ou is her middle name
O n my shoe she chews and chews
U ntil I make her stop.
Sarah Bergin, Grade 5
Coffeen Elementary School, IL

Horses, Horses

Horses, horses, watch them run
Around the field one by one.

Horses, horses, quick as light
Come in colors dull and bright.

Horses, horses, pretty and sleek
Some are bold and others meek.

Horses, horses, fun to ride
Through the meadow, far and wide.

Horses, horses, aren't hard to find
They are always on my mind.

Falabella, Pinto, Thoroughbred, and Dale
They're beautiful from head to tail.

Horses, horses, big or small
You can bet I like them all!
Emily Mears, Grade 4
Stonegate Elementary School, IN

Jake

There once was a boy named Jake
Who liked to eat things that he'd bake
He'd make pumpkin pie
With whipped cream piled high
He'd give them to friends to take
Jacob Monroe, Grade 5
Bethel Lutheran School, IL

Autumn

I am outside, what do I see?
I see leaves of all colors
They are lying on the ground
I see fresh morning dew
It has settled on the tips of the grass

I am outside, what do I hear?
I hear the whistling wind
It is whistling to me
I hear the stiff leaves
They crunch under my shoes

I am outside, what do I feel?
I feel the cool breeze
It slowly moves around me
I feel the rays of sun
They warm my face form the cool wind

I am outside, what is all this?
This is autumn
It is beautiful
Corrine Callaway, Grade 6
Peoria Academy, IL

If I Was a Pencil

If I was a pencil,
I would let each
And every lead break
So my owner could sharpen me.

If I was a pencil,
She would sharpen me,
And sharpen me,
Until I was small and free.
Annai'D Leonard, Grade 5
Edison Elementary School, IL

Mom

Mom
pretty, nice
soft hair, loving, beautiful
hardworking, kind-hearted, intelligent
Mom
Priya Patel, Grade 4
Neil Armstrong Elementary School, IL

True Friends

True friends
Friends 'till the end
They never stop fun and laughing
They get a shoulder to cry on when they're sad
True friends

Kierstin Girdler, Grade 4
Warren Central Elementary School, IN

Snow

When you see snow fall
you will see, hear, feel, think and play.
When it first falls you think it is milk, cotton.
You hear the snow
Crunch
You feel the snow cold
You will see the snow
Fall.
You can make a snow man
You can melt snow
You can feel snow.

Jose Suarez, Grade 5
Lincoln Intermediate School, IL

Soccer Game

Dribbling down the sidelines like a puma chasing its prey.
Creating fancy moves to weave past the defenders
as a needle making its way through yarn.
Getting in ready position to shoot.
Feeling nervous pressure
like five hundred pound weights in your head replacing a brain.
Trying to ignore the roar of the crowd.
Screaming, shouting, booing.
One touch on the ball and bam!
The ball soars through the air like a rocket in space.
It hits the back of the net.
Score!
That is a soccer game.

Olivia Westrich, Grade 4
Walden Elementary School, IL

I Can Make a Difference

I can make a difference by doing what is right.
I will try to do my best every day and night.

When I am all done with school I want to help fight crime.
My job would be to protect the globe most all of the time.

Drugs are bad and could hurt us all.
That's why I want to work with the law.

So when I grow up and decide what to do.
I will work very hard to protect ones like you!

Hunter Moreland, Grade 5
Dee Mack Intermediate School, IL

What Am I?

I get a new friend each school year,
Trapped inside me is their biggest fear.

I am dark and empty as can be,
Except for the mirror hanging in me.

I am slammed shut every morning and night,
At 8:00 a.m. and 3:00 p.m. it hurts quite!

I am holding coats and bags all day,
Finally at night I let my dreams take me away.

Guess what I am. Dare to try?
The secret is locked away…what am I?

Andi Schmidgall, Grade 5
Dee Mack Intermediate School, IL

Chocolate Love

C ome near my chocolate and you'll be sorry
H eat it up, I'll drink a cup
O h my gosh, chocolate flowers I'll eat them for hours
C ocoa trees, get on your knees and collect some
O h man, my chocolate melted in the pan
L ick chocolate lollipops
A taste of heaven for 7/11
T ackle the taste don't let it waste
E very bite is a creamy delight

Angelica Arreguin, Grade 5
Benjamin Franklin Elementary School, IN

Autumn Life

My life is like autumn.
The leaves are bright and colorful.
It makes the world look joyful and friendly.
The perfect warmth makes me feel like I can do anything.
My family connects it all.
They are my life.
Family is warmth, colorful, and bright.
My life is like autumn.
The perfect warmth of the sun.
The rainbow of leaves.
The blue sky.
I have a beautiful life.
My life is like autumn.

Peyton Bykowski, Grade 6
Daniel Wright Jr High School, IL

Fall Sports

Look out! Here comes the Super Bowl.
The baseball playoffs are on a roll!
The basketball season is coming up.
There are so many sports I'm about to blow up!
My back is up against the wall,
Because all of these sports are played in the fall!

Jesse Smith, Grade 4
Chrisney Elementary School, IN

Halloween

So many different faces
Hulk, Spiderman, Venom
Candy from different places.

Alaijah G. Gonzalez, Grade 6
Jane Addams Elementary School, IL

Nature

Skies so blue, grass so green
I can't believe that this his happening
I look around and all I see
Is nature growing yippy
Birds are flying,
Squirrels are climbing
Dogs are barking
Cats are meowing
Flowers smell so good
Kids playing how much fun
Till I think about what is happening
And it is nature
It's so pretty
It's so fine
It's happening all year round
It's colorful
It's fun
It's everlasting life
Nature

Ashley Calandra, Grade 6
South Middle School, IL

Slumber Parties

Slumber Parties —
Pizza, Pop, and secrets
Fun, friends, and staying up late
Games and boy talk
Slumber Parties

Haley Smith, Grade 5
Pleasant Lake Elementary School, IN

Girls and Boys

Girls
Happy, playful, talking
Volleyball, basketball, golf, baseball
Playing, talking, listening
Working, busy
Boys

Ryan Harper, Grade 6
Perry Central Elementary School, IN

Katie

Katie
Friendly, pretty
My friend, playful, gentle
Fast worker, kind, trustworthy, nice
Not vain

Paige Tobeck, Grade 4
Warren Central Elementary School, IN

Arizona Desert

I'm a tourist.
My eyes will tell you that I'm good at taking pictures of amazing creatures.
I'm wearing a pair of tennis shoes, shorts and a tan T-shirt that is very comfortable for walking around in like fur on a bobcat.
I came from Galesburg, Illinois where I was born and I still live here today.
Behind me is a backpack which I use to hold my items, like a first aid kit and camera.
Sometimes I like to take pictures of my friends when they're being goofy.
I long for the days when it's warm but not hot.
I look forward to seeing amazing creatures.
I wish Arizona wasn't so hot.

Cianna Fairow, Grade 6
Churchill Jr High School, IL

Arctic Fox

Lodging in the frigid cold,
Farther north than all the rest,
it must be cold without a coat, but their pelt is quite more than enough
Its snow-white coat is attractive, though their purposes not for beauty,
for these deceivers are not arrogant,
as dwelling in the heart of malevolent cold is not simple.
Sharp beings know a striking white can be the best hiding place,
So why not hide in its fleece?
It's more than the heat of a hot fireplace,
it is a coat of beauty and protection.
It has even grown shoes on the bottom of its feet,
how original, ingenious, these scavengers,
all will agree.
When the heat returns, to keep a high-quality hiding place,
it outgrows its beautiful white pelt and buys a new brown fleece.
They are not picky eaters; scavengers as such like to hoard amounts of food,
when there is plenty, keeping track that every feast is enough.
Only at hopeless times do these deceivers show their sly side,
they take advantage of food, from polar bears, cheating on them all.
Coincidentally, this being is not evil, it will thankfully take leftovers
from the polar bears.

Eveline Liu, Grade 5
Highlands Elementary School, IL

The Brain

The audacity and capacity of the human brain.
If you think about it, it's pretty insane.

You've got numerous amounts of brain cells, that tell your body what to do.
And if you really think about it, that's what makes you, you.

Drinking and smoking, no way!
They burn billions of brain cells every day.

Would you really like that price to pay?
When you're eating your way through Harvard's L.A.

So listen to your brain, because it knows all.
What do you think tells your body to grow so very tall?

Davide Behr, Grade 6
St Joseph School, IN

The Mountain

As we drive on the dirt worn driveway
I unhook the ancient looking gate
Down the driveway sits a welcoming log cabin
Right next to the enormous mountain

When I walk down a path
Happiness and pure joy pour through my heart
Up the path I can hear the rushing of water
Birds are whistling lovely tunes as I trot up the path

Where the path ends
A beautiful white water rapid starts
Surrounding the river
Stand towering evergreen trees

As I near the cabin
I smell steaks roasting on a huge grill
The scent of evergreen trees fills my nose
Life on the mountains is a wonderful life

Mattea Lewis, Grade 6
Dee Mack Intermediate School, IL

Fall

Scary costumes on Halloween.
Halloween.
Movies all the time.
Good food on Thanksgiving.
Colorful leaves on the trees.
A light jacket to wear.
The light breeze in your face.
Piles of leaves to jump into.
So many decorations to hang,
Spending time around the fireplace,
Having quality time with your family.

Kyle Garner, Grade 5
William B Orenic Intermediate School, IL

The Winter Show

The Winter Show
has begun.
    Spectacular Snow
    Blows by to get the
audience excited.

    Wonderful Wind has joined
    Snow to blow the guests away,

        Cold accompanies his friends,
        To relieve us from all that heat.

At last the color white blinds us as it
prepares us for winter. You might think the
show is over but it's not. The show has just
begun it will end in spring.

Nkem Ekwunife, Grade 5
Walker Elementary School, IL

Star

Oh I am so tired
All night working to keep the sky bright
But soon it will be okay for tomorrow is a new day
I will rest and my mom, the Sun, will come out and play
Sometimes I am tired but it's okay
I love to help you see at night because,
When I see you look up and smile at me
I get a feeling of delight

Allison Gish, Grade 6
Helfrich Park Middle School, IN

The Tetons

The trees and their cool breeze
The cicadas chirp
My water
Cold in my mouth
The mountains and valleys stretch before my eyes
Like a set game board
Rivers rush in the distance
Leaves dance along the wind
Soft as a whisper
The view is wonderful
And now
My hike is over

Erin Luck, Grade 5
Stanley Clark School, IN

Hot Summer Day

It's a hot summer day I can feel the beat.
I can feel the really hot heat.
And I am here in my seat.
It is a hot summer day!

I go swimming in the lake.
I went home and cooked some cookies that's no fake.
I bring food to the beach so I can bake.
It's a hot summer day!

I love to go fishing that's what I do.
At night the owls go ho ho.
People sing at the beach and I go boo.
It's a hot summer day!

Also when people sing and I get sick.
I always find a big huge tick.
I always bring my brother Nick.
It's a hot summer day!

I am here playing in the sand.
With my biggest fan.
Listening to a band.
It's a hot summer day!

Rebecca Antonucci, Grade 4
Coal City Intermediate School, IL

Spooky Things

Spooky nights, spooky days, don't know what will happen in any ways.
Every day is filled with light, every night is filled with fright.
Spooky stories to be told, spooky houses trying to be sold.
Weird candy to give out, to little children, who choose to shout.
Yet you think this scary, spooky holiday is Halloween, but the chance is no.
So, don't be scared to come join me at the door, because soon you'll be the one who's saying "So?"

Lile Soliunas, Grade 4
Peter M Gombert Elementary School, IL

Life

Through the woods like an Indian, I feel yet the breeze of the clear and fresh wind that yet I cannot see. The bushes sway back and fourth to the movement of the soul and spirit. I am alone yet not alone. I feel the world circle day after day. As I wander silently through the woods, the only sound, I hear of is the leaves crunching, the birds chirping, and the sun brighten only to cause a sudden thirst of breeze. My family is alone, yet right beside me standing calmly. I fly through the open eyed sky. In the day the eye awakens its fragile lashes, then they close to the bright yellow and orange sunset. Brown as chocolate my skin, yet white as snow my heart and soul. Tenderness blinds my feelings. Roughness takes the lead by flowing through my blood. I challenge my feelings by bringing it out on the air surrounding me. One by one each day I feel yet the breeze of the clear fresh wind that yet still it is impossible for me to see.

Jadelyn Mathis, Grade 5
Grandview Elementary School, IN

He, the Hero

He walks balanced and sturdy, with a determined look,
Though his sleek black-and-white suit makes him flow smoothly on the hard earth below.
His dark eyes glitter brightly, smiling softly on the world around him.
Others watch him stare out to his task, and he bravely dove to it.
He came back out from his daring chore with a proud look in his eyes.
The others dove in, happily relieved for his helpful task.
The fellow penguins were happy, and the one heroic penguin did his chore of seal-watching.

Libby Carnell, Grade 6
Batesville Middle School, IN

The Winner

I see the balloons
rising higher and higher.
I wave in excitement as the crowd sways in time and chants my name
"Kendall, Kendall, Kendall."
I hug my dog, Shadow.
She looks like a shadow pressed up tight against my leg.
Her fur feels soft and fluffy on this cold crisp night at the fair.
I feel her steady breathing.
A man announces my name with radiance.
Behind us, I see the tough treacherous terrain and aggressive agility that we had to endure.
A man hands me a soft, silky blue ribbon.
A gold medal gleams in the sun.
I see and smell the country.
The bright moon shining on the far off water is my spotlight.
I gleam inside as the man hands me my trophy.
I know where I will put it.
The weather is rainy,
But I don't care.
I am a winner.

Kendall Sharpe, Grade 5
Stanley Clark School, IN

The Roller Coaster Ride

Her clothes were new and her hair was done,
she was strapped in the tram, anticipating some fun.
As she rode down the hill,
she held up her hands ready for the thrill.
She came to a tunnel that looked low to sight,
her eyes got red, her face turned white.
As she rode through the darkness toward the light,
she came to the end there was no more fright.
She went around the curve up over a hump,
she heard in the distance Thump, Thump, Thump.
She looked at her passenger and asked what to do,
he said to her I have no clue.
As the tram jerked to the side,
she knew it was the end of the ride.
As she giggled and laughed and enjoyed the ride,
she thought I want to ride again
I need to find someone to sit beside on the roller coaster ride.

Lavada Carroll, Grade 5
Perry Central Elementary School, IN

Guitars

Guitars are cool
Metal strings shaking
The musical arts one-of-a-kind tool
Glass and windows breaking

Gibson Les Paul
Very loud sound
I want them all
To carry around

From concerts to homes
From beginner to master
Lessons to super domes
My fingers get faster

Eric Clapton and Slash
Jimmi Hendrix and their bands
They play in a flash
They were born with guitars in their hands

Randy Stark, Grade 5
Trinity-St Paul Lutheran School, IL

A Moment in Time with a Butterfly

There it is my butterfly I call it
It is so peaceful so calm I wonder
Where it's going follow it I say
Follow it today and see what it seeks
Say that's nifty the butterfly went home
I saw his family his family is bright
I know his mother now his father brother too
Now I say good-bye I say good-bye to you

Emily Peterson, Grade 5
Booth Tarkington Elementary School, IL

All About My Family

My family is very active
We are very tactive
My mom's shopping comes first that's the worst
After shopping I'm ready to burst
That's my family they're the best

Dance, basketball, and softball are the best
My sister is a pest
My dad is always my coach in sports
I'm so active on the basketball courts
That's my family they're the best

My mom likes to support me at games
We both like spots the same
My sister is the greatest sister
My sister is very good at cutting paper
That's my family they're the best

Makenna Emerson, Grade 4
Coal City Intermediate School, IL

Horses

We sat upon your ancestor's backs,
For hunting,
For fighting,
For fun.
You got killed in our cruel wars.

And yet, we still wanted more.

We took you from your wilderness home,
Where you ran free,
Brushing the ground,
Like a paintbrush on canvas,
Arching your neck and sliding through the cool breeze.
When I look into your eyes,
I see sadness,
And pain,
But yet something else,
A glimmer of hope,
That someday you will be,
Without blinders,
Without saddles,
Without riders,

That one day you will run carefree in the world.

Emily Mu, Grade 5
Highlands Elementary School, IL

Pennies

There once was a man named Lenny,
Who collected a lot of pennies.
He ate a penny one day.
And all the people shouted "hooray."
Then he said, "Never again will I eat a penny!"

Kimberly Reglos, Grade 4
St Peter Catholic School, IL

My Curious Dog

I have a curious little dog
Who likes to get in trouble?

She'll get in the garbage,
Sniff in your shoe,
And tries to eat carpet.

Even though she is so silly,
I love her no matter what.

She loves to play
And loves to love.

She is just the cutest dog
You will ever see.

And that's my Cloe.
Shelby Seigneurie, Grade 5
Perry Central Elementary School, IN

Snow

Snow is fun and cold
You watch it go down and down
Till it hits the ground
Ferris Ingraham, Grade 5
Walker Elementary School, IL

Elements in Life

The earth and the air,
The high and the low,
The sea in its depths,
and the fire below.

The circle of life synthesizes all four.

Life has a road
a path, a stream

The air is for breathing
for living, it seems

The fire is a triangle
needing heat, air and a spark.

The water, the creeks and the rain
give life when we drink.
And with stability from the earth,

These are the elements
and those are their gifts.

Life reposes on these.
Alexis Kottoulas, Grade 5
Keystone Montessori School, IL

Snow

Snow, falling from the sky.
Impatiently waiting to come down.
Ready for adventure.
Ready for kids to jump right in.
Ready for all those snowball fights.
Ready for the creation of snow angels.
Excited to hit the ground.
Snow, falling from the sky!
Joshua Dixon, Grade 5
Walker Elementary School, IL

Football

There are lots of different sports,
A ton of different sorts.

But my favorite one of all,
Has to be football.

I'm not too fond of basketball,
I'm not too fond of baseball.

Even though football is very hard,
And a lot of times I get scarred.

Don't try to change my mind,
Because all I will do is whine.

My favorite sport is football,
Even though sometimes I fall.

The point I have been making to you,
Is, yes I've really thought it through.
Cole Wiegand, Grade 5
Dee Mack Intermediate School, IL

Puppies

Puppies so cute and fine
Oh, he got bit by that prickly pine.

He nibbles and nibbles
Oh, he's playing that fiddle.
Carson Smith, Grade 4
Veale Elementary School, IN

Me

B right
R ighteous
E xcellent
N oble
D angerously fun
A mbitious
N ifty
Brendan Sutherland, Grade 5
St Jude Catholic School, IN

Saturn

Spinning, spinning,
Around and around
I shan't be on too long
I am spinning on and on
Looking at planets
So big and so round
From here to there
Jade Larson, Grade 4
Bailly Elementary School, IN

Fall Is Here

Fall is here
Leaves starting to change
Falling — falling out of the trees

Thanksgiving is near
Starting to get cold

Deer starting to come out of the wood
Deer starting to eat uncut beans

Wild turkeys strutting and gobbling
Trying to find a mate

All the animals sense fall in the air
Knowing winter is approaching!
Tabitha Lasher, Grade 5
Perry Central Elementary School, IN

School

School
I wish it had a swimming pool.
That's what makes it cool.
Do you think it should have pools?
I do!
If school had a swimming pool.
It will make me say "school rules!"
With lots of tools for the Janitor.
Amarii Johnson, Grade 4
Lincoln Elementary School, IL

Seeing Life

Look out your window
Feel the breeze
Smell the air
Watch the leaves fall from trees
Look out your window
See nature
See its beauty
See its life
See its type of sadness and happiness
See what life's like.
Chris Paris, Grade 5
Perry Central Elementary School, IN

Birds

Birds are feathery,
Their skin is leathery.
They lay their eggs in trees,
Their nests are hidden with leaves.

Branden Yagelski, Grade 5
Washington Township Elementary School, IN

After College

What will I do after college?
After college I will be as free as a bird.
To teach God's word,
To those who haven't heard.

What will I do after college?
I will start my career,
And sing to those who want to hear,
About him who I hold in my heart so dear.

What will I do after college?
I will use my voice,
To help others make a choice.
From up above,
God pours out his love.

What will I do after college?
Whatever troubles may come,
I will not fear,
For my God is always near.

Amanda Jacobs, Grade 6
Christian Life Schools, IL

Lost in a World Above

Lost suddenly in a world above,
Seeing nothing but a dove,
He put me on his back and we went away,
In two hours he became my best friend,
Though I would never say,
I was sad because I knew this day would come to an end,
I wondered if I would see him again,
Slowly we went down on the grass,
I ran around and found a coin made of brass.

Looking up to the sky,
Seeing someone waving from high,
So the dove and I flew up there,
To get the biggest scare,
The wicked witch of the east,
She was known as the beast,
We ran for so long,
Soon from the town we heard a gong,
They knew she was coming,
I found out I was dreaming,
The gong was just my brother drumming,
And the flying was just the water steaming, from the shower.

Taylor Vacala, Grade 6
St Matthias/Transfiguration School, IL

Seasons

Seasons, seasons it's all about seasons
Summer, winter, spring, and fall
Spring — playing in the sweet smelling rain
As the farmers begin their work planting in fields wide
Summer — sitting in the shade with a cool lemonade
The farmer works to water his crops
Autumn — school starts again
Backpacks full with supplies
Farmers harvest the work they prepared for
Winter — sledding in the hills so steep
As the farmer takes a much needed sleep

Hannah Kraus, Grade 6
Crown Point Christian School, IN

My Great Grandmother

She always had a smile on her face
She was never in disgrace
She always loved making chocolate chip cookies
She never remembered the team of Rookies

She had supper ready for us when we came
When she was there, there was no one to be blamed
She always had good food
When she was in the mood

She always had some time to play
With me outside in her yard all day
I will always miss my great-grandmother
She only had one brother

She was always very sweet
But she was so very neat
My last great-grandma that was still living
I will never forget her because she was so giving

She loved me and I loved her
I will never forget her cat that would never purr
The one thing I will always remember
Is all of the fun we had in December.

MacKynzee Balbach, Grade 6
Nancy Hanks Elementary School, IN

Fall

The leaves are falling.
Little boys screaming.
Little girls weeping.
It is Halloween and no one can stop it.
House drowned with decorations.
People scaring all over town.
Costumes with colors of red, blue, and black.
Skeletons walking the streets.
It's Halloween and I wish it never ended.

Cory Turnbo, Grade 5
William B Orenic Intermediate School, IL

I'm Late

My sister made me late
Being late is what I hate
I'm late for my game
I hope she feels shame
I had to sit the bench
But winning was a cinch

Caleb R. Gramman, Grade 5
St Michael School, IN

Girls Before Boys

Girls before boys
That's how it should be
'Cause girls have cool curls
And boys have scraped knees.

Girls are gonna win,
'Cause we know how to go
Girls are gonna win
'Cause we know what to know.

Boys are gonna lose
'Cause all they think about
Is violence and sports
And lots of video bouts.

So, girls before boys,
That's how it should be,
'Cause girls have cool curls
And boys have scraped knees.

Angeliki Moussetis, Grade 4
Peter M Gombert Elementary School, IL

My Dad

Dad you're always here
When I am scared
You help me out
When I have doubt
You know Dad
You're all I think about
You put a roof over my head
I have a pretty nice bed
Dad you're mine
And that's just fine.

Abby Strack, Grade 5
St Jude Catholic School, IN

The Holidays

The holidays are near.
When we are with our families.
When everyone is here.
We all laugh and cheer.

There is room inside
The hearts that love them most.

Ariana Quintana, Grade 5
Edison Elementary School, IL

Fall

Fall is a time when the stern oak says its farewells to its last leaf.
Then along comes the wind.
It swirls around the red orange leaf as it swiftly falls to the hard dry ground.

Fall is a time when the temperature slowly drops and the days get shorter.
Out come the "winter" jackets, mittens, gloves, and that scratchy old scarf!

Fall is a time when pumpkins are carved and all you hear on October 31 is...
"Ding dong! Trick or treat!!"

Fall is a time when rakes are out to sweep and cradle up the delicate leaves and then,
Whoosh! A colorful rainstorm forms.

Morgan Wozniak, Grade 5
South Elementary School, IL

When I Get a Dog

When I get a dog I will walk him each and every day.
When I get a dog I will whisper promises and secrets in his ears
When I get a dog I will play with him each and every second.
When I get a dog I will only give him food that's good for him.
When I get a dog I will spoil him with love.
When I get a dog I'll do as much good as I can to protect him.
When I get a dog I will always miss him when I'm gone on long trips.
When I get a dog I will never care if he's clumsy as an ox and a goat.
When I get a dog I will love him no matter what.

Rachel Ford, Grade 6
Christian Life Schools, IL

I Am From

I am from juicy apples from the orchard,
And watching every last tear
Crying and crying until I can't breathe,
And dealing with pain and lingering fear

I'm from going against the rules,
But trying to do what's right
I am from cold winter days
And long summer nights

I am from the tears that have taken turns spinning down my face,
And going into the unknown
Missing my sisters at college
From spending hours with them on the phone.

I am from who, what, when and where
And never going back,
Being told to think about what I have
And never what I lack

I am from memories, hope and love
And not just believing in what I could see
I am from family and friends,
Much less I, myself and me

Jackie Harris, Grade 6
Northwood Elementary School, IN

Me and Hannah*

Hannah that I like so much, we play together and have fun.
She's really great she's number one.
Let's go Hannah and have fun.
I like Hannah so very well,
We are friends that is swell.
If there's a problem we work it out,
We are friends and that's no doubt.
We'll never fight, that is true.
What if you fight, what would you do?
We always laugh and play,
I would never run away!

Annamarie Gorski, Grade 4
Coal City Intermediate School, IL
*Dedicated to my friend Hannah Batuzich

Soccer

I am a soccer player
I wonder if I am going to win the game
I hear many goals
I see other teams on the field
I want a new soccer ball
I am a soccer player

I pretend that I am a professional soccer player
I feel the grass
I touch the soccer ball
I worry I will not win the game
I cry when we win a tournament
I am a soccer player

I understand if we lose a game
I say other teams almost win against us
I dream of a gold soccer ball
I try to be a good soccer player
I hope to be the best soccer player
I am a soccer player

David Melendez, Grade 4
Meadow Lane School, IL

Cotton Candy

Hey, my name is Natalie.
I love cotton candy.
Sticky, gooey,
Soft and chewy.
Think of this,
I would never miss.
Hot pink,
Light blue ink,
Orange fizz.
Gee Whiz!
It is so much fun.
Cotton candy is #1!

Natalie Rokosz, Grade 5
Washington Township Elementary School, IN

When I Become a Ninja

When I become a ninja I will defeat all of my enemies
When I become a ninja I will conquer Superman
I will be better than the Teenage Mutant Ninja Turtles
When I become a ninja I will be as famous as Hannah Montana
When I become a ninja I will glorify God
When I become a ninja I will be awesome!

Leah Caraotta, Grade 6
Christian Life Schools, IL

Truth and Lies

What is Truth?
It really is a stunning thing.
And though humans are a genius creation,
we still like to lie.
But what are Lies?
It's a flower with closed buds,
refusing to accept the truth inside.

But then, again,
How do we find the Truth?
We use our perspectives,
of course.
But then,
if our perspectives change,
does the truth change with it?

Confusing me daily,
making me think and ponder,
trying to figure the answer out.
Hard to wrap a mind around
and find an answer.
But still, persistently, I ask,
What is Truth and What are Lies?

Joy Chiu, Grade 5
Highlands Elementary School, IL

Jessica Brown

We played together every day.
On the swings, on the ground.
We had play dates.
We walked around a friendly part of town.
As we walked home one day,
I turned around and went away.
She turned around and said good-bye.
As she walked across the street,
a screech of brakes and lots of smoke.
I turned around, my heart was broke.

Sitting by her bedside in that gray hospital room,
holding her hand soft and cold.
She looked at me and faintly smiled.
She said, "Don't worry."
Her final words, her final breath.
Gone…

MacKenzie Binkley, Grade 6
Perry Central Elementary School, IN

Christmas

Sled rides
Coats made of animal hides
Snow is white
Children's delight
Hot chocolate feels good
Children play in the neighborhood
Fire feels good
Flowers don't blossom
Sarah Clinton, Grade 4
Veale Elementary School, IN

If I Were a Dog

If I were a dog,
I would run.
I would chase a ball.
I would have fun.

If I were a dog,
I would walk every day.
I would eat.
I would play.
Evelyn Ortega, Grade 5
Edison Elementary School, IL

If I Was a Dog

If I was a dog,
I would chase a ball.
I would eat.
I would play with you all.

If I was a dog,
I would bite.
I would sleep.
I wouldn't fight.
Eduardo Guadarrama, Grade 5
Edison Elementary School, IL

Looking at the Sky

A day in fall
the geese are flying
for the winter.
Sun is bright and blinding
the sky is blue with clouds
differing in shape and size.
Planes fly over head
flying through the clouds.
Vultures fly in circles
finding prey.
Cardinals fly and are gone
for the winter to the warmth.
Helicopters fly through the sky
like swift birds.
James Harris, Grade 6
Milltown Elementary School, IN

The Dog

A funny creature is the dog,
He is tall when he hops to the log

When the dog spots you in bed,
He quickly pounces on your head

He noisily crunches his food,
When he is in a really good mood

He's as big as a rhino,
but he's no big dino

When a car comes rushing by,
The dog follows to say good bye
Sarah Preflatish, Grade 6
Perry Central Elementary School, IN

Football

F ootball is the best!
O ur team is good.
O nlookers cheer for our team.
T ouchdown!
B est team is the Toppers!
A pass, a catch,
L eaping for the goal line,
L eaving is the worst part.
Cheyenne Snyder, Grade 5
Coffeen Elementary School, IL

Shoes

Big shoes
Little shoes
Long shoes
Wide shoes
Narrow shoes
Tennis shoes
Soccer shoes
Basketball shoes
Baseball shoes
Football shoes
So many shoes
Evan Adkins, Grade 5
Perry Central Elementary School, IN

My Parents

P atient
A bsolutely caring
R espectful
E verlasting love
N otable
T houghtful
S tupendous
Cameron Gillman, Grade 5
St Jude Catholic School, IN

Santa Claus

Christmas is icicles hanging off trees.
They look like sticks.
Christmas is flakes of white snow.
Santa comes and says "ho, ho, ho."
Every year on December 25
The jolly old guy stops by
With his reindeer that fly.
If you stay awake to see him
He will not come
But if you sleep you'll wake to a treat.
When he comes he drinks warm milk
And cookies you leave him to eat.
He has two lists, he checks them twice.
Hope you're on the one that says nice!
There are presents under the tree.
I think I see one for me.
When the presents are all unwrapped
Don't be sad because he'll be back!
Kaylie D. Tanis, Grade 4
Meadow Lane School, IL

Snow

Snow is white,
Snow is bright,
Snow is going to fall tonight,
Snow on the trees,
Snow on the ground,
Snow falling all around.

My brothers and I decide to play,
on this very icy, cold day.

Time to come inside
from the storm we will hide.

Sit by the fire's glow,
now it's time to relax and lay low.
Nicholas Verta, Grade 5
St Daniel the Prophet School, IL

Dying

Why do we have to die?
Why can't we live?
Do our hearts just stop beating?
Do our bodies just give up?
Does God just say, "Time for you to go?"
Why don't we get a sign of dying?
Why is dying so effective?
Why is dying so easy?
Why is dying in human nature?
Why is it so serious?
Why does death happen so often?
Symiah Williams, Grade 5
Edison Elementary School, IL

I Am

I am funny and annoying.
I wonder about space.
I hear Ackalay screaming in fright.
I see people flying on broomsticks.
I want a Wii (ah man).
I am funny and annoying.

I pretend I'm a rock star.
I feel the weight of the world on my shoulder.
I touch the sun.
I worry about the end of the world.
I cry about dead puppies.
I am funny and annoying

I understand about war.
I say that we all get mad.
I dream of being rich.
I try out for basketball.
I hope for an end to war.
I am funny and annoying.

Alec Turner, Grade 6
Helfrich Park Middle School, IN

Used

You said that it was deep
That made my heart skip a beat,
I thought this feeling would last
But you got angry way to fast,
You know I still care
Even the circumstances just aren't fair,
I would still do anything to be with you
But I guess your words weren't true,
You hurt me and now I feel used
Now my confidence will be forever bruised,
I don't know why I still like you anyway
You see me make eye contact and look away,
So I'm trying to forget about what we once had,
But whenever I see you with her I still get mad.

Espy Ramos, Grade 6
Harding Grade School, IL

Ocean

Covering most of the Earth.
I am salty and fun.
I push and pull on the sunny sand,
leaving behind shells that have washed away years ago.
Sometimes I get lonely, but not all the way.
People visit me all the time.
I have the silver glistening moon, at my side.
All sorts of creatures live inside me.
They swim and play as if there were no time or day.
The sun looks so pretty when it sets on top.
The day is over, but not for long.
I am the ocean.

Destinee Loyd, Grade 6
Helfrich Park Middle School, IN

I Am

I am cool and handsome
I wonder when the war is going to end
I hear things about my friends that other people tell me
I see ghosts floating when I look around
I want a frog
I am cool and handsome
I feel like I just want to cry
I touch the angels when I reach up
I worry about the war
I cry when I think of my grandma
I am cool and handsome
I understand my grandma died when I was little
I am not scared of ghosts
I dream that I can fly
I try to do my best in school
I hope to live for a long time
I am cool and handsome

Jeremiah Garretson, Grade 5
Walker Elementary School, IL

Midnight Attic

As you walk in, silent is all
Step by step, you hear the creaking wall
Seeing things from early on
Reminds you of memories from when you were gone
Suddenly, you hear a sound
It makes you think you need to turn around
As you're walking back, you see a light from the moon
And it tells you that you need to leave soon
This midnight attic adventure has been fun
You hope to come again after morning sun

Emily Bruin, Grade 4
Stonegate Elementary School, IN

Halloween

Halloween will give you a fright!
You'll get scared every Halloween night.

You will have lots of fear.
When you see people disappear.

Everyone is in for a scare.
Because you may end up in a ghost stare.

Don't count to two.
Then someone might follow you.

So when you go out.
Make sure you stick to your route.

Remember if you scream.
You could see an evil beam.

Katie Sand, Grade 4
Summit Elementary School, IL

Laughter

Gift from God
Giggle, smile
Sadness vanishes
The world illuminates
Laughter
Amy Gooderum, Grade 6
Tri-West Middle School, IN

Snow

Snow sheet covers Earth
Children sing as home they go
Frostbite stings my face
Fabian Najera, Grade 5
Walker Elementary School, IL

Autumn

Autumn is here,
What a wonderful year,
Leaves changing colors,
Falling to the ground,
Crisp, cool nights,
Fall time, the most beautiful of all!
Phillip Taylor, Grade 5
Perry Central Elementary School, IN

Santa

There is a place way up north.
I once went there a long time ago.
I met a man with a white beard
who laughed with a ho ho ho.
He danced with his wife
and ate with his elves.
He told stories of all that he would do.
There is a person way up north
and I believe in him too.
I call him Santa, how about you?
Nicholas Reid, Grade 5
St Daniel the Prophet School, IL

Fall

Fall is here in November
Every fall I will always remember.
Here is all I can say
Having fun every day
The leaves outside are falling down
Now they're always going to be brown.
Fall is here always great
It is a good time to celebrate
When fall is over the leaves are gone
Now it is ready for dawn
Bedtime is here now
Winter is here for the wolves to howl
So the next fall that I see
Is great for you and me.
McKenzie Elverd, Grade 5
Perry Central Elementary School, IN

Rams Run

The Rams are running in basketball against the Saint James Raiders.
The ball is tipped and there we are.

The game was rough
Rough as sandpaper
5 players fouled out

Everyone was excited when we called "Time out."
It was tied 30-30

We ran out
Saw 5 seconds left
Heard the crowd

I got the ball
Dribbled up
Felt it leave my hands when I shot

The buzzer buzzed wildly buzz buzz
It was halfway there

It went in with a "swoosh"
The crowd ran onto the court like unleashed dogs.
We won, we won, we won.
Jonathan Kopp, Grade 6
Our Shepherd Lutheran School, IN

A Penny in a Pocket

As I sit by the fire-pit drinking my herbal tea
I look outside and see all the opportunities that wait for me.
I think to myself, "Why am I so fortunate when others have less?"
I have more than I need I must confess.
I see a man standing in the freezing rain
His whole outlook on life was surely plain.
So, I want all of you to see everything outside of thee.
As I sit by the fire-pit drinking my herbal tea,
I look down at my solid gold locket
And think of those who only have a penny in their pocket.
Kristin Lynn Scriven, Grade 6
Emmanuel-St Michael Lutheran School, IN

Fun Months

January the snow is still here sometimes you can wear it
February is the time when Valentine's rhyme
March is when snow starts to melt and when it also tilts
April is the part when April Fool's starts
June is when you shout and play about
July is the fourth and also my birth
August is the time when butterflies fly and kids watch them fly to the sky
September is when some leaves fall when some people say they would wait and stall
October's when there's schemes when some laugh, but also scream
November's the time of Thanksgiving Day when turkeys are on the table all day
December's when the Ice Hogs play and my sister has a wonderful day
Olivia Wilkens, Grade 5
Forreston Grade School, IL

Snow

Snow is white,
Snow is bright,
Snow is such a lovely sight.

Snow is icy,
Snow is cold,
But in March it gets old.

Snow looks like a white cloth,
Soft, fluffy, and warm,
Makes you want to bundle up in a winter storm.

Snowballs from snow,
Snowmen from snow,
Snow is fun anywhere you go.

Jordin Pearson, Grade 5
St Daniel the Prophet School, IL

I Am

I am a blue sea and pure gold
I wonder how a bird got its wings
I hear the ocean whispering to me
I see the palm tree and candy canes
I want to stop war
I am a blue sea and pure gold

I pretend to be a runway model
I feel fur and diamonds
I touch money
I worry that my candy will get stolen
I cry when I see other kids with their grandma
I am blue sea and pure gold

I love my mom and dad
I believe in magic
I dream made of water pebbles and pearls
I try not to be a litterbug
I hope to be a fashion designer
I am blue sea and pure gold.

Shaelyn Lord, Grade 5
Walker Elementary School, IL

The Sport of Basketball

The fans are yelling
The players are running
We pass, we shoot
We score, we score, we score
Bang! The fans are yelling, they shoot and it's blocked
As I dribble I can taste the Gatorade in my mouth.
And smell the hardwood floors
I can feel the soft round ball
This is why I love the sport of basketball

David Popoola, Grade 5
Stanley Clark School, IN

Basketball

Basketball is the very best sport
I like the way you dribble up and down the court
When you hit a big three
You hear the crowd yell yippee
Now its half-time, time to take a break
You're so tired its tough to stay awake
Then the bell rings and you know its time for more
When you come out the crowd is even louder than before
You start off doing very, very good
Better than the other team ever could
But then the enemy starts coming back
They seem to be good at doing that
At the end of the quarter its 42-43
But the opposing team is in the lead
You are down by two with 1 second to go in the last quarter
You steal the ball and you shoot a half-courter
The whole crowd goes silent in a hush
As the ball goes through the net you hear a big swoosh

Zach Zoglman, Grade 6
Nancy Hanks Elementary School, IN

Leaves

Leaves gliding with grace
away from trees that held them
to be hills of leaves.

Antonio Presutti, Grade 4
Frank H Hammond Elementary School, IN

My Perfect Poem

This is a poem
A perfect poem
Just for you and me
I write this very neatly
Just for you to see
During the day and in the night
Everything is so lovely and stars so bright
I think I know why
Because my perfect poem is a great sight!!

Marianna Aspuria, Grade 5
St Daniel the Prophet School, IL

Christmas Love

Snow on the ground
You listen, but there's no sound
Children marvel at each little flurry
When out in the snow a gathering squirrel scurries
The kids are eager to open their presents
While the air fills with a gingerbread essence
The children are in their beds sleeping tight
They know very well they will get a visit tonight
Santa's coming and bringing toys
Little dolls and Christmas joys
So this I offer to kids short and tall
Peace on Earth good will to all

Emma Lyn Comer, Grade 6
Allen J. Warren Elementary School, IN

Michael Jordan

Michael Jordan had no hair
but could still glide through the air
he was very tall
and was amazing at basketball
Joseph Kennell, Grade 6
Bethel Lutheran School, IL

Orange

I was eating an orange
When I hit my door hinge
I threw a fit
So I walked downstairs to sit
And saw some porridge.
Charles W. Harner, Grade 4
Shoals Elementary School, IN

Jesus

J oyful
E ucharist
S upreme
U nderstanding
S avior
Joe Gervasio, Grade 5
St Jude Catholic School, IN

Notre Dame

What is Notre Dame?
A college
A sports team
A Catholic Church
A symbol of Mary
Notre Dame is my team.
Greg English, Grade 5
St Jude Catholic School, IN

Sister

Sister
cute, loving
nice, cheerful, fun
beautiful, smart, funny, helpful
Sister
Neha Patel, Grade 4
Neil Armstrong Elementary School, IL

Purple

Purple is smooth and silky.
Purple is a flying butterfly in the spring.
Purple is a juicy grape.
Purple is a frilly sweater.
Purple is a relaxing shade.
Purple is a sleeping bird.
Purple.
Samantha Schultz, Grade 5
Henryville Elementary School, IN

Imagination

Imagination,
is a gift,
Believe in it,
love it,
use it,
hope you get more,
If you don't,
it just might,
fade,
away.
Brittney Shambaugh, Grade 5
Churubusco Elementary School, IN

Friendship

I love my friends with all my might
They are the ones who changed my life
They are the ones who are there for me
They are the ones who make my day
They are like pizza
Some are thick, some are thin
But any way they are my friends
Abby Niemeyer, Grade 6
All Saints Academy, IL

Boys

Boys are…
Thoughtful
Silly
Wicked
Evil
Super
Cheerful
Breathtaking
Adventurous
Great
Inefficient
Peaceful
Exciting
Enjoyable
Mayra S. Arteaga, Grade 5
Lincoln Intermediate School, IL

Punished

P unished
U nbelievable
N ever fun
I mpossible
S tressful
H aving no excuses
E ncouraging…Not!
D oomed!
I just hate being…punished!
Kaylee Blum, Grade 5
Pleasant Lake Elementary School, IN

Zucchini Lunch

Yesterday I ate
A zucchini breakfast lunch
With my family
Ricardo Camacho, Grade 5
Edison Elementary School, IL

Difference

Angel
White, kind
Floating, not killing, singing
Halo, soft, horns, rough
Falling, killing, shouting
Red, mean
Devil
Breanna Book, Grade 5
Forreston Grade School, IL

Friend

Loving, caring
Thoughtful, protecting, fun
Guiding, sharing, mean, angry
Nasty, rough, fighting
Cheating, rude
Foe
Nathan Kriech, Grade 5
St Jude Catholic School, IN

Baseball

Cheers fill the air
The love of the game is everywhere.

They hit a homerun
And the crowd is having fun.

The crowd just can't wait
For him to step on home plate.

Hooray hooray they won the game!
And he was the hero with all the fame!
Myranda Fox, Grade 5
Forreston Grade School, IL

Christmas

C arolers
H omemade goodies
R ed and green
I cy snow
S tars
T rees with lights
M istletoe
A ngels roam the sky
S anta's sleigh bells
Mandy Porter, Grade 5
Dee Mack Intermediate School, IL

The Holocaust

The Holocaust
I wonder what it was like to be in the Holocaust.
It makes me appreciate my life more and more.
Not having to hide
Being able to go to school.
Eating as much food as I want.
I wonder what it would be like to wonder if I still have a
family or to have my life taken away or the last thing
I see is the gas chamber.
Having nowhere to go after the war.
Trying to find any trace of my family.

Brianna Rodgers, Grade 5
Benjamin Franklin Elementary School, IL

The Gym

The kids of St. Daniel had gym class in a church basement.
This was not proper placement.

A new building would be good.
That was understood.

This project needed money,
So bad it wasn't funny.

The children cried and cried
The parish tried and tried.

Where will we play?
Our sports equipment has no place to stay.

We had a Dollars 4 Dans bash.
It raised lots of cash.

Quick, look outside,
The gym has been built with St. Dan's pride!

Jacob Petraitis, Grade 5
St Daniel the Prophet School, IL

Artifact

Eyes staring into space as if deep in thought,
Carefully carved curls covering her shoulders,
Chest puffed out like a brave warrior,
Cracks running down an amber arm
As if she's been dropped once or twice.
Maya figurine reminds us of the past.

Kiersten Rowe, Grade 6
Knox Community Middle School, IN

Stones

I live in a hollow tree.
Black is my favorite color because my friends are all black.
My job is to be skipped across the pond.
It hurts when people try to smash me.
It is HARD to be a stone.

Michael Porter, Grade 6
Trinity Oaks Christian Academy, IL

Babies

Babies here babies there babies everywhere
Jan, Feb, March, April, May, June, July
Babies are born every day of the year
Sleeping, crying, pooping, eating
They do all this very much
They need very good care
They need all they can get
It is hard caring for babies
If they fall they need help back up

Sammi Endicott, Grade 5
North Knox East Elementary/Jr High School, IN

Pretty Flowers

You can smell the flowers.
They are in the spring.
They are in the summer.
They are beautiful things.

When winter comes they're sleeping.
When spring comes they wake up.
They blossom and bloom
My favorites are sunflowers and buttercups.

Brandon Sharp, Grade 5
Coffeen Elementary School, IL

Squirrels

Squirrels gliding through the air
Flying over trees that crack
Swishing down through the babbling brooks
Scrambling through the swaying leaves
All the colorful and green
Falling nuts go splash in the new mud
in the water in the brooks
That over flows when it rains
The squirrels hide as it pours
It is cozy and warm inside
Cold freezing outside
Fighting over nuts in their little holes
Kicking and screaming oh what a fuss.

Dakota Curl, Grade 6
Milltown Elementary School, IN

Football

I love football, it's my game.
When I get the ball, all I hear is gain.
But, when I'm on defense, I usually get a sack.
It's better when the quarterback tries to backtrack.

I'd like to intercept a pass, I think it would be great.
If I want to catch a ball, I'd have to dominate.
I really love football, I think it is the best.
Running, jumping, passing, it's better than the rest.

Dylan Gray, Grade 5
Coffeen Elementary School, IL

Student's Feelings

When I am sad
I feel like the genius
Who got an F.

When I am afraid
I feel like the soldier
Called to arms in Iraq.

When I'm nervous
I feel like an actor
Who forgot their lines in a play.

When I'm angry
I feel like a nuclear bomb
About to explode in Japan.

When I am confident
I feel like Albert Pujols
About to bat against a rookie.

Austin Scott, Grade 6
Dee Mack Intermediate School, IL

The Big Bird

I have giant wings,
and I am brown and white.
In the sky I shall be.

Anthony Martinez, Grade 4
Rose Hamilton Elementary School, IN

Gems

Shimmering in the sun
A piece of topaz lies quietly
Waiting to be carried
In a warm pocket

Riding the water
A chunk of sapphire relaxes
Awaiting the safety
Of a child's bedroom

Dug in the ground
A piece of emerald sleeps
Waiting to be revealed
For its symbol of beauty

Weight crushing it
A chunk of amber
Waits for this turtle's belly
To get off of him

Displayed in a shop
A slice of amethyst
Waits to see the world
And its treasures

Nathan Wojcik, Grade 5
Walker Elementary School, IL

Rosa Parks

R osa got on the bus from work,
O n the seat in the front she sat.
S itting just minding her own business,
A nd got arrested for refusing to move.

P anicked because she thought she didn't do wrong.
A rguing for her right to sit anywhere she pleased,
R ights for the blacks was all she asked for,
K indness and equality was all she wanted.
S aying "no" to riding buses so this foolishness would come to a stop.

Jazmine Torres, Grade 5
Benjamin Franklin Elementary School, IN

An Ode to Going to My Baboo's House

Oh, Baboo oh Baboo,
I love coming to sleep over at your house.

Oh, Baboo I like the way you buy me new pajamas
and tuck me in and fall asleep with me a little bit
And make me waffles for breakfast again and again!

Oh, Baboo I like to come over when Bones is there.
He always has big hair and says funny things like he don't care.

Oh, Baboo when I come over lil Jer is there too.
I like when he plays piano and lets me watch him play,
and lets me play his game cube all day
Until he is ready to play Madden.
Oh, Baboo when I come over Jess is there too!
Jess is the best. She baby-sits me and is always super nice to me.

Oh, Baboo when I come to your house I bring my mom too.
So she can make us dinner and play games with us and take our pictures too!

Oh, Baboo I love coming to your house!
It's soooooo much fun!
I'm going to come there every Friday night from now until doomsday,
Because I love you Baboo and all the fun things we do.

Gaje Willis, Grade 5
Allen J. Warren Elementary School, IN

Kayos

Kayos
Cute, cuddly, gray, and white
A cat family
Lover of Kristen, picnic table, Kaire (sister)
Who feels independent, strong, frisky
Who needs a family, a home, a mother
who fears cars, meaner cats, and people sneaking up on her
Who gives comfort, happiness, and loving pride
Who would like to see more food, the inside of the house, and less cats
Resident of Indiana
Fenwick

Kristen Fenwick, Grade 6
Helfrich Park Middle School, IN

If We Were the Same

Imagine if we were all the same
If we all had the same hair,
If we all had the same skin,
If we all had the same personalities,
If we all had the same possessions,
If we all had the same feelings,
If we all had the same ideas,
If we all had the same opinions,
If we all knew the same things,
There would be no adventure,
No color to the world.
Then there would be no Martin Luther King,
No Helen Keller nor the Wright brothers,
No Benjamin Franklin or Plato,
There would not be a single thought
To come up with computers,
Cameras, award winning stories or TV's.
Life would be a dead end, nothing new, nothing old,
But we are not all the same, and I'm glad,
We're different, unique in our own way,
And it's a good thing.

Madison Gee, Grade 6
Keystone Montessori School, IL

Wintertime

It's the most wonderful time of the year.
Everyone telling you be in good cheer.

Give happy greetings to friends that appear.
It's the happiest season of the year.

Bells are clanging, and children are singing.
People are merry, carols are ringing.

Hear the voices singing, "Let's be jolly."
While you deck the hall with boughs of holly.

Now this is something you might want to hear.
Seasons greetings, have a happy New Year!

Mackenzie Etienne, Grade 6
Perry Central Elementary School, IN

Chocolate

C hocolate is sweet
H ot and soft
O nly milk chocolate
C rispy and hard
O r white chocolate
L ovely, yes
A lways sweet, not bitter
T asty, tasty, tasty
E very time is better

Daniel Serna, Grade 5
Benjamin Franklin Elementary School, IN

Basketball

You walk in the gym, feel the emotion.
Such a big gym, only you in the colossal room.
You get a leathery ball, start to dribble.
When you dribble the ball makes a
sound almost like a heart beating.

Your eyes see the hoop. You pick up the ball.
You shoot. It goes up…"thud." You missed.
You pick up the tree bark colored ball again.

You dribble back down the court.
You stop at the free throw line.
You shoot "swish." It goes in, you can
sense the sweat. You sense something else,
it's the school's basketball coach. In a faint voice
you hear, "Welcome to the team!"

Mattison Gardner, Grade 5
Lincoln Intermediate School, IL

I Can Make a Difference

I can make a difference by saving the plants and trees.
So listen to this message, please.
We all need to save the rainforest.
This is probably for the best.
Take a look at all the animals' faces.
Do you really want to destroy their birthplaces?
If you pollute the Earth's air,
It will create a frightening nightmare.
I hope this Earth you will defend,
And that, my friend, is the end.

Daniel Cobb, Grade 5
Dee Mack Intermediate School, IL

Colts

The Colts are my favorite team
I even see them when I dream.

The uniforms are blue and white
The Colts are going to shine tonight.

When Payton's in as quarterback
The team will never lack.

Bob Sanders he is really cool
So don't be a fool.

If he comes your way you're gonna get hit
You better be wearing your helmet.

The record stands at 8 and 0
Tonight we will make it 9 in a row.

The Colts are Arizona bound
No better Super Bowl champs will be found.

Anna Molloy, Grade 5
St Jude Catholic School, IN

Change in Season

The cold wind blows through the dark black night as a single silver eye stares down from endless space and then disappears behind a single gray cloud it covers up the glowing eye and then it emerges from the dull mist and disappears once more, its cold stare freezes the air and not a living soul dares to wake on this frosted night then suddenly the sky lights up and it is the first day of a new season the beautiful warmth of spring, winter is over, daylight shatters the clouds AND I COME OUT TO PLAY...

Madeleine Costello, Grade 4
Peter M Gombert Elementary School, IL

Seasons

Fall has come, now is the time for raking and playing in leaves. The evergreen still looks proud with pines, but other trees look sad, looking forward to another spring. Winter is now upon us, a blanket of snow has covered the land and people are putting up the Christmas trees and having fun. Also, at this time many families celebrate Christmas; what a great time of year. The snow melts, and spring is here! This is the time of blooming flowers and birds in the air, and children will soon be out of school. The long wait is finally over for the trees, they now have leaves growing from their branches. Families are going on outings and playing at parks. Now comes my favorite season of all, summer. School is out and children are free to enjoy the warmth of summer with their families. Now is a time of great leisure. It is a time to spend with family and make memories that will last a lifetime. These are the seasons of the year.

Neal Wrobel, Grade 5
St Rita Catholic School, IL

In My Winter

In my winter I skate.
In my winter I skate and play in the snow.
In my winter I skate, play in the snow, and shovel snow.
In my winter I skate, play in the snow, shovel snow, and drink hot cocoa.
In my winter I skate, play in the snow, shovel snow, drink hot cocoa, and get Christmas presents.
This is my winter, and when it is over I'm sad, but then I notice it's almost summer.
And then I get days at the pool and days at the beach.
All fun in the sun, and that is how I like it.

Claire Dickerson, Grade 4
Peoria Academy, IL

Christmas

C andy, Christmas, cookies and coughing, crispy, coldness, and comfy couches.
   Cheery fires, and chestnuts roasting, caramel apples, and the stove all a-glowing.
H appy holidays, wish you the best!
R iding along in the horse-drawn sleigh, so snowy and fresh.
I cy and freezing, the perfect weather.
S nowflakes a-falling as light as a feather.
T ime to tell stories of Christmas weather, long, long ago that brought people together.
M erry feasts and dancing with family and friends.
A n absolutely wonderful holiday with all kinds of cheer, Merry Christmas to all, it's coming near!
S nowing and sneezing, and cookies and cream, all of these things make the best Christmas for you and me!

Lucy Thomas, Grade 6
Corpus Christi Elementary School, IN

Neptune

N eptune is now the farthest planet from the Sun.
   It used to be the second farthest, until Pluto's life as a planet
E nded. Neptune is the coldest planet because it is the farthest
P lanet from the Sun. Its average
T emperature is -328 degrees F. This planet is made up of an icy core
U nderneath water and the gaseous surface that surrounds
N eptune. There is a large storm on Neptune that disappeared in 1994, then came into
E xistence once more, but in a different hemisphere.

Mallory Hill, Grade 6
Pinewood Elementary School, IN

Love Is…

Love is not far away, Paris, or Rome
Love is not evil, cruel, or harsh
Love is not lonely, being apart, or weak.

Love is in the heart, the soul, and mind
Love is goodness, kindness, and gentleness
Love is friendship, togetherness, and strength.

Love is you
Love is me
Love makes perfect harmony.

Katie Parsons, Grade 6
Tri-West Middle School, IN

Fall

The wind in your face,
The leaves are falling,
They are all different colors,
They look like a rainbow.
You jump into a pile of leaves,
You rake them back up and jump back in,
Then winter comes with its cold winds and icy snow.
Oh how you miss fall,
But don't worry,
It will come again.

Alex Neal, Grade 6
Stanley Clark School, IN

Autumn

Wind blows leaves off trees,
A wonderful autumn breeze,
Winter is coming.

Aubrey Stoll, Grade 5
North Knox East Elementary/Jr High School, IN

Be Strong

Dance, like nobody's watching.
Sing, like nobody's listening.
Laugh, like everyone's laughing with you.

Just do what you want, as if there were no rules.
Make jokes, like you're the funniest person.
Live, like you always wanted.

Give, like you're giving your heart.
Love, like your hearts never been broken.
Just have fun, as if you've never been sad.

Trust, like you've never been lied to.
Dream, like you've never had a nightmare.
Believe, like you'll always have miracles.
Imagine, like everything revolves around you…

And know that you're loved.

Carly Oakes, Grade 6
Harding Grade School, IL

Holidays

The holidays are a great time for families to get together.
It's always a peaceful day, no matter the weather.
There's a lot to be thankful for.
Eating with the ones we adore.
Taking vacations for fun.
Sitting outside enjoying the sun.
Kids can't wait for Santa Claus to come.
Open presents and have a little fun.
New Year's is the time to start the year clean.
It's one whole year so kids try not to be mean.
We might go fishing with our fishing rods.
But most importantly spend time with God.

Jonathan Robinson, Grade 4
St Matthew School, IL

School

School is so cool,
even though it makes me drool.

I like to do work,
as I give my teacher a smirk.

I love to go to PE,
I always giggle with glee.

Lunch is always delicious,
though it does make me suspicious.

I love to do math,
it leads me on the right path.

I love to go on breaks,
school gives me a headache.

My teachers are so nice,
I think they're made of sugar and spice.

I like to hang out with friends,
they are friends on which I can depend.

Michelle Thompson, Grade 6
Emmanuel-St Michael Lutheran School, IN

Happiness

Happiness is overrated
That's what I think
To talk
To sing
To laugh
To cry
You're always happy because
Deep inside
Happiness is overrated

Hannah Dobrowski, Grade 5
Booth Tarkington Elementary School, IL

The One Thing

The one thing with girls
Is that they chase after boys.
They say that they love them
But they treat them like toys.

The one thing with boys
Is that they mature later.
They stick food up their nose
And then shoot it at the waiter.

The one thing with parents
Is that they are the boss.
And when we break our things
They say it's our loss.

The one thing with the world
Is that there is hatred about.
The devil had started it
With his pointed tail and snout.

The one thing with everyone
Is that we are different.
But no matter what people say
We are all equivalent.

Amanda Newmark, Grade 6
Marie Murphy School, IL

Let Us Remember

Let us remember…
The day that I was welcomed
  to a world of peace.

Let us remember…
God is always beside us
Watching children grow.

Let us remember…
Love grows in a gentle spirit
Not one filled with hate.

Olivia Knight, Grade 4
Churubusco Elementary School, IN

My Dogs

My dog is black
he is nice to other people.
We bought him from my
Dad's country, Mexico.
The dog's name is Ruby.
It is fun to play with him.
In 2006, I got a new dog,
it's name is Lala.
Ruby and Lala play together.

Brian Olmos, Grade 5
Glen Flora Elementary School, IL

Christmas Night!

Christmas is here
So let's give a big cheer!

Get the stockings and lights
Don't be scared of heights

Get the candy canes
And set the choo choo trains,

Get the Christmas tree
Boil some "hot tea"

Set out a plate of milk and cookies
SHHH!!! Go to bed it's night
And make sure the bed bugs do not bite!

Elli Mendenhall, Grade 4
Summit Elementary School, IL

Deer Hunting

I went deer hunting
and the deer were
run, run, running and playing.
I shot a deer and he took off
running into the creek.
He went across the creek and died
I was really, really happy
that I got that deer
he had really, really big
antlers on him
I got home and told
mom that I got a deer
a really big deer and so
we went and got it
and took him home with us
and hung him up.

Blake Patton, Grade 5
Gard Elementary School, IL

On a Cold Morning

The leaves were rustling in the wind.
The branches started to bend.
I grabbed my coat and jacket.
My dad grabbed the hatchet.
I ran down the street.
I could hear my heart beat.
My mom started crying.
I thought she was dying.
I ran in the house.
As quiet as a mouse.
It turns out the TV was on loud.
Then I heard a big pound.
On a Cold morning.

Bailey Fidler, Grade 6
Milltown Elementary School, IN

Sad to Happy

Sad
Lonely, mad
Stabbing, shooting, living
Vietnam, Iraq, Gettysburg
Sleeping, daydreaming, listening
Free, angels
Happy

Minka Stukenberg, Grade 5
Forreston Grade School, IL

Fall

F un season
A ll kids come out to play
L ittle kids jump in leaves
L oving kids invite lonely
  kids to play with them.

Maria Petrillo, Grade 6
South Middle School, IL

Jonathan

J umps a lot
O ver and over I call my mom
N ot a good drawer
A mazing good
T he book I'm reading is *Spiderwick*
H ave a scar
A good speller
N ot a good poet

Jonathan Huron, Grade 4
Warren Central Elementary School, IN

My Mommy

My mommy
is loving
My mommy
is caring
My mommy
is as sweet as a cup of sugar
My mommy is a secure blanket
My mommy
is as serious as can be
My mommy
is the queen of England to me
My mommy
is a fragrant flower
My mommy
is a nice grandma
My mommy
is my mommy
no matter what
I am glad my mommy
is not a mummy

Kailey Fox, Grade 4
Veale Elementary School, IN

Good Night

You gaze silently into the sky.
A shooting star whizzes by.
The star twinkles, oh, so wise.
"Good night, good night," he seems to cry.

He grins and you do, too.
He is just the star for you.
You drift off to sleep in a happy way.
That is the story to tell today.

Julia Wang, Grade 5
Sycamore School, IN

The Cafeteria

The cafeteria is like a jungle
The cafeteria is like a mad house
The cafeteria is like a zoo
The cafeteria is like a loud concert
The cafeteria is a place to eat
The cafeteria is like a flock of noisy geese flying closer to you
The cafeteria is a place to talk to your friends.

Alex D. John, Grade 5
Lincoln Intermediate School, IL

Fall

Fall is the time to rake,
instead some women like to bake.
I say that with all of my might.
In fall I also love to fly my kite,
I fly it even though, I have to hold it tight.
This is all I say to you,
please take my word and love fall too!

Ellen Kolb, Grade 5
St Michael School, IN

A Day in Spring

I love to watch and smell the flowers,
I could always do it for hours.
Outside I can find something to do every day,
I could do it in almost every way.
In the spring I like to swing,
And I hear the birds start to sing.
The trees, the trees such a pretty sight,
I blow the leaves away with almost all my might.
I spy the trees swaying,
The kids are all playing.
This moment seems like it is almost past us,
Even though it is moving like molasses.
The clouds pass by so white and fluffy,
And here comes the bunnies so white and fluffy.
It is so sunny outside,
And not so sunny inside.
A day in spring is finally here!

Jessica Will, Grade 6
St Patrick School, IN

Movies

Movies
Drama, action
Entertaining, exciting, watching
Funny, hilarious, fairy tale action
Films

Amber Tolson, Grade 5
Washington Township Elementary School, IN

In the Forest

On a trail, in a forest am I
Twelve robins chirping in the trees
Leaves blowing softly in the breeze
A doe standing, watching
The smell of fresh, crisp autumn air
The bark of a tree under my hand
A fallen tree to my left, the doe to my right
Nothing but nature
Nothing but nature

Nicole Gorman, Grade 5
Stanley Clark School, IN

Uncontrolled Losses

The trees are cut down.
Animals lose their homes forever.
Land is not pretty.

Matthew Rogers, Grade 5
Benjamin Franklin Elementary School, IL

God Is Great

God is great,
God is almighty,
God is the one for me,
God is busy as a bee but has time for me,
God is better than a present or a toy,
he is the greatest gift of all,
God is the right present for you,
God is better that a dog or a cat
God can give you a trip to Heaven,
Where there are many gifts for you.

Jonathan Yang, Grade 6
Christian Life Schools, IL

Drugs Destroy Dreams

Do you dream of living a life with good health?
Do you dream of living a life of great wealth?

Do you dream of a life filled with fun?
Do you dream of living a life relaxing in the sun?

Do you dream of a life that is good?
Do you dream of living a life as you know you should?

Don't let drugs destroy your dreams.
Definitely take time to enjoy life's cream.

Matt Hovey, Grade 5
Dee Mack Intermediate School, IL

Indiana Birthday

I ndependent
N ew
D eciduous trees
I nterstate highways
A nd so graceful
N o one can take the land
A nd never boast or brag

B eautiful
I f the flag drops
R ed white and blue
T he colors
H ave to go
D on't let the flag drop
A nd always stand tall
Y ou should be here!

Bailey White, Grade 4
Scipio Elementary School, IN

Nolan

Nolan
Smart, funny, cool, trustworthy
Brother of Noelle and Noriel
Ice cream, soda, talking
Who feels sad when friends leave
Who needs video games
Who gives money to the poor
Who fears death
Who would like to see Niagara Falls
Who lives in a big house
Dalman

Nolan Dalman, Grade 5
St Jude Catholic School, IN

Smile

My smile shines through the night
Sparkling, glistening, and shinny
I will brighten up your day!

Samantha Kulak, Grade 6
Jane Addams Elementary School, IL

A Frightening Fear

Fear is like…
a controlling pain,
a freezing darkness,
a bad dream.
Fear is like
storming out frightness
getting a cavity
remembering all of your life
Fear is like
losing someone, watching sharp pain
losing your brain,
Fear

Jhai Herendeen, Grade 4
Churubusco Elementary School, IN

Monster School

A school when monsters play
It is not a lovely day.
In class monsters are shooting spit balls!
Some monsters are even screaming so you can hear it in the halls!
In the cafeteria some monsters are good as they slurp their soup.
Some monsters are rude and they just burp their soup.
At recess monsters squiggle and giggle as they play many tricks.
Some monsters even play pickup the sticks!!!
On the bus monsters are playing video games.
Some monsters are calling other monsters lame names.
Monsters are monsters just how they will be.
We'll just have to face it you and me.

Jessica Simpson, Grade 4
Fox Creek Elementary School, IL

Thanksgiving

On Thanksgiving we are so grateful for the blessings God gave us;
freedom to pray, a bountiful land and Jesus to save us.
Thanksgiving is a time for families to be together.
We laugh and joke and talk about the weather.
We remember Thanksgivings from the past,
and always wish the day would last and last.
Grandma just keeps on cooking such good food,
while the dads watch football and begin to brood.
The children are running and screaming and playing.
"Watch out for that vase!!" the moms are all saying.
Thanksgiving is also a time of feasts,
with the table full of holiday treats.
There is turkey and stuffing and potatoes, too;
green beans and cranberries — but just a few.
We pass all the food around the table.
Bowl after bowl until arms are not able.
The table is so loaded you would think it would break.
Stomachs are full and starting to ache.
I get so full I just sit back and sigh.
But there is always room for another slice of pie.

Alex Fortmeyer, Grade 6
Emmanuel-St Michael Lutheran School, IN

Naniwa

At my favorite sushi restaurant,
I see the familiar waitresses showing us to the table.
I pass the worn-down brown carpet with Chinese lettering on it.
I watch as the chef carefully pours the soy sauce
so that no one piece of the eel roll has more sauce than others.
I smell the steam wafting up from the beef-teriyaki
and wonder how the chefs make it so good.
I hear the knife chopping through the crab
to cut it to just the right size for my spicy dragon roll.
I savor the scrumptious spicy tuna roll burning holes in my mouth.
I have enjoyed the greatest meal I have had for months.
And I relax for I am content.

Matthew Scott Finkel, Grade 6
Chicago City Day School, IL

Cats vs Dogs

Cats
Small, playful
Running, jumping, playing
Fluffy, frisky, crazy, funny
Licking, dripping, biting
Cute, cuddly
Dogs

Elizabeth Follis, Grade 5
Washington Township Elementary School, IN

Skiing

People coming from everywhere
faces glistening in the sun,
Blades scratching the ice
as they razor their way,
Moguls waiting to be skied on
by a black diamond expert.

Snow flying everywhere
as someone rapidly turns,
Teenagers on ice rails
trying to impress their friends,
Tired ski groups waiting to get hot chocolate,
But everybody's leaving
as they hurry to their hotels.

Christopher Vergara, Grade 5
Walker Elementary School, IL

The King

the buck
so graceful
in the forest so vast
in a snowy white December
while searching for food under a blanket of snow,
the king of the forest
stands alone

Sydney Goffinet, Grade 6
Perry Central Elementary School, IN

My God

Singing, praising, teaching, learning. My God is the owner.
Praising Him with love and honor. My God is the owner.
Go to Him with any problem. My God is the owner.
He made me live to spread the word. My God is the owner.
He loves me when I do wrong. My God is the owner.
He died upon a wooden cross. My God is the owner.
He had great pain so that we could live. My God is the owner.
He owns His people and the world. My God is the owner.
He owns the heavens and the angels. My God is the owner.
I am his servant and I bow to him. My God is the owner.
He shed His blood for all our sins. My God is the owner.
I hope I live with Him one day. My God is the owner.
He is my only God.

Alivia Held, Grade 5
North Knox East Elementary/Jr High School, IN

Friends

Friends are always there for you
Through the good times and the bad
Playing pool and shooting hoops
There is no way we could be sad

Friends are good secret keepers
Even when it's hard to do
They try to never lie and cheat
But sometimes we just do

Friends are good at letting things go
They are quick to comfort and easy to forgive
They always know what is wrong and how to make it better
To tell you the truth without friends I could not live.

Emily Taylor Fox, Grade 6
Emmanuel-St Michael Lutheran School, IN

Indiana

Indiana is great to me
and I think everyone should always be
living in Indiana.
I want to live in Indiana forever
and if you don't you'll never be the one for me.
The four seasons create a beautiful landscape
with the flowers in the spring, the snow in the winter,
the leaves in the fall, and the green grass in the summer.
Indianapolis is just the right size.
It has all these great places
like the children's museum and a great big mall.
It has lots and lots of farming and all the corn you need
you can always find a place to grow your crops.
Indiana is such a great place
you'll always find what you are looking for
and find everything you need.
Indiana is so awesome
Indiana is really great
Indiana will always be great for you and me.

Olivia Rent, Grade 4
Stonegate Elementary School, IN

Juice Williams

Juice gets to run the play,
Making his move every Saturday.

Doing the option making the play,
If he gets tackled he'll throw it away.

When he goes back for a pass,
He'll look for someone open in mid-grass.

When he scores a touchdown he'll jump up and down,
Putting them up by sundown.

Bryce O'Neill, Grade 5
Dee Mack Intermediate School, IL

Sports

I like playing sports,
Such as football.
But sometimes it hurts,
When you fall.

I like playing basketball,
But hockey, not at all.
I practice so much,
The field is where I abide.

I have a good time,
My team plays well.
Our coach does not have to yell,
If we lost, it would be a crime.

Noah Blunier, Grade 5
Bethel Lutheran School, IL

Thankful Thanksgiving

Family eating
celebrating together
thankful offerings

Madison Day, Grade 4
Rose Hamilton Elementary School, IN

Bad Days

Bad days are everywhere
Filled with doom
Coming down like rain.
Heads are filled with sorrow
All night and day.
People cry
Oh no no.
Living in the dark
And never seeing the sun.
Never seeing love
In day or night,
Yes, bad days are here.

Michelle Atwood, Grade 6
Milltown Elementary School, IN

Working with People

When we work with people.
You have to be caring and joyful.

Don't be a liar.
Or else you will be a fighter.

When you have a ball.
Make sure you share with all.

Don't be rude.
Or you will be in a bad mood.

Autumn Dunn, Grade 4
Summit Elementary School, IL

The Ducks

Ducks fly in the deep blue sky
They fly there and they get tired.
They spot the blue ocean below
They see some colorful fish.
They soar down gracefully to eat
They missed the fish and get nothing.
The ducks stop to rest a while
A small dog barked and scared them off.
They soar gracefully to a pond
They get some sleep for a night.
They eat food for a day or so
They're gone for a whole season now.
They came back for the summer
Amazing graceful ducks there is.
They might get shot and be eaten.

Misty Bye, Grade 6
Milltown Elementary School, IN

I Like…

Dogs
but not when they're wild.
Cats
but not when they scratch.
Games
but not when they're boring.
Army
but not when they get you.
Cars
but not when they're slow.
Movies
but not when they're chick flicks.
Books
but not when they're horrible.
Pizza
but not when there are mushrooms.
School
but not when you have homework.
Snow
but not when it gets snow in your boots.

Chris Minnick, Grade 5
Churubusco Elementary School, IN

The Heart of Nature

One cannot see,
But knows it exists.
The heart of nature,
Is falling behind,
The ice is melting,
The heat is rising,
The Earth is turning,
Every second of your life.
(Global Warming)

Caitlin Riley, Grade 6
Daniel Wright Jr High School, IL

Moods

Sad
Sad is a mood,
Sad is plain.
Sad is a plain mood,
A mood so plain and crude.
Are you in a sad mood?
Or Happy,
A mood which is bright,
It has such might.
With a lot of light!
Or Mad,
If you're mad this is very bad.
You can catch it like chicken pox,
If you're lucky put it in a box.
Then toss it out the door,
Oh, you will have such galore
For getting rid of that mood!

Erin McCreedy, Grade 5
Perry Central Elementary School, IN

Christmas

Christmas is white
and when I'm dreaming it makes
me bright.

With stockings, cookies, and
families so dear, and the love of
Christmas that we all share.

From family to friends and
cousins, so we can say blessing for
all and the family so dear.

The white is in the winter's
day and we all celebrate
a wonderful Christmas
Day.

Jazmyne Crites, Grade 4
Fox Creek Elementary School, IL

My Mom

Oh she is an excellent cook
She gets her recipes from books
We eat good dinners together every night
Conversation is enjoyed with every bite
Missing dinner gets us "the look"

In the kitchen she will bake
A chocolate frosted cake
My mom is as peaceful as a dove
She always passes around her love
There is joy in all she makes

Max Provan, Grade 6
St Colette School, IL

Thanksgiving

T ime of thankful tidings
H as always been a happy holiday
A lmost always has apple pie
N o one will ever eat squash without nutmeg
K anned kranberries kan taste good
S weet potatoes taste sweet with cinnamon and sugar
G od's great time of remembering giving thanks to Him
I always like the taste of turkey
V ery vibrant for various reasons
I 'm impressed by the incredible smells in the kitchen
N o one seems to notice our nontoxic centerpiece
G reat to be gathered at the table in a group.

Michael Monroe, Grade 5
Bethel Lutheran School, IL

When I Get My iPod

When I get my iPod
I'll tell you what I'll do
I'll listen to it day and night
Until my face turns as blue as the sky.

When I get my iPod
I'll load up every song I have
Which there were only 82
My parents will get ticked at me
Cause listen to my iPod is all that I will do

When I get my iPod
Or if it finally breaks
That's usually what they do
I'll pout and moan and complain a bunch
Until Mom says "Luke…Hey, it's time for lunch"

Luke Goodrich, Grade 6
Christian Life Schools, IL

Freedom

America, taken of their rights
Its patriots transformed to slaves
But our brave citizens of America
Inspired by the crimson flag that waves
For their goal was to take back their rights
America fighting to be free
What they had was confidence
With glory in their sight
For Washington called the win
That America was victorious in war
So joy crossed through their country
For so high did they soar
With the Declaration of Independence
America walking from the dilapidated coliseum
Walking the glory road
Glad that they won their freedom

Dregory Williams, Grade 5
Benjamin Franklin Elementary School, IN

I Like My Life

I like
Pizza
But not with sausage
Shopping
But not with my evil brother and sister
Movies
But not when they're rated R
Boys
But not the nerds
My TV
But not when my mom comes in and says it's time to go to bed
Playing softball
But not when we lose the game
Football
But not when I play
Animals
But not when they try to bite
Going outside
But not in the winter
Meeting new people
But not when I have to say "bye"

Chayenne McRoberts, Grade 5
Churubusco Elementary School, IN

Halloween

Halloween will give you a scare
You may get a chocolate pair
When you go door to door
You will get lots more
When you are done you will trade with Andy
A sucker will come in handy
If you need more to Randy
If you love bubble gum
You will say yum yum
When the clock strikes 12:00
You will hear the bells

Anthony Marconi, Grade 4
Summit Elementary School, IL

Winter Days

I like to play in the snow
When it is very cold.
I like the blue skies
When I get to ski on ice.

I think the bare trees are cool
And most of the time we don't have school.
It's very cold when you go to bed
But days are colder just ahead.

When the wind comes and blows
And the temperature is twenty below,
You bundle up to go out and play
So you have a fun day.

Bradley Hill, Grade 5
Coffeen Elementary School, IL

Trout

Trout live in big streams
Trout hide from their enemies
They can't hide from me
Abe Brueggemann, Grade 5
St Jude Catholic School, IN

Autumn Leaves

The leaves are falling off the trees,
Because of a slight breeze.
The leaves are whirling.
The leaves are curling.
Dylan Russin, Grade 4
Meadow Lane School, IL

Chicago

A city full of laughter,
Games parks and fun,
People playing on the beach,
Or tanning in the sun.

The Sears Tower stands so high,
A building nearly,
As tall as the sky.
Buckingham Fountain's freezing the air,
The most beautiful city of all,
I swear.

But looking closer,
What do you see?
Nothing but wasteland,
A garbage spree.
Homeless resting
In every park,
Where depressed street dogs
Just sit there and bark.

Through every building, every hall,
Illinois precious gem,
May not be precious at all.
Sarah Hill, Grade 4
Butterfield School, IL

Nature

The birds are singing,
The river is roaring loud,
It's beautiful here.
Monica Allman, Grade 5
St Jude Catholic School, IN

Christmas Time…

Christmas is a time of year
Where we all come together and…
Share and be nice to
each other and more…
Rebecca Dowell, Grade 5
Lincoln Intermediate School, IL

Winter Feeling

As winter falls, the trees go bald and the wind gave me a quiver.
My hat points tall, covering ears and all, while the snow gives me a shiver.
The Christmas feast, with all the goods, with a turkey my dad got from the woods.
As the sky went dark, turning into night, Santa made his Christmas flight.
Finally it comes, the day has begun showing a gleaming sun.
I ran downstairs with bloodshot eyes. I saw presents, I saw a lot!
Susie Jeziorowski, Grade 5
South Elementary School, IL

Riding My Go-Cart

Tires screeching, dirt flying and laughter all around.
Kids screaming and cheering.
Mosquitoes are coming we must put on bug spray.
I can feel the wind in my face and the happiness within me.
The light post gleaming as if it were the sun.
The vibration makes me go up and down.
The steering wheel turning left to right, over the hills we go.
The dirt flying in our faces.
I feel brave when I am in the go-cart with all the things I've done.
It's time for me to go and say goodbye to the dirt.
I'll be back another time to enjoy this experience again.
Christine Mai, Grade 5
Stanley Clark School, IN

Don

Funny, strong, loving, and caring
Relative of a talkative daughter
Lover of the Chicago Cubs, Dallas Cowboys, and me
Who feels he can dance, he's never wrong, and he's the king of the world
Who needs shelter, food, water, and me
Who fears heights, losing me, and losing the ones he loves
Who gives me love, happiness, and Hacienda
Who would like to see himself become a millionaire,
meet Kim from Dancing With The Stars,
and me growing up to be an intelligent girl
Resident of a crazy family
My Daddy
Haley Turpin, Grade 6
Helfrich Park Middle School, IN

Winter Wonderland

Snow is a white substance that has a little fuzzy feeling
That lets you leap in the air with joy and laughter
Making snow angels
Step in snow, jumping and laughing in snow
Never eat snow if it is a different color than white
With the ice slippery and gray
You can go down the slide really fast like a car going down the track
Landing in a funny position with a smile, grin, mad, glad, joy, and a doomsday face
It just makes you go wild
Snow lands here and there
Every year it will come back the winter wonderland, and that is what I call snow
Christian Washington, Grade 5
Walker Elementary School, IL

Camping

You see the trees and the land,
You see the sun setting and the water glimmering
With glee, you see and feel the rough and smooth rocks,
You hear the water, and your breath, and the birds singing.
To me, this is a perfect moment.

Malik Oudghiri, Grade 5
Stanley Clark School, IN

Things You Like

Stripes or dots, whatever you like
Scooters, skateboards, or a bike

Trees and bees and butterflies
Or making fresh mud pies

Orange juice, lemonade, or fruit punch
Or just a crunchy sandwich for lunch

Lizards, cats, and dogs
Or catching slimy frogs

You may be young, you could be old, too
But the things you like will always bring joy to you

Claire Buchanan, Grade 5
Dee Mack Intermediate School, IL

Jack My Cat

Jack my cat is cute, but trouble!
Loads of trouble.
Like getting stuck in the dryer or into sugar.
Jack my cat is evil like his brother.

He's jumped into water not knowing what it is.
He climbs the curtains so high…
I have to get a chair.
Jack's evil like his brother.

The good thing is he always calms down
If he doesn't, he's a clown.
But when he does lie down,
He isn't such a clown.

Ellyssa Dougan, Grade 4
Fox Creek Elementary School, IL

Christmas

C hrist is born on Christmas day.
H ollies are put up in the hallways.
R eindeer bring Santa to town.
I ce is everywhere, so be careful.
S nowy days are fun for sledding.
T ogether we gather to celebrate His birth.
M any joyful carols are sung.
A ngels come down to give a sign Christ is born.
S kiing and skating are fun for family day.

Amber Stoops, Grade 6
Corpus Christi Elementary School, IN

The Place to Be

Some people are world travelers,
Some people never stay,
But as for me,
I don't want to go away.
Fort Wayne is my home,
It's a great place to live.
A great thing about Fort Wayne is
Everyone likes to give.
The parks are all well kept,
You can tell by the way they look.
The ACPL is a great library,
You can check out any book.
At the coliseum,
There's a lot to go to,
Baseball, basketball, and hockey,
You can imagine the workers have lots to do.
Fort Wayne is always fun,
So as you see,
When you want to have a great day,
Fort Wayne is the place to be!

Zach Panning, Grade 6
Emmanuel-St Michael Lutheran School, IN

Brothers

B ossy
R idiculous a dork
O h boy he's weird
T he boy who is tied with the weirdo of the house
H as dork friends all through school
E xcept for one [his girlfriend]
R iding motorcycles is a hobby for him
S uper silly

Ashley Sweet, Grade 4
Scipio Elementary School, IN

Girls Basketball

Referees shouting foul plays here and there.
The crowd's going wild because they care.
Twelve just ran across the lines,
While number two whines,
"Don't carry the ball,
If they see you they'll make a call…"
At the end who'll take a shouting?
But whoever does will go home pouting.
The winning team will adore their coach,
As the losing team will be hard to approach.
Number seven just made a good play,
Some think that she'll save the day.
Even though she forgot her shirt,
Fourteen just made a basket, OH! and it looks like it hurt!
She's limping around clutching her knee,
While I'm sitting on the bench just glad that's not me.

Kaylie Johnson, Grade 6
Dakota Elementary School, IL

Leaves

The leaves are falling from the trees.
They whirl around in the breeze.
Whenever I play in the leaves,
Somehow they always make me sneeze.

Carly Hayes, Grade 4
Meadow Lane School, IL

Fall

Summer is not here,
Fall is near.
I am having fun
Playing in the sun.
Off the trees
Fall the leaves.

Cody Bolin, Grade 4
Chrisney Elementary School, IN

Basketball Game

You're running down the court
with your head held high.
On and on you go as you are to fly
The hoop comes in view
and you go up to shoot.
WWOOSSHH it goes in
for the ear splitting cheer.
You jump up and down
while they carry you on.
For you are the champion
who scored the last point.
Think of what could have happened
like not hitting the last point.
Think of what could have happened
at the basketball game.
WOW you are now in the hall of fame
to joyfully rest in peace.
Someone else will take your place
to join in for the basketball team.

Marie Schwartz, Grade 5
Perry Central Elementary School, IN

Audrey

Audrey
Caring, loving, helping, demanding.
Sister of Marc.
I like volleyball, dogs, and cheering.
I feel sad when someone dies.
I need ice cream every day.
I give love to everyone.
I fear spiders.
I would love to see Hannah Montana
I live in a loving home
Roland

Audrey Roland, Grade 5
St Jude Catholic School, IN

The Dog

There once was a dog
that followed me home
I told him to leave
but he wouldn't leave me alone!
I threw a stick
into the bushes
I told him to fetch
and hoped he'd never come back
The very next day
I saw him again
That time he looked so cute
so I decided to keep him.
Then the owner came
and took him back
I thought he was gone forever
The very next day
I saw him again
I cheered in delight
We then lived together
forever and ever

Daniel Zou, Grade 4
Butterfield School, IL

Carissa

C urious girl
A wesome person
R adiant as can be
I ntelligent in school and out
S uper nice
S urprisingly considerate
A nimal lover

Carissa Hollin, Grade 5
Forreston Grade School, IL

Tiger

My unique fur,
  helps me not be seen
  in the grass.
Why do I turn white?
Don't I run so gracefully?
When I am running,
  the grass and dirt feels so
  good on my paws.
I hate it when people try to
  hunt down me and my friends.

Kaitrin Colby, Grade 6
Sacred Heart Elementary School, IL

Ice Cream

Many different flavors
Vanilla, cherry, blueberry,
  A very sweet snack.

Anthony Talavera, Grade 4
Jane Addams Elementary School, IL

Keegan

K eeps away from trouble
E ats a lot
E ducational student
G iving person
A chieves work
N on-complicated

Keegan Akins, Grade 5
Forreston Grade School, IL

The Golden Pear

Golden blossoms fade away
  Happiness drifting astray

Broken trees as black as night
  Then you come into the light

  You see misery no more
  You see birds begin to soar

You smell around you, fresh air
  Then you see a golden pear

You eat the pear you're far along
And all your misery fades to song.

Jasmine Feder, Grade 6
Stanley Clark School, IN

It's Christmas!

It's Christmas morning
Outside, snowflakes are falling
"Mom, Dad, come quick!"
I hear myself calling

The spicy smell of gingerbread
Wafts through the air
And as I admire our Christmas tree
I hear wrapping paper tear

Now for the presents
All the electronics and toys
Should I open the tiny one
Or the one that makes a funny noise

Last night was the night
That Santa Claus came
Spreading joy to all children
Was the way he achieved his fame

Now I go to have fun
And spread Christmas cheer
But it will all soon be over
I can't wait until next year.

Haley Schueler, Grade 5
Butterfield School, IL

Saturn

S aturn has 7 magnificent rings. Saturn
A lso has 59 moons. Its nickname is Lord of the Rings. Saturn's
T emperature is always
U nder zero degrees. Saturnus,
R oman god of harvest, is for whom Saturn is
N amed.

Allison Wirt, Grade 6
Pinewood Elementary School, IN

Roses of Blue

The smell of a rose
Feels like a pillow of fluff.
Different colors blue, red, white and yellow.
Soft thin pedals smooth as silk.
Stem, thorns of red poke like needles.
Roses of blue.

Clayton M. Vestal, Grade 5
Lincoln Intermediate School, IL

Kittens

Kittens
Clean, tiny
Playing, snuggling, sleeping
Lazy, furry, playful, energetic
Barking, running, fetching
Excited, hyper
Puppies

Lacey Williams, Grade 5
Washington Township Elementary School, IN

War

Starting as a country,
Upon country disagreement,
Turned ugly and rotten,
It travels like a contagious disease.
Families turned against each other,
Because of beliefs.
Love is smashed.
The battle begins.
Bullets strike the air,
As if to say,
"We hate you all."
Time passes.
Life as we know it had ended,
So why had the duel not ceased?
Friends perish,
In the silvery moonlight.
Out of the gloom, a ghostly flag is raised,
It's finished.
Many decades later we look back,
And remember the horrors that had happened,
During the war.

Aly Murray, Grade 5
Highlands Elementary School, IL

Pillows

You always look so comfy
all the time you make me want to go to sleep
all day long I see you with your leather feathers
and your soft pillowcase
so please pillows stay soft.

Mark Hallman, Grade 5
Allen J. Warren Elementary School, IN

Ode to My Fefe

Black as the moon night.
White as the morning daylight.
Fefe, mi perrita.

Her tongue soaking wet.
It drips like rain.
Her wet kisses on my cheek.
They feel like wet waves.
Fefe, mi perrita.

Her paws on mud
As she looks around.
She squashes her paws right down to the ground
Fefe, mi perrita.

Fefe, I will always treasure you.
Yo le amo con todo mi corazon.
Mi perrita, Fefe.

Michelle Magdaleno, Grade 5
Walker Elementary School, IL

Sisters

Little sisters think they're so tough
but all they do is get in your stuff.
They sneak in your room and make it look like a bomb hit
it almost makes you want to vomit.
The world thinks they're cute with their ribbons and curls
but there's nothing meaner than little girls.

Jesse Aders, Grade 5
Perry Central Elementary School, IN

The Fall Nature

Orange, red, yellow, and a little green leaves
Are in the season of fall.
You can taste all those wonderful treats at Halloween.
When Thanksgiving comes you taste the ham and turkey.
You can smell the wrinkly, dry leaves.
Sometimes you can hear the birds that are migrating.
The chilly air makes you want to put on a jacket.
The leaves crunch under your feet when they dry up.
You play with them and rake them to jump in.
Or you could rake them then put them in bags to make money.
The sky is the most pretty blue.
It is the season of football and basketball.
I love fall.

David W. Horn Jr., Grade 4
St Matthew School, IL

Autumn Leaves

Autumn leaves float to the ground
Painting hills with vibrant colors
Like a rainbow caught on the ground
Waiting to break free
Autumn leaves that do stand out
Like some dirt on white tile flooring
A sparkling gem in a garbage heap
Noticed by all
Autumn leaves that children play in
Jumping in the giant leaf piles
As leaves spray up in a shower of sparks
Oh, what fun!

And whether you like them or not
They will come every year
A bug you can't get rid of
Buzzing and buzzing around your head.
Michelle Marasigan, Grade 5
Thomas Dooley Elementary School, IL

Summer

Swimming in the sun
With a slight breeze in the air
Blowing through my hair.
Skyler Barrett, Grade 5
Churubusco Elementary School, IN

Our Classroom

In our classroom
I can hear the tappety-tap
of the students pencils.

I can smell the dust of the
chalk and the chalk eraser.

We can see the teacher
writing in cursive on the chalkboard.

I can feel the roughness
of the wood on our desk
because of past students
writing on our desk.
William C. Carnes, Grade 5
Lincoln Intermediate School, IL

Birthday

B est day of your life
I s a special day for you
R ain never comes
T he day when you have a lot of fun
H ave a lot of friends over
D o whatever you want
A day for fun
Y ou make everything special
Harley Shepherd, Grade 4
Scipio Elementary School, IN

Thanksgiving

Thanksgiving is a time when family comes around,
Where aunts, uncles, cousins, and grandparents can be found.
At the Thanksgiving dinner, the turkey is served,
We say our thanks, and then eat the bird.

We play games like checkers and chess,
To win all the games, we all do our best.
There is so much to be thankful for at this Thanksgiving time,
The cold wind outside makes the wind chimes chime.

We're happy and joyful and we don't want to fight,
We all say what we're thankful for on this beautiful Thanksgiving night.
After the party, music, and games, we say our good-byes,
But right before we leave, we all eat delicious pumpkin pie.
Kaylee Lockenour, Grade 5
Dee Mack Intermediate School, IL

Why My Dad Loves Me

I wish he would listen and do things the first time I ask him.
Like picking up his room.
I wish he would pick up sticks in the yard.
I always tell him he's smart, but he never listens.
He's good at math, but he thinks that he's not.
He knows he's smart when it comes to science.
He makes things harder than they are.
Especially when it comes to math;
He makes problems harder, by adding more steps.
I love it when he does his homework.
It might take him a while, but he usually gets a good grade.
I love it when he reads to me.
I hate it when he doesn't go to bed on time.
Then he's really tired in the morning.
Then he doesn't want to wake up and sometimes misses the bus.
He's never late for school.
I like the fact that he doesn't have a lot of homework.
These are some good and some bad reasons why I love him.
Garrett Vincent, Grade 6
Dee Mack Intermediate School, IL

The Year

January is very cold with snow. Back to school we go.
February, shorter than all the rest. But Valentine's Day is best.
March is when my birthday falls. Grandma's is the 12th and we do call.
April is a month of spring. Snow melts and birds do sing.
May is when we play outside. We camp, have fires, and 4-wheeler ride.
June is when school is out. We love this time and we do shout.
July is when firecrackers pop. My brother and I cannot stop.
August is when football starts. I love to play and do my part.
September is Labor Day. The last long weekend we play.
October has my brother's birthday. He is older than me they say.
November brings out guns to shoot. Deer, squirrel, and hats and boots.
December is my favorite, you see. Because we have a big Christmas tree.
Jacob Cunningham, Grade 5
Forreston Grade School, IL

Christmas

Every Christmas we put up the Christmas tree.
Then we put decorations on.
We put the angel on the top.

Each Christmas we make Christmas cookies.
My family and me make them with cookie cutters.
They are so delicious.

On Christmas we make eggs, biscuits, and bacon for breakfast.
I make it into a sandwich.
It is so yummy. My mom thinks so, too.

I like playing in the snow.
I like sledding down it.
I like having snowball fights.

After playing in the snow I have hot chocolate.
It tastes nice and warm.
My sister has it too.

I love opening presents.
I can't wait to see what I get.
Then I play with them as much as I can.

Alex Browning, Grade 4
Fox Creek Elementary School, IL

Moving Through Time

Let me help to mend your heart
you've been through such hard times
I want you to be cheerful again
when you hear those beautiful wind chimes

It makes you sad to think about
the good times just never last
but sometimes just be happy
and remember that joyful past

The little thing that started this
it makes me so angry
I really want to unleash on something
but this feeling is stuck in me

It is keeping us from seeing each other
as much as we really want
It's surely succeeding in one thing
putting us upon a haunt

Rileigh Roberson, Grade 6
Northwood Elementary School, IN

Walter Payton

The Chicago Bears had Walter Payton.
When they needed a score he never kept them waitin'.
All they asked was just one score.
But he ended up scoring a whole lot more.

Jacob Qualkenbush, Grade 5
Washington Township Elementary School, IN

Baseball

It's the top of the first inning,
Kaleb is up to bat.
It's low, inside, ball one.
Here's the pitch right down the middle
He swings, it's a ground ball left field.
He rounds first going to second.
Left fielder throws as the runner goes to third
He goes all the way!
HOME RUN!
And the first run is across.

Kaleb Nevers, Grade 5
Lincoln Intermediate School, IL

Ta'Liska

Ta'Liska
Adorable, cutie pie, loving, sweet
Relative of my heart
Lover of family, food, toys
Who feels happy, in charge, like the cutest baby in the world
Who needs a lot of attention, someone to play with, and love
Who fears being alone, falling, the vacuum cleaner
who gives slaps, earaches, and love
Who would like to see people, mother, me
Resident of two families
My Niece

Ambria Wright, Grade 6
Helfrich Park Middle School, IN

My Cat, Teddy

M y cat, Teddy, is so cute.
Y ou see, he's black.

C an you see him run?
A cat came by and attacked him,
T oo scared to come out from under the porch.

T wo days later he came out and got attacked again.
E veryday that happened, until he ran away.
D id he run away?
D oes he still love us?
Y ay! We found him hiding in the attic!

Kendra Hirsch, Grade 5
Coffeen Elementary School, IL

Respect

R esponsible is what you should be
E njoy the things you see
S elf-control is nice too
P ositive is what you should do
E steem is one too
C are for each other too
T rustworthy can be good so tell me what you should

Kaliha Robinson, Grade 4
Summit Elementary School, IL

New York, New York

When I go to New York, I will go to the city.
I will see everything there is to see.
When I go to New York, I will find that the city is as busy as a bee.
There are as many people as there are stars.
I will never count them all.
When I go to New York, I will see the Statue of Liberty.
It is so big, it is taller than me.
It is so big and green from the sea, it is very unique.
When I go to New York, I will visit the Empire State Building, the largest building in New York City.
When I go to New York, I will go to Times Square.
From the restaurant Planet Hollywood, to all the shops, you can't miss a thing.
When I go to New York, I will finish my day.
I've seen so much, that when I leave, I will want to come back.
New York is a great place to be!

Emily Bremmer, Grade 6
Christian Life Schools, IL

The Winter Trip Outside

Going outside is like being on a stage. The snowflakes fall silently as though breathless of your performance. The moon high above is like a spotlight, highlighting your beautiful steps. The snowman is like the conductor, his thin arms swaying in the wind to the tune of the music, seeming to conduct an invisible orchestra. The chill from deep within is like the nerves of being on stage. Then, when you are inside your warm home, it is like that wonderful feeling of being done with the performance. But there is another feeling. A feeling of wanting to go again, to be outside and on stage.

Madelyn Smith, Grade 6
Corpus Christi Elementary School, IN

Thanksgiving

T hanksgiving
is when people give thanks for everyt **H** ing they have.
It was made a holiday when a lot of tr **A** velers came here so
they could worship God. The E **N** glish were not letting the Pilgrims worship
Their God, so they **K** icked the Pilgrims out.
The Pilgrims went to America. **S** o
the people who did this were called Pil **G** rims.
They ran into a tribe who were called the **I** ndians. They taught them how to get food.
The Pilgrims were **V** ery grateful.
They gave thanks with the **I** ndians,
and the Pilgrims had a feast. **N** ow,
Thanksgiving is a national holiday. **G** ive thanks for everything you have!

Ajay Jayakar, Grade 4
Frank H Hammond Elementary School, IN

Untitled

I jump up and down looking at the roller coasters towering above me making never ending twists and turns.
Each roller coaster requiring a line as long a two hour wait.
I can hear people screaming and roller coasters coming to a stop, making a loud "BANG!"
I can smell the fresh salty water around me,
I can also smell food and beverages, and sweets of all flavors.
I can taste my juicy hamburger as I chow it down for lunch.
I can feel the sweat on my hands as I was going down a roller coaster
Holding on to my harness for dear life and screaming "Aaahhh!"

Mario Manta, Grade 5
Stanley Clark School, IN

Dog vs Cat

Dog
Hunting, barking, sleeping
Small, cool, tall, lean
Prancing, leaping, sneaking
Soft, quiet
Cat

Jordan Carr, Grade 5
Washington Township Elementary School, IN

Emotion

I love rock and roll!
With its heart-to-heart songs
About real lives of joy and sorrow
Rockin' good music
With drums that are phenomenal
They keep the band in rhythm
It makes the music keep an awesome beat

Megan Willemin, Grade 6
St Joseph School, IN

Lion

You're so furious and so unique in your own way
You're the king of the jungle some people might say.
I adore you in so many ways.
Some ways I might not be able to explain.
You have courage and so do I
But when I'm in a difficult situation I might cry.
Oh, oh lion, you are so divine.

Jayda Jones, Grade 5
Allen J. Warren Elementary School, IN

Gizzie

Even though he was just a dog
It felt like he was a part of the family
Because you were in the family longer than I was
When you died I didn't even see it coming
At least not when I was at school
But it wasn't hard to figure out
When I came home from school something didn't feel right
I went in my room and there my mom was
Sitting by my door crying
And right then and there I knew what she did
She brought him to the vet to get a shot
But it wasn't an ordinary shot it was to put him asleep
Even after what she did I was still kind of glad
Because I know why she did it
And she did it for the right reasons too
She did it because he was biting too much
if she wouldn't have done it
Something really serious could have happened
If you wouldn't have been biting
Then we wouldn't have been put through all this pain

Alexis Schwoeppe, Grade 6
Nancy Hanks Elementary School, IN

My Dog Champ

My dog Champ was a good dog.
He ran away when I was sleeping.
That was terrible.
I was looking for him
But I couldn't find him anywhere.

I miss our walks together.
I miss our movies and games.
I love when I'm feeling down
You will make me feel happy again.
I see a dog like you and when I say Champ
The dog says nothing.
Then I knew that wasn't my dog.

Kenny Poyser, Grade 5
Walker Elementary School, IL

Final Destination

Loving,
Caring,
Kind,
Wishes to grow up,
Dreams of making the world a better place,
Wants to feed world hunger,
Who wonders what lies beyond the earth,
Who fears death,
Who is afraid of murder,
Who likes boys for who they are,
Who believes in spirit.
Who loves cooking and baking,
Who loves to watch football.
Who loves school, spends lots of time with friends.
Who loves people who are very kind.
Who plans to be a writer.
Who plans to get married with kids.
Who plans to get my doctor degree.
Whose final destination is heaven.

Mikhaila Builta, Grade 5
Forreston Grade School, IL

Wind

The wind whistles like a train in the distance,
Moving sometimes fast and slow,
No one knows when it's going to come,
Until you hear the whistle in the air.
Coming at you with no care.

Hannah Wilson, Grade 6
Trinity Oaks Christian Academy, IL

The Great Lions

The great broad kings lie around,
The wicked wild settles around, but some still roam.
The great kings' bright brown glistening eyes light the night.
But soon the bright light goes away to start another day
And the King of the wild sleeps.

Brandon McCay, Grade 6
Knox Community Middle School, IN

Christmas

C hristmas is about family.
H appy Holidays!
R espect everybody.
I nstead of being mean, be nice.
S hall we dance?
T ime for opening presents!
M erry Christmas!
A re you bringing the ham?
S hall we kiss under the mistletoe?

Alex Hamm, Grade 6
Holy Family Catholic School, IL

My Dogs

My dogs are playful
Chase, catch, fetch
Vader and General
Make me safe…

Vanessa Perez, Grade 4
Jane Addams Elementary School, IL

Fall Fun

Halloween is in the fall,
And I'm having a ball!
I should use a smoke machine
On Halloween.
As you trick or treat
You will get something sweet.
You hand out some snacks
And get all relaxed.
You'd better be careful
When you eat some candy,
Cavities aren't dandy!

Zach Litkenhus, Grade 4
Chrisney Elementary School, IN

The Musical

Voices ringing others singing,
In just 3 more days…

People cheering
No one is fearing
Death or the devil,
In just 2 more days…

Many crying
About Jesus
Dying in just 1
More day…

Stunned and amazed
Walking through the fields of maize
Jesus Christ has risen, only tonight.

David Vornholt, Grade 6
Our Shepherd Lutheran School, IN

Woolly Mammoths

Lumbering brown mountains,
In a landscape of white,
creatures with features
of solid gold
Walking with logs,
Noses like whips,
Teeth miles long.

These tall brown mountains
Stood straight and tall
until rains of danger
Eroded them down to
Drifting grey clouds
In a landscape of white.

Maxwell Lowery, Grade 4
Highlands Elementary School, IL

Books

There are many kinds of books
Ones with adventure and fishing hooks
Horror with deep mystery
Nonfiction with history
Fantasy with magic balls
Mystery with twisting halls
Books with fascinating facts
World Record Books with great attacks
Explorers of the great outdoors
Elevators dropping many floors
Cars that are manufactured
Bones in the body that may be fractured
Thick woods hiding a shed
Famous quotes and things that are said
Go and find your favorite
and go ahead and savor it

Olivia Smithhisler, Grade 4
Stonegate Elementary School, IN

Scary

S oon kids will
C ome with candy bags
A nd costumes
R eady to raid candy and
Y ell with glee

Ellie Anton, Grade 4
Bailly Elementary School, IN

Train on Track

On the big steel train
Set a large green crane.
The long stretch of the track
The track laid way back.
The steel train was always in the rain.

Grant Hischke, Grade 5
Bethel Lutheran School, IL

Autumn

Leaves everywhere
Cold wind blows
Mist in the air
Rain falls on my nose
Autumn is here

Cassie Carullo, Grade 4
Bailly Elementary School, IN

Shoes

You always need me when you go out.
I get stepped on,
all the time.
I come in all different shapes and sizes.
I hate when I'm shoved in a box!
A lot of the time I wish I was
much, much taller.
Sometimes I get dirty in snow and mud.

Jeanne Disis, Grade 6
Sacred Heart Elementary School, IL

War

War is like a ghost.
It comes and goes,
with or without warning
it takes us by surprise;

The color for war is black
upsetting and dejecting,
but one war we cannot outrun
is the one we find in ourselves.

Santos "Carlos" Rivera, Grade 6
Keystone Montessori School, IL

Winter

As I walk through a world of white.
I wonder does winter ever end.
My hands are as red as a piece of bark.
I shake like a leaf on a tree.
I throw snowballs at my friends.

Nick Piane, Grade 6
Stanley Clark School, IN

If I Were a Dog

If I were a dog,
I would like to be small,
And like little bones,
And also like to play ball.

If I were a dog,
I would be nice,
And like the sunshine,
But not like ice.

Kristian Martinez, Grade 5
Edison Elementary School, IL

Trees

I gaze at the trees
And see that nature has bloomed
My heart is there too

Linnea Carr, Grade 5
Benjamin Franklin Elementary School, IL

Christmas Winter

The Christmas season now is here,
Winter cold and Christmas cheer.

People open presents all around,
A little girl plays with her merry-go-round.

Christmas is the time of noel,
Listen and you hear a Christmas bell.

Only one problem on the other side of town,
One little boy sits with a frown.

His Christmas spirit has not been found.

Colin Rafferty, Grade 5
St Daniel the Prophet School, IL

Thanksgiving

T hanking people.
H ow do you cook the turkey?
A unt Beth is coming.
N ow Saint Nicholas will be coming.
K icking back and enjoying the day.
S ometimes snow is here.
G ive and be rewarded.
I am stuffed with wondrous foods.
V isiting relatives.
I love that my grams and gramps are coming.
N ow go have some fun.
G od bless everyone.

Brock Wiegand, Grade 5
Dee Mack Intermediate School, IL

Variety

At night I like to read a book
About *Peter Pan* and *Captain Hook*
Robin Hood and *Jaws*
I love to read them all

I'm reading *Alice in Wonderland*
Next *Treasure Island*
Then *Heidi* and *Frankenstein*
Black Beauty and *Antigone*

When I get
Into my bed
I know I'll wake
To read again

Elijah Virgil, Grade 5
Bethel Lutheran School, IL

Life

Life is like a roller coaster of twists and turns.
Life is like an adventure that can take you anywhere.
Life is a waterfall flowing into a river.
Life is as crazy as a pig chasing a bear.
Without life nothing would be here.
Life is something we thank God for giving us.
Life is an amazing thing.
I am so glad we are here.

Katelyn Utecht, Grade 6
Christian Life Schools, IL

A Day in the Life

Blue and purple skies at night,
it's time to say goodnight.
You will get hugs and kisses,
you close your eyes and pray at night.

Now it's morning time, you say good morning,
you change your pants and shirt.
You see your school bus, then you're off to school.
You listen to your teacher, and you get to work.
You learn in class, then you get homework.
You get on the bus, they take you home.
Then, you do your homework.
Now it's the afternoon,
you ask your mom can you go outside?

When you come in, it's nighttime,
you eat dinner, then you take a bath.
When you're done, you brush your hair,
then lay down and watch a movie.

Then you will fall asleep,
and say goodnight

Danielle Wiedman, Grade 4
Glen Flora Elementary School, IL

When Fall Comes

When fall comes, leaves turn orange, yellow, red, and brown,
And then they go down.
Down, down off the trees,
Down, down go the leaves.
It gets cooler in the season,
I don't know why, what is the reason?
You don't know why?
Oh well, let's have pumpkin pie.
Raking the leaves, raking the leaves,
Do you like raking leaves?
I sure do.
I'm jumping like a kangaroo.
I'm jumping into the leaves,
I'm jumping into the leaves.

Dregan Pike, Grade 4
Chrisney Elementary School, IN

Dolphin

Graceful creatures of the sea
Roam the Watery Kingdom below us.

Leaping out of the
Shimmering water and
Diving back under the
Wondrous, Deep Blue Wall of
Shining Glass.

In the water,
They fear nothing.

The intelligent sea creatures
Dance their graceful dance,
Shooting deeper quietly.

The magnificent sea roamers
Wander around the Glittering sea
Looking for some
Last minute Prey
Before the Sun
Fades away
And goes to Sleep.

Helen Sun, Grade 5
Highlands Elementary School, IL

Cupcakes

Cupcakes are fun to make.
Grabbing and snatching,
Pouring and mixing,
Rolling and fixing,
Put it in the oven
and the munching
and crunching
will begin.

Lindsey Wisniewski, Grade 4
St Matthew School, IL

Ode to…Madden 07 Play Station 2

I click on play now
My heart pounds
With excitement
As I create my own team
I play games
One by one
Now I'm on the biggest stage
It's the Super Bowl!!!
I'm down in the fourth quarter
But I'm the comeback kid
Down by two
I kick a field goal
3,2,1
It's good!!!
I'm the Super Bowl champ!!!

Ben Rogan, Grade 5
Walker Elementary School, IL

Shopping

Hollister is my favorite place to shop
When I'm shopping I never want to stop
There is always new trends to shop for
It is never time to go out the door
Oh no it is time to go
I bought a really cute shirt with a bow
My feet are killing me right now
It's been a long day shopping now it's time to go lie down

Kaitlin Dotson, Grade 6
North Knox East Elementary/Jr High School, IN

Playstation

Playstation
When you play this you will need hand-eye coordination.
To be a winner you must keep playing with lots of determination.
It's all around our nation.
You can get addicted because of all the fascination.
Some people think it's horrible but I think it's a wonderful creation!
I have a dog that likes it, she's a Dalmatian.
It gives some people an inspiration.

Jennifer Miller, Grade 6
Emmanuel-St Michael Lutheran School, IN

Friendship

My friend and I were playing, down by the school yard,
But then she stopped and told me, "I have to move very far."
I sat down on the slide and started to talk to her
I told her, "Next year is going to be berserk."

She went inside; I followed, and told her, "There has to be a mistake,"
Then she told me, "We have to find another way."
"How are we going to talk to each other?"
I said, "Let's go ask our mothers!"

Our mothers thought of some ideas, but then I thought of one,
The next day I told her, "We could send each other letters, after school is done."
She said that it could work and then we both said yes,
So then after, we became very happy friends.

Veronica Bernabe, Grade 6
St Matthias/Transfiguration School, IL

In the Garden

In the garden you see the flowers
Dancing in the wind.
The birds flying gracefully in the air.
You see the animals that have come to enjoy the beautiful garden.
You hear the birds singing.
Chirp chirp chirp.
The big buzzing bees buzzing around from flower to flower.
Buzz buzz buzz.
The wind rustling in the leaves.
You can smell the beautiful fragrance of all the flowers.
All you see, hear and smell,
all blend together as the harmony of a beautiful, peaceful garden.

Sarah Hosinski, Grade 5
Stanley Clark School, IN

Over the Meadow

Over the Meadow so sweet and soft
Over the Meadow leaves fall and color the ground
The wind blows and trees rustle
The birds fly south with dreams of summer
Over the Meadow Thanksgiving awaits
As sweet as the Love it gives

Logan Benink, Grade 6
Christian Life Schools, IL

Too Old

David Beckham is too old
By someone he should be told;
He had his time
David is past his prime.

Luke Soliday, Grade 5
Washington Township Elementary School, IN

Which Color

Not dull not dreary
But sweet and cheery

I smell the posies and roses
It makes the girls tingle at their noses

And mm the taste of frosting on the cake
It's so good it makes me quake

Then there's the bubblegum
Everyone's expression will be yum

Now when you go to the store go down the Barbie aisle
You'll see the same color go on for a mile

I can hear the laughter of everyone
They have no trouble having fun

Boy, this color really makes you think
Oh, I know, it's *pink*

Jessica Lee, Grade 6
Dee Mack Intermediate School, IL

Sometimes

Sometimes you are mad.
Sometimes you are sad.
Sometimes you are mean.
Sometimes people think you look green.
Sometimes you are nice.
Sometimes you act like mice.
Sometimes you are silly.
Sometimes you act like a goat named Billy.
Sometimes you are just insane
Sometimes you are just plain.

Adrianna Linne, Grade 5
Perry Central Elementary School, IN

The Machine

There was a very small girl,
In a very big world,
Who had to make a machine.
It was mostly black, some blue,
And a little bit of green.
Her machine was dirty,
Her machine was sturdy,
And it did nothing she wanted it to do.
But in the end she figured out it needed batteries to move.

Ashley Wax, Grade 4
St Matthew School, IL

Nature

Nature is fantastically filled with happiness,
there are beautiful things galore,
but forests are getting torn down,
until there are no more.
Please don't kill the trees,
save a whole bunch of them,
save animals and plants,
both the leaves and the stem.

It is just so sad,
that everything's torn down,
all the beautiful wildlife,
dying into the ground.
We need to save Mother Nature,
and all the things inside,
we all want to rescue it,
that's a fact that you can't hide.

Grow some trees and a lot of plants,
until you can't fit anymore,
and once you see how amazing it is,
you will faint to the floor.
…it's sad though, all those trees dying…

Nick Perozzi, Grade 6
Daniel Wright Jr High School, IL

Presents

I saw an elf on a cold winter day,
helping Santa on his way.
The elf helps him put presents down the chimney
When they are done,
They hop on the sleigh
And old Rudolph is on his way.

Dylan Rauch, Grade 6
Herrick Grade School, IL

Ricky Carmichael

The thing we like about Ricky Carmichael
Is he rides a motorcycle.
When he has a blast,
He usually is going too fast.

William Hartman, Grade 5
Washington Township Elementary School, IN

This Is Sports

I like basketball.
I'll tell you why.
When I jump so high.
It feels as if I could fly.
I love baseball.
It makes me smile.
When I hit the ball.
It looks as if it travels a mile.
I like football.
It gets me going.
When I am running my sweat starts flowing.
I like all sports.
They are cool.
Next year I will get to play for St. Matthew School.

David Taylor, Grade 4
St Matthew School, IL

My Rock

Though I sit upon a little rock
I have a treasure with a lock
The treasure in my rock on my little dock

I know now that people don't really care
Because all I do is fix their hair
They know I have a treasure but don't know where

They look around but didn't find it at all
They searched for it even in fall
Also they searched for it in every hall

They finally found it at last
My birthday had already past!
And they DIDN'T find it FAST!

Melody Showalter, Grade 6
Francis Granger Middle School, IL

The Sailfish

The yellow and brown sailboat, which used to glide
through the waves of Lake Michigan,

now sits buried under the sand next to green
dunegrass. This little sailfish, made in

1962, is now taking a long nap in the
sand!!!

Jack McNeil, Grade 5
Benjamin Franklin Elementary School, IL

Index

Author Autograph Page

Author Autograph Page

Author Autograph Page

Author Autograph Page

Author Autograph Page

Author Autograph Page

Author Autograph Page

Author Autograph Page

Author Autograph Page

Author Autograph Page

Author Autograph Page

Author Autograph Page